1994

9 Pieces

6-2000

INTERMEDIATE
NEW TESTAMENT
GREEK

INTERMEDIATE

NEW TESTAMENT
GREEK

A LINGUISTIC
AND EXEGETICAL
APPROACH

RICHARD A. YOUNG

BROADMAN
& HOLMAN
PUBLISHERS

Nashville, Tennessee

4210-59
0-8054-1059-7

Dewey Decimal Classification: 225.48
Subject Heading: Bible. New Testament // Greek Language
Library of Congress Card Catalog Number: 94-8694

Composition and diagrams by Kelby Bowers,
COMPublishing, Cincinnati, Ohio.

Library of Congress Cataloging-in-Publication Data
Young, Richard A., 1944– .
Intermediate New Testament Greek : a linguistic and exegetical
approach / by Richard A. Young.
p. cm.
Includes bibliographical references and indexes.
ISBN 0-8054-1059-7
1. Greek language, Biblical—Grammar. 2. Bible. N.T.—Language,
style.
I. Title.
PA817.Y68   1994
487'.4—dc20   94-8694
                                                                          CIP

Contents

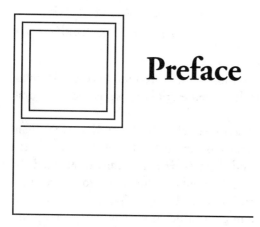

Preface

In keeping with my intent to write an exegetically based textbook for use in intermediate Greek classes, I have found it necessary to deviate from most intermediate grammars in several areas.

First, this text is not a grammar in the traditional sense. Traditional grammar is confined to the surface structure of a language: the forms and structure of words (morphology) and their arrangement in phrases and sentences (syntax). It does not concern itself with possible skewing or mismatch between surface structure form and deep structure meaning. Traditional grammar has also been confined to sentence analysis, without taking into consideration how literary and situational contexts influence meaning. Because conventional sentence-based grammar studies only one aspect of the communication process in isolation from all other aspects, it is unable to make definitive statements concerning meaning.

The objective of students in seminary Greek classes, however, is to use Greek in exegesis of the New Testament. This text is designed to help students by augmenting traditional grammar with insights from modern linguistics. Its purpose is to train students to become exegetes, not merely grammarians. It is an exegetically based treatment of topics normally discussed in intermediate grammars of New Testament Greek.

Most grammars have delved into exegesis to a certain degree, often with a disclaimer that what they are doing is not grammar. For example, Moulton (1978:72) remarks that the study of subjective and objective genitives is not a matter of grammar but of exegesis. The same holds true for the interpretation of adverbial participles and tense functions. This text makes no such disclaimer. It is committed to the exegetical process and seeks to link grammar, semantics (meaning), and exegesis. In working toward this goal, it incorporates linguistic models that have proven to be profitable in uncovering the meaning of a discourse. Among those models are a modified transformational grammar, propositional analysis, genre criticism, semantic structural analysis, pragmatics, speech act theory, and discourse analysis.

Second, this text follows the descriptive school of linguistics rather than the historical school. Many grammars assume that what a particular structure meant before the koine period dictates what it means when used by New Testament writers. The historical school therefore tends to be prescriptive, a notion shunned by modern linguists. The descriptive school, on the other hand, recognizes that usage in context determines meaning, not prior usage. Thus, among other aspects of syntax, this text promotes the five-case system rather than the eight-case system with its predetermined assumption of what each case represents.

Third, this text interacts not only with the grammars but also with recent commentary literature, periodical literature, monographs, and dissertations. Acquainting students with exegetical debates in literature regarding the meaning of syntactical structures will caution them about making dogmatic grammatical interpretations and will sharpen their exegetical skills. This interaction will also demonstrate how the study of Greek is exegetically significant and will provide a glimpse into current research and trends.

Fourth, this text will give students an appreciation of the dynamics of language and language analysis. Language evidences vast amounts of synonymy between forms, where the same sense is conveyed by several different constructions. Also, a single form may evidence a wide variety of meanings. Alerting students to these features will help them avoid the pitfall of a puristic, inflexible notion of language implied by simpler grammars. All now recognize that H. A. W. Meyer's dictum that εἰς with the infinitive always means purpose is incorrect ([1884] 1979:59). However, there are many other forms that students are led to assume always have a single meaning. Our knowledge of language is still evolving. Do the morphological tags that are associated with tense, for example, signify time at all? There is evidence that this once ironclad rule is crumbling. Moreover, certain syntactical categories are debatable, others are tentative, and hardly any are as clear cut as the labels suggest. The state of the art is simply not as settled as most grammars imply. Categories, interpretations, and former ways of understanding can be challenged. Hopefully this text gives a more realistic view of language.

Fifth, this text makes three assumptions about the meaning of any given passage: (a) meaning is inextricably bound together with the author's intent;

(b) meaning of any part (whether lexical or syntactical) cannot be discerned in isolation from the entire communication act; and (c) there is often a skewing between surface structure form and intended meaning. This grammar seeks to integrate these ideas into the exegetical task. The integration is brought together with the discussion of discourse analysis in chapter 17. The method of discourse diagraming outlined in chapter 18 (semantic structure analysis) is considered by many to be the most exegetically profitable approach. The text also sets forth thought-flow diagraming as a fast, practical type of diagraming for exegesis. It does not, as several intermediate grammars do, present word-by-word line diagraming as an exegetical tool.

I have chosen to frame the discussions in the traditional format rather than by semantic functions at the chapter level for pedagogical reasons. This will help to make the transition into linguistic concepts as transparent and painless as possible. The format therefore presents the material according to the recognized parts of speech with grammatical and semantic functions listed under each form. This may give the false impression that one can analyze the meaning of each part independently from the whole and then add the pieces together to arrive at the meaning of the text. The student should recognize that the semantic functions and examples listed under each form are derived from usage in particular contexts and can only be applied by considering the larger context in which the form in question is embedded. The basic unit of analysis must be larger discourse units, such as paragraphs, not individual words or grammatical constructions.

Perhaps a word is in order concerning the title. By using "New Testament Greek" I do not mean to imply that the Greek of the New Testament is a peculiar form of Greek, such as "Hebraistic Greek" or "Holy Spirit Greek." Neither is the Greek in the New Testament typically koine. Rather it represents a variety of forms of koine Greek, ranging in style from refined to colloquial. This lack of uniformity should caution the careful exegete against thoughtlessly applying the semantic function of a linguistic item characteristic of one writer to another.

I recommend that students begin reading the introduction for an overview of how Greek fits into the exegetical process. After that, the chapters do not have to be followed in order. Although the text has followed the traditional order of nominals before verbals, I have found that the most effective approach is to begin with participles, infinitives, and then nominals. This gives a good introduction to deep structure clause formation, semantic relations, and the notion of skewing between form and meaning. A systematic reading program should be assigned in addition to the exercises so that students can be allowed to use English versions and Greek helps with the exercises. Answers are often dependent on reading the wider context, something that would be very difficult for second-year students restricted to the Greek text. Moreover, the exercises focus on sharpening interpretative skills rather than on vocabulary or morphology.

It is hoped that those who use this text will do so with a mind that is willing to challenge what is said, as well as to be challenged by new ideas. Our knowledge of how language works (and especially Greek) is still imperfect. There are always new perspectives that shed additional light on language meaning. The common assumption that everything in Greek scholarship has already been accomplished has stifled a generation of Greek research and needs to be abandoned. My desire is that the thoughts gathered together in this book will encourage further research and understanding of the biblical text.

I owe a debt of gratitude to those who have sought to break the bonds of grammatical tradition and to integrate Greek scholarship with insights from linguistic theory, many of whose works are listed in the bibliography. I owe a special thanks to my acquaintances at the Summer Institute of Linguistics, and especially to John and Kathleen Callow, whose lectures in Greek discourse analysis did much to inspire this work.

Abbreviations

acc.	Accusative case
AV	Authorized (King James) Version
BAG	Bauer, Arndt, and Gingrich, *A Greek-English Lexicon of the New Testament*
Barclay	William Barclay, *The New Testament: A New Translation* (1969)
BDF	Blass, Debrunner, and Funk, *A Greek Grammar of the New Testament and Other Early Christian Literature*
BW	Brooks and Winbery, *Syntax of New Testament Greek*
dat.	Dative case
DM	Dana and Mantey, *A Manual Grammar of the Greek New Testament*
gen.	Genitive case
Goodspeed	Edgar J. Goodspeed, *The New Testament: An American Translation* (1923)
JB	*The Jerusalem Bible: New Testament* (1968)
LXX	The Septuagint
Moffatt	James Moffatt, *The New Testament* (1935)
NASB	*New American Standard Bible* (1973)
NEB	*The New English Bible* (1970)
NIV	*New International Version* (1984)
NJB	*The New Jerusalem Bible* (1985)
NWT	*New World Translation of the Holy Scriptures* (1961)
NRSV	*New Revised Standard Version* (1989)
Phillips	J. B. Phillips, *The New Testament in Modern English* (1972)
pl.	Plural
REB	*The Revised English Bible* (1989)
RSV	*Revised Standard Version* (1971)
sg.	Singular
TEV	*Today's English Version* (1976)
TR	*Textus Receptus*
UBS	United Bible Society
Weymouth	Richard Francis Weymouth, *The Modern Speech New Testament* (1903)
Williams	Charles B. Williams, *The New Testament in the Language of the People* (1966)

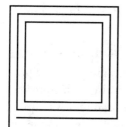

Introduction: Language Study and the Exegetical Task

The primary reason for taking a course in New Testament Greek is to use it as a tool to interpret the biblical text in a more precise and meaningful way, that is, in the exegesis of the New Testament. The term *exegesis* refers to the careful, meticulous, and thorough interpretation of a literary work. Exegesis should be contrasted with two close synonyms: interpretation and exposition. Interpretation is simply the act of explaining the meaning of something. Exposition is the act of presenting a concept in a clear, lucid manner. The word "exegesis" carries with it a connotative value not present in the other terms: that of a rigorous and exacting study.

The connection between language study and exegesis seems rather obvious. Language is the medium of communication. Therefore to understand what is communicated one has to understand the language used. We study Greek grammar and syntax to understand the language used in the New Testament and presume that this knowledge will automatically open the door to the meaning of the text. This atomistic or fragmentary approach lacks the explanatory perspective that can only come when language is studied as part of an entire communication act. The atomistic approach reflects the reductionistic approach to knowledge that characterizes a mechanistic world view.

The Communication Act

The first thing an exegete must do is to step back from the text to see the entire picture. We will observe that there is a speaker, a purposeful transmission or exchange of ideas, and an audience. We also observe that this exchange takes place in a real-life setting. Both the audience and situation influence the formation of the utterance. Sometimes the speaker chooses (subconsciously) to omit some pertinent information because he or she presumes the audience either knows the information or can discern it from the situation. The speaker may also express part of the message in a way quite foreign to the usual meaning of the words and syntax used. For example, at a formal dinner party, one would not say "Give me the salt," although this expresses the meaning, but rather "Can you pass the salt?" If one were to exegete the latter expression, one would say that the speaker is inquiring about the ability of another person to pass the salt. Obviously, mere analysis of the words and syntax will not yield the intended meaning. Meaning cannot be discerned apart from considering the entire literary and situational contexts. The communication act therefore is one interconnected whole.

The meaning of an utterance is conveyed through the interaction of many components. Language is merely one part of the whole process, a part that cannot be isolated from other parts if the intent is to discern meaning. This has significance for the study of Greek syntax. It would be questionable to assert that the aorist tense, subjunctive mood, genitive case, first class conditions, or any other aspect of Greek grammar means anything by itself. Without a context all we can say about each aspect of Greek grammar is that it has a range of possible meanings, some of which are more common than others.

Furthermore, how a particular part functions (especially particles and conjunctions) is often determined by levels of discourse higher than the sentence, that is, by the structure of the paragraph or section. This is also true of the choice of tense in narrative material, the position of elements in the sentence, and even the use or nonuse of the genitive absolute in narrative. Thus the constraints of higher discourse levels help determine the choice and meaning of parts on the sentence level.

Implicit and Explicit Information

One point touched on above is the subconscious selection of the parts of the message that need to be expressed. Of course, the entire message is needed if the audience is to understand the meaning (or if we are to understand what a New Testament writer said). However speakers never say everything. They allow as much as possible to be inferred from the immediate situation, shared experiences, shared knowledge, cultural mores, and prior statements in the same and related discussions. Why say something that is obvious and insult your audience's intelligence? Or why take the time to define your terms when they are obvious from the situation? People may not be too economical when it comes to money, but when it comes to speech activity, they tend to be extremely frugal. They say just enough to be understood in light of the situation, allowing the audience to compare what was said with the context and their own knowledge and to draw the proper inference. Hopefully, through this process the audience will arrive at the intended meaning.

The information that is expressed in the surface structure of a language is called *explicit information*. The information that is left unsaid is called *implicit information*. Implicit information is more common with informal, conversational speech than with formal speech. There are three kinds of implicit information: (a) information that is indirectly expressed in the surface structure by means of figures of speech, idioms, rhetorical questions, grammatical ellipses, and the like; (b) information that is presumed by the speaker to be common knowledge between speaker and audience; and (c) information that is understood only because the communication was spoken in a certain cultural and social context. Implicit information is just as much a part of the meaning of the communication as explicit information. Thus the interpretation of Greek words and syntax is often dependent on information that is not explicit in the text.

Form and Meaning

Another point touched on in the discussion of the communication act is the lack of strict correspondence between form and meaning. It is obvious from the example about passing the salt that there can be mismatches between form and meaning. Knowing the form of a language (the grammar and vocabulary) does not necessarily imply that we know the meaning. This noncorrespondence between form and meaning is called *skewing*. Skewing may be due to the influence of the social context, but it is more often due to the conventions and constraints of a specific language. For one not skilled in the language, an expression that evidences skewing may appear ambiguous, as total nonsense, or as something quite different from what was intended. Yet the skewing normally does not present a problem for the original audience. This is why we can say one thing and mean something else (and get away with it).

Examples of skewing abound in the New Testament. Among the more obvious types are idioms and figures of speech, where there is little correspondence between form and meaning. The meaning is understood because it is a convention of a particular language. For example, in a West African language the idiom "my sleep lives" means "I am sleepy." In Mark 5:23 Jairus told Jesus that his daughter was "having lastly." The AV correctly interprets the idiom as "at the point of death." Also when Jesus said that Lazarus sleeps, He did not mean that Lazarus went to bed, but that he died (John 11:11). The words and grammar of such expressions cannot be interpreted literally, for they involve a skewing between form and meaning.

Although not commonly recognized, a less obvious type of skewing occurs when one form can express more than one meaning. This may involve lexical items, such as the word λόγος, or grammatical items, such as the genitive case, which can have two dozen different meanings. If the same form can convey a variety of different meanings, then there simply cannot be a one-to-one correspondence between form and meaning. To identify a Greek noun as a genitive does not guarantee that we know what it means. Does ἡ ἀγάπη τοῦ Χριστοῦ in 2 Corinthians 5:14 mean our love for Christ or His love for us? This not only illustrates skewing but also shows that information beyond the lexical and grammatical level is needed before we can make any definite statement regarding the meaning of the expression.

Another type of skewing occurs when one part of speech is used for another. Greek nouns, for example, may be used for verbs. When Paul said in Ephesians 6:19 "that a word might be given to me in the opening of my mouth" (literal Greek), he did not intend for the noun "opening" to be taken as a noun (his oral cavity). He meant for it to be taken as a verb: "that utterance may be given unto me, that I may open my mouth boldly" (AV). The problematic phrase "hearing of faith" (Gal. 3:2) probably has two nouns used as verbs, "they heard and they believed." Also, articles may be used for pronouns, infinitives for nouns, and nouns for adverbs, as when the disciples "feared a fear" (Mark 4:41). They were not afraid of fear, but they feared exceedingly. Even the main verb may be used as an adverb and the participle as the main verb. When Paul said, "I do not stop praying for you," he meant, "I pray for you very often" (Col. 1:9; cf. TEV).

In addition, one sentence type may be used for another. We often use questions in place of commands ("Can you close the door?" means "Shut the door!") or statements in place of commands ("It's rather drafty in here" means "Shut the windows!") In the New Testament, rhetorical questions are often equivalent to statements. For example, "What shall it profit a man if he should gain the whole world and lose his own soul?" (Matt. 16:26) conveys an emphatic negative declaration, "It will surely not be of any lasting benefit if a person gains the whole world and loses his soul."

Surface Structure and Deep Structure

One way of analyzing the skewing in language is to posit a deep structure that corresponds to the intended meaning of an utterance and a surface structure that represents how that meaning is expressed. The *surface structure* pertains to the actual spoken or written symbols of the language; for example, the words and sentences you see when you pick up a piece of paper with writing on it or the words you hear as people speak. There is a definite structure to the words and sentences we use. The discipline that studies the surface structure of a language is called *grammar* (which includes morphology and syntax). The term *deep structure* refers in general to that which underlies the surface structure. Some recognize only one level of deep structure and equate it to meaning. Others see two (or more) levels of deep structure, equating only the deepest level with the full meaning of the communication act.

We will recognize two deep structures. First, the conceptual deep structure refers to the total meaning of the communication act. The speaker chooses to utter part of this meaning through the linguistic deep structure to the surface structure; the rest is left unsaid, expecting the audience to draw the proper inference in light of the context. The conceptual deep structure is universal to everyone in the world. It is only as these thought patterns are expressed in the conventions of a specific language that they appear different. Second, the linguistic deep structure is formed with the basic word order of the speaker's language in very simple patterns. This simple structure then is transformed into the complexities of the surface structure.

We should note that the skewing between surface structure and the linguistic deep structure is rarely a total skewing. Some correspondence usually remains between deep structure and surface structure as the meaning is expressed. This even pertains to idioms. The surface structure provides clues about what the speaker meant. The interpretative process that we must undertake is similar to that of the audience. The probable meaning is arrived at as the idioms and figures of speech are unraveled, the implicit information is supplied, the peculiarities of the specific language are decoded, and the contextual inferences are drawn. Then all this information is pieced back together into a unified, related whole. The main complication in the process is that no two people share the exact same pool of experiences and knowledge. The further removed the audience is from the time and place of composition, the greater the difficulty in interpreting meaning. This gap is a special problem in biblical interpretation.

Semantics and Pragmatics

Semantics is the study of language meaning. Philosophers study semantics because they need to ascertain the meaning of words in the premises of logical arguments. Linguists also study semantics. In the past they too have focused on restricted segments of language, as for example with lexical semantics, which is the study of the relationship between individual words and what they represent. Contemporary semantics, however, is becoming more concerned with the total meaning of communication in everyday situations.

The meaning of an utterance cannot be determined merely by adding up the supposed meaning of individual words and pieces of grammar. Meaning can only be determined by viewing the communication act as a whole. Each part contributes information to the whole, while at the same time being modified by the presence of other parts. Thus semantics must be concerned with a wide range of interacting linguistic and extralinguistic data.

For example, the way something is said affects the meaning, as when emphasis is added. Compare "*John* bought a book" and "John bought a *book*." The former clarifies that it was John (not Mary), and the latter clarifies that it was a book (not a magazine). Voice inflection can be reflected somewhat in written Greek by fronting elements before the verb. The way words are arranged (syntax) also affects the meaning. Compare "*Only John* bought the cookies," "John *only bought* the cookies," and "John bought the *only cookies*." In addition, the situational context of the words affects the meaning. For example, the sentence "It is hot" means something entirely different if it were uttered by a person traveling across the Sahara desert, by a thief who just stole a car, or by a mother warning her child not to touch the pan on the stove. The latter would be a statement being used for an imperative,

"Do not touch the stove." This leads to another aspect of semantics: the way a speaker uses the words has a bearing on the meaning. For example, a wife might say to her husband "The car is dirty." If the husband simply nods his head in agreement and continues to read the sports page, he will probably exasperate his wife. She meant her statement to be taken as a command: "Please wash the car."

Some distinguish between semantics (what the words and grammar mean) and pragmatics (what the speaker meant by them). If meaning is based on authorial intent, however, then it cannot be divorced from how the speaker used the language. That is, semantics includes pragmatics. *Pragmatics* generally refers to how extralinguistic elements (including speaker's intent) influence meaning.

This brief overview of the role of language in the exegetical process is intended to lay a foundation for meaningful Greek study. We must study the New Testament documents as a communication, and any communication involves the interplay of a variety of interconnected components. Studying grammar (morphology and syntax) in isolation as a system unto itself is of dubious exegetical value.

Nominative, Vocative, and Accusative

The case suffixes on nouns, pronouns, adjectives, articles, and participles help to indicate the relation of that particular word to the rest of the sentence. In English this is accomplished by word order and prepositions. For example, in the sentence "The man is writing a letter to his servant," we know that "man" is the subject and "letter" is the direct object because of their placement before and after the verb, respectively. We also can determine that "servant" is the indirect object partly because it is preceded by the preposition "to." In Greek, however, these relations are signaled by case markers: γράφει ὁ ἄνθρωπος ἐπιστολὴν δούλῳ αὐτοῦ. In this sentence, the nominative case ἄνθρωπος indicates subject, the accusative case ἐπιστολήν indicates direct object, and the dative case δούλῳ indicates indirect object. Translation into English will require a change in word order and often the addition of prepositions.

There are five different case forms in koine Greek: nominative, genitive, dative, accusative, and vocative. These five case forms are often said to express eight distinct ideas. Some, therefore, hold to a five-case system (based on form) and others to an eight-case system (based on function).

Five-Case System (Form)	Eight-Case System (Function)
1. Nominative	1. Nominative (Designation)
2. Genitive	2. Genitive (Description)
	3. Ablative (Separation)
3. Dative	4. Dative (Interest)
	5. Locative (Location)
	6. Instrumental (Means)
4. Accusative	7. Accusative (Extension)
5. Vocative	8. Vocative (Address)

9

Advocates of the historical school of linguistics contend for the eight-case system because originally there were eight distinct case forms in the Indo-European language group, each expressing a different idea (cf. Robertson 1934:446–49). It is argued that case is determined by function, not by form. The historical school of linguistics, however, falls prey to the fallacy of the prescriptive view of language; this teaches that a prior notion establishes the correctness of grammar. The eight cases of the historical school fit neither the form nor the usage of koine Greek. Koine Greek displays only five forms and dozens of functions. The current trend, following the descriptive school of linguistics, maintains that usage is the sole plausible guide. Thus the five-case system is preferable because it is based on the five existing case forms in koine Greek. Formal distinctions between certain cases had long since eroded away by the time of the Hellenistic period, with their case functions being taken over by other case forms (e.g., the dative taking over the functions of the instrumental and locative). The same is true in English. At one time English had six case forms, but most modern linguists do not recognize six cases today; they only recognize the three that correspond to the inflected forms of certain pronouns: I (subjective), my (possessive), and me (objective).

It seems best therefore to view case as a category in the inflection of nominals; case along with word order, prepositions, and context help establish the relation of that nominal to the rest of the sentence. The word *nominal* refers to a word or word group that functions as a noun. We should be cautious about generalizing the form/function categories in the above chart. The idea that a certain form must convey a certain function is often misleading. For example, the attempt to force certain nominals with a genitive form into either a descriptive or separation mold could easily result in misinterpretation. The actual usage of nominals far exceeds the five or eight general categories. The following discussions are based on the five inflectional forms existing in koine Greek.

Nominative Case

Subject Nominative

When the verb is in the third person, the subject is often designated by a noun or other construction in the nominative case. The term *subject* is difficult to define. It could be defined as the noun phrase that functions as one of the two main parts of a sentence about which something is said in the predicate. In other words, it is the topic of the sentence. The subject is not always the agent that produces the action of the verb (e.g., passive constructions).

A subject noun phrase can be constructed in various ways using the nominative case: for example, (1) with a noun, with or without an article, as in Mark 1:13 οἱ ἄγγελοι διηκόνουν αὐτῷ (the angels were ministering to him); (2) with an adjective, with or without an article, as in Matthew 11:5 τυφλοὶ ἀναβλέπουσιν (blind people receive their sight); (3) with a participle, usually with the article, as in John 3:36 ὁ πιστεύων εἰς τὸν υἱὸν ἔχει ζωὴν αἰώνιον (The one believing in the Son has eternal life); (4) with an article and δέ, as in Matthew 16:14 οἱ δὲ εἶπαν (and they said); (5) with an article and a prepositional phrase, as in Matthew 24:16 οἱ ἐν τῇ Ἰουδαίᾳ φευγέτωσαν εἰς τὰ ὄρη (let the ones in Judea flee to the mountains); or (6) with a relative clause, as in Matthew 10:38 ὃς οὐ λαμβάνει τὸν σταυρὸν αὐτοῦ καὶ ἀκολουθεῖ ὀπίσω μου, οὐκ ἔστιν μου ἄξιος (The one who does not take his cross and follow after me is not worthy of me).

A subject noun phrase can also be constructed with forms not in the nominative case, such as with an articular infinitive (Rom. 7:18), with a ἵνα clause (Matt. 10:25), or with a ὅτι clause (Mark 4:38).

Predicate Nominative

The nominative case noun that functions as the complement of a copulative verb is called a *predicate nominative*. The predicate nominative will either identify (John is the president) or qualify (John is a president). It should be distinguished from a predicate adjective (The ball is red), which employs an adjective in the predicate instead of a noun. The verb is usually a form of εἰμί, as in 1 John 4:8 ὁ θεὸς ἀγάπη ἐστίν (God is love); sometimes γίνομαι, as in John 1:14 ὁ λόγος σὰρξ ἐγένετο (the word became flesh); and occasionally ὑπάρχω, as in Luke 8:41 οὗτος ἄρχων τῆς συναγωγῆς ὑπῆρχεν (This one was a ruler of the synagogue). There are two nominatives in each of these sentences: a subject nominative and a predicate nominative. In general, when there are two nominative case nouns, the articular noun is the subject (this will be further developed in chapter 4). The predicate nominative can be formed with other types of noun phrases, such as

ὁ θεὸς ἐστίν ἀγάπη

with a participle, as in Matthew 13:20 οὗτός ἐστιν ὁ τὸν λόγον ἀκούων (This is the one hearing the word).

Nominative of Apposition

Apposition occurs when one nominal is followed by another that explains or identifies the first one by giving more specific information. The two nominals are usually of the same case, whether nominative, genitive, dative, or accusative. An example of a nominative of apposition is Mark 2:7 τίς δύναται ἀφιέναι ἁμαρτίας εἰ μὴ εἷς ὁ θεός (Who is able to forgive sins except one, namely, God?). The word εἷς (one) is in the nominative case and is followed by ὁ θεός, a nominative of apposition. In Romans 1:1 Παῦλος δοῦλος Χριστοῦ Ἰησοῦ (Paul, a servant of Christ Jesus) the nominative δοῦλος is in apposition to Παῦλος. Occasionally a nominative case nominal may be in apposition to a noun in an oblique case (Rev. 1:5; 2:20; 3:12; 20:2; some of these could be interpreted as nominatives of appellation).

Nominative of Address

About sixty times in the New Testament a nominative case noun is used to designate the person being addressed. The nominative functions like a vocative: Luke 8:54 Ἡ παῖς, ἔγειρε (Child, arise) and Ephesians 5:25 Οἱ ἄνδρες, ἀγαπᾶτε τὰς γυναῖκας (Husbands, love your wives). The nominative and vocative forms of παῖς and ἄνδρες are the same. Here they must be nominatives, since vocatives do not take articles. The nominative of address is usually preceded by an article (exceptions include Matt. 9:27; 15:22; John 12:15).

The nominative ὁ θεός in Hebrews 1:8 has been interpreted several ways. Most interpret it as a nominative of address: ὁ θρόνος σου ὁ θεὸς εἰς τὸν αἰῶνα τοῦ αἰῶνος (Your throne, O God, is for ever and ever). This interpretation attributes deity to the Son. Westcott (1974:25–26) argues that it is a subject nominative (God is your throne) on the basis of the sense of Psalm 45:6 in which it would be "scarcely possible" that the king of Judah should be addressed as God. The meaning would be that his kingdom is founded upon God (cf. Goodspeed, Moffatt, NWT, NRSV margin). A third option, which Turner (1963:34; 1965:15) suggests is only remotely possible, is for ὁ θεός to be a predicate nominative (Your throne is God). Although all three are grammatically possible, only the first is contextually plausible because it harmonizes with the theme of the section (i.e., the exalted Christ).

Nominative of Appellation

When a proper name or title is mentioned, it is sometimes placed in the nominative case instead of the case expected by the construction (as in Matt. 1:21). This usually occurs after verbs of naming and calling, such as the passive voice of λέγω and καλέω: Luke 2:21 ἐκλήθη τὸ ὄνομα αὐτοῦ Ἰησοῦς (His name was called Jesus). Ἰησοῦς is in the nominative case rather than accusative as one might expect. Some examples cited in grammars could be construed as apposition or predicate nominatives. For example, Ἰωάννης in John 1:6 could be taken as a predicate nominative after an understood ἦν· ὄνομα αὐτῷ Ἰωάννης (his name was John).

Perhaps this use of the nominative case resolves the problem in Revelation 1:4 where a nominative follows the preposition ἀπό: χάρις ὑμῖν καὶ εἰρήνη ἀπὸ ὁ ὢν καὶ ὁ ἦν καὶ ὁ ἐρχόμενος (Grace to you and peace from the one who is and the one who was and the one who is coming). Turner (1963:230) suggests that the divine name ὁ ὢν καὶ ὁ ἦν καὶ ὁ ἐρχόμενος "may have been regarded as indeclinable in Greek" (cf. Rev. 1:8; 4:8; 11:17; 16:5). Moffatt (1974:337) concurs, saying it was done "to preserve the immutability and absoluteness of the divine name from declension." Charles (1920:10) calls John's use of the nominative in Revelation 1:4 a deliberate violation of the rules of grammar. Yet it can only be a violation if grammar is viewed prescriptively. With a descriptive view of grammar, it merely illustrates the range of expression that koine Greek tolerates. Thus John's use of the nominative is not a mistake in grammar.

Names in the ancient world often coalesced with the bearer of that name; the person was what the name designated. It is conceivable then that on occasion the passive "was named" or "was called" approaches the meaning "to be" (BAG 1957:400) and could be so translated. For example Luke 15:19, 21 οὐκέτι εἰμὶ ἄξιος κληθῆναι υἱός σου (I am no longer worthy to be your son) (cf. Matt. 2:23; 5:9; 1 Cor. 15:9; 1 John 3:1.) For a parallel between "shall be" and "shall be called" see Luke 1:32. Perhaps this could partly explain the use of nominatives in such constructions.

Nominative Absolute

The designation *nominative absolute* refers to nominative constructions that show no grammatical relationship to other elements in the sentence. This function is also called *independent nominative*. The nominative absolute appears in various situations.

Exclamations—Exclamatory interjections function to call attention to something or to express one's emotions. Exclamations can be formed by using the nominative case, as in Mark 3:34 Ἴδε ἡ μήτηρ μου καὶ οἱ ἀδελφοί μου (Behold! My mother and brothers). The nouns μήτηρ and ἀδελφοί are in the nominative case, not the accusative. Therefore they cannot be the objects of a command to look (cf. John 1:29; 19:5, 27; Rom. 7:24; 11:33).

Titles of books—Nominative case nouns without predicates are used to designate the titles of books: Ἡ Καινὴ Διαθήκη (The New Testament). One example is Mark 1:1 Ἀρχὴ τοῦ εὐαγγελίου Ἰησοῦ Χριστοῦ υἱοῦ θεοῦ (The Beginning of the Gospel of Jesus Christ, God's Son). Cranfield (1959:34–35) lists ten interpretations of this verse and its relation to what follows. He takes the verse as a short title for the contents of 1:2–13. Most, however, understand it as the title of the whole book. Taylor (1952:152) notes that the words "point far beyond the story of the Fore-runner and admirably sum up the substance of the Gospel." Since it is a title, a full stop (period) should be placed at the end of the verse and no verb inserted. Another example is Revelation 1:1.

Salutations of letters—Colossians 1:1–2 Παῦλος ἀπόστολος Χριστοῦ Ἰησοῦ . . . χάρις ὑμῖν καὶ εἰρήνη ἀπὸ θεοῦ πατρὸς ἡμῶν (Paul an apostle of Christ Jesus . . . grace and peace to you from God our Father). Both Παῦλος and χάρις καὶ εἰρήνη are in the nominative case without predicates. To render this ancient formula for opening salutations more readable in English, it is plausible to insert "from" before Paul's name (showing its parallelism with the "to"). However, inserting a verb, such as "writes" or "sends" is just as unnecessary as inserting a verb on the mailing label of a package. The same is not true of the nominatives χάρις καὶ εἰρήνη. Since they are part of an invocation for divine blessing, they could be considered subjects of an implicit verb, such as the optative of εἰμί (May grace and peace be to you), or perhaps as objects (May God grant you grace and peace).

Cleft construction—A cleft construction is a focusing device that high-lights information at the beginning of a sentence that is repeated later in the same sentence. The nominative case is used for this emphasized information regardless of the case of its referent in the sentence: Revelation 3:21 (The one who conquers, I will give him the right to sit with me; cf. Matt. 10:22; Acts 7:40; 1 John 2:24). It would dissipate the rhetorical value of the construction to view these nominatives as being in apposition to other elements and thus merely explaining them. This construction is usually called hanging nominative or pendent nominative *(nominativus pendens)*.

Proverbial sayings—Verbs are sometimes omitted in proverbial expressions, leaving an unattached nominative (An eye for an eye, a tooth for a tooth). Many proverbs are specific to a certain culture and may require the insertion of a verb to make sense in English. Thus it is proper to transform the first participle in 2 Peter 2:22 into the verb of the first stanza and insert a verb for the second stanza, "A dog returns to its vomit, and a pig that is washed goes back to wallow in the mud." The nominatives κύων (dog) and ὗς (pig) become subjects of the inserted verbs. Also the expression ὁ δρασσόμενος in 1 Corinthians 3:19 becomes "He catches . . . " rather than "The one who catches. . . ."

Adverbial Nominative

Occasionally a nominative noun functions adverbially. In Mark 6:39 Jesus commands the people to sit down "in groups" (συμπόσια συμπόσια). The words should be considered nominative rather than accusative because of the πρασιαὶ πρασιαί that follows. In Matthew 15:32 and Mark 8:2 Jesus had compassion because the people had remained with Him "for three days" (ἡμέραι τρεῖς). Turner (1963:231) suggests that those expressions involving time may be due to an ellipse of a verb (and it was three days; cf. Luke 9:28).

Vocative Case

The only syntactical function of the vocative is direct address. The noun in the vocative case names the person or thing being addressed, either by personal name, title, or descriptive phrase. Matthew 27:46 θεέ μου θεέ μου, ἱνατί με ἐγκατέλιπες (My God, my God, why have you forsaken me?).

Mark, however, translates the Aramaic using the nominative of address: Mark 15:34 ὁ θεός μου ὁ θεός μου, εἰς τί ἐγκατέλιπές με.

Semantically, the vocative conveys various nuances. It can show the speaker's attitude toward the person(s) spoken to. For example, it can show respect, "I am not mad, most excellent Festus" (Acts 26:25); strong displeasure, "God said to him, 'Fool! Tonight your soul will be demanded from you'" (Luke 12:20); affection, "My little children, these things I write to you" (1 John 2:1); or gentleness, "Daughter, take heart" (Matt. 9:22). The latter could be understood as "He gently spoke to her. . . ." The vocative can also highlight certain qualities of the person or group being addressed which are transformed from a deep structure clause into the vocative. For example, "O you of little faith" (Matt. 6:30) expresses the deep structure clause, "You have little faith" (cf. TEV). For further discussion, see Barnwell (1974:9–17).

The interjection ὦ occurs seventeen times with the vocative, primarily in Luke and Paul's writings. Sometimes in Acts ὦ with the vocative may be regarded as a classical formality and omitted in the translation: Acts 1:1 ὦ Θεόφιλε (O Theophilus; cf. Acts 18:14; 27:21). More often, however, it conveys emphasis or emotion: Mark 9:19 Ὦ γενεὰ ἄπιστος (O faithless generation). Jesus here expresses sadness at the people's lack of faith. Because ὦ with the vocative is the exception in koine Greek, but was the norm in classical, Zerwick (1963:11–12) suggests that there is usually a reason for it, such as to express deep emotion on the part of the speaker. Thus it casts "light on the state of mind of Our Lord and of His apostles" (cf. BDF 1961:81).

Accusative Case

Accusative of Direct Object

A direct object is a noun (or noun phrase) denoting the person or thing that receives the action of an active transitive verb, participle, or infinitive. A transitive verb is one that takes an object; intransitive verbs do not. For most verbs, the direct object is in the accusative case: Mark 1:31 ἤγειρεν αὐτήν (He raised her). Other verbs will take objects in other cases. In John 10:27 there are three verbs, each taking a direct object in different cases: τὰ πρόβατα τὰ ἐμὰ τῆς φωνῆς μου ἀκούουσιν, κἀγὼ γινώσκω αὐτὰ καὶ ἀκολουθοῦσίν μοι (My sheep hear my voice, and I know them, and they follow me).

Double Accusative

Certain verbs take two accusative objects to complete the thought of the verb. Verbs that fall into this category include: (1) verbs of speaking, such as διδάσκω (John 14:26), ἐρωτάω (Mark 4:10), αἰτέω (Mark 6:22), and ἀναμιμνῄσκω (1 Cor. 4:17); (2) verbs of dressing, such as ἐνδύω (Matt. 27:31), περιβάλλω (John 19:2), and ἐκδύω (Matt. 27:31); (3) verbs of naming, such as ὀνομάζω (Luke 6:14), καλέω (Matt. 22:43), and λέγω (Mark 10:18); (4) verbs of giving, such as ποτίζω (1 Cor. 3:2), and φορτίζω (Luke 11:46, also cognate); (5) verbs of thinking, such as ἡγέομαι (Phil. 3:7); (6) verbs of sending and presenting, such as ἀποστέλλω (1 John 4:14), and παρίστημι (Acts 1:3); and (7) verbs of making and appointing, such as ποιέω (Matt. 4:19), καθίστημι (Acts 7:10), τίθημι (Heb. 1:2), and ἔχω (Acts 13:5). The double accusatives of these verbs fall into two subcategories.

Personal and impersonal objects—Mark 6:34 ἤρξατο διδάσκειν αὐτοὺς πολλά (He began to teach them many things). Both αὐτούς and πολλά are accusative case direct objects. They are sometimes called "accusative of person" and "accusative of thing" (cf. Heb. 5:12).

Direct and predicate objects—Luke 19:46 ὑμεῖς δὲ αὐτὸν ἐποιήσατε σπήλαιον λῃστῶν (But you have made it [to be] a den of thieves). The second accusative σπήλαιον is considered a predicate accusative or object complement after an understood copulative verb (cf. John 15:15; Rom. 4:17; Jas. 5:10).

Cognate Accusative

A cognate accusative is an accusative noun that has the same stem as the verb, as reflected in the English translation of 2 Timothy 4:7 (I have *fought* the good *fight*). It can be the direct object, an accusative of manner, an accusative of oath, or part of a double accusative. An example of a cognate direct object is Matthew 6:19: Μὴ θησαυρίζετε ὑμῖν θησαυροὺς ἐπὶ τῆς γῆς (Do not treasure up for yourselves earthly treasures).

An example of a cognate accusative of manner is Matthew 2:10 ἐχάρησαν χαρὰν μεγάλην σφόδρα (They rejoiced exceedingly). Χαράν cannot be considered a direct object because χαίρω is intransitive. The χαράν expresses how they rejoiced (i.e., joyfully), with μεγάλην and σφόδρα intensifying the adverbial idea. Williams translates the expression,

"They were thrilled with ecstatic joy." The φόβον in Mark 4:41 is also a cognate accusative of manner: ἐφοβήθησαν φόβον μέγαν. It is not that they feared a great fear, as if φόβον were the object, but they feared with awe and terror at the possibility of a divine visitation. It could be rendered "They were terrified." The cognate accusative is sometimes said to convey emphasis, but perhaps any emphasis comes from adjacent words, as in the above examples. Often there is no emphasis (see Mark 2:4; Luke 2:8; 1 Pet. 5:2; 1 John 5:16).

Cognate accusatives can also be constructed with synonymous expressions rather than with identical stems (e.g., 1 Pet. 3:6). This is also observed with the cognate accusative of oath (e.g., Luke 1:73; Jas. 5:12).

Accusative of Oaths

An *accusative of oath* names the person or thing that guarantees an oath or vow. When objects are used they are normally substitutes for personal beings. The verb will convey the idea of swearing or taking an oath. The word "by" is commonly inserted in the English translation. Mark 5:7 ὁρκίζω σε τὸν θεόν (I adjure you by God) and James 5:12 μὴ ὀμνύετε μήτε τὸν οὐρανὸν μήτε τὴν γῆν μήτε ἄλλον τινὰ ὅρκον (Do not swear, neither by heaven nor by earth nor by any other oath) (cf. Acts 19:13).

Accusative Subject of Infinitive

The accusative noun or pronoun that functions semantically as the subject of an infinitive is usually called an *accusative of general reference*. It is so called because grammatically it is not a subject. However, it is a subject of the deep structure kernel clause. Semantically then there is nothing amiss in calling it a subject. In Mark 1:14 Μετὰ δὲ τὸ παραδοθῆναι τὸν Ἰωάννην (After John was arrested) the accusative noun phrase τὸν Ἰωάννην is the subject of the infinitive παραδοθῆναι.

Problems sometimes arise when the infinitive also takes an accusative object: Philippians 1:7 διὰ τὸ ἔχειν με ἐν τῇ καρδίᾳ ὑμᾶς. This could be rendered two ways: "Because I have you in my heart" or "Because you have me in your heart," depending on whether the subject of the infinitive is με or ὑμᾶς. Those who contend for the first option (Vincent 1979:9; Lightfoot [1913] 1953:84; cf. AV, NIV, REB) appeal to the context (v. 8) and Greek word order (the subject generally comes before the object in Greek). Those who favor the second option (Hawthorne 1983:22–23; cf. NEB) also appeal to the context (vv. 6–7) but dismiss Greek word order because of its irregularities. It would be somewhat odd for Paul's confidence in them to be based on his affection for them. Thus it might seem that the second option is preferable.

However, when an infinitive takes both an accusative subject and object, the subject normally precedes the object (Moeller and Kramer 1962:25–35). It is only when the author wants to emphasize or focus on the object that it is moved before the subject (Reed 1991:1–27). The object-subject order is to be considered as a marked order; for example, an intentional variation in word order that conveys additional meaning, such as emphasis or topicality. Examples of the marked order include Matthew 16:15 and John 1:48. Over ninety percent of the cases, however, demonstrate the unmarked order of subject-object. A clear example is 1 Corinthians 7:10–11 παραγγέλλω . . . ἄνδρα γυναῖκα μὴ ἀφιέναι (I command that a husband not divorce his wife). The previous verse spoke of the other option, that of the wife leaving her husband.

Adverbial Accusatives

Manner—An adverbial accusative of manner modifies a verb by telling how something is done. Often the adverbial accusative is translated with an adverbial prepositional phrase, as in Revelation 16:9 ἐκαυματίσθησαν οἱ ἄνθρωποι καῦμα μέγα (Men were burned with a great fire). In Mark 5:23 an accusative adjective is used adverbially: παρακαλεῖ αὐτὸν πολλά (He earnestly beseeched him). The accusative πολλά is translated as the simple adverb "earnestly." Jairus did not ask the Lord many things, as if πολλά were the object. Only one thing was on his mind—his dying daughter, for whom he earnestly beseeched the Lord. Other accusative adjectives that function adverbially include μόνον (Mark 5:36) and πρῶτον (Matt. 6:33).

A special type of manner involves comparisons using the accusative of τρόπος (way, manner), as in Matthew 23:37 (I have longed to gather your children like a hen gathers her brood) and 2 Timothy 3:8 (just as Jannes and Jambres), or τὸ δὲ αὐτό, as in Matthew 27:44 (in the same way the robbers who were crucified with him mocked him) and Philippians 2:18 (You too should rejoice in the same way). These comparisons should be considered manner, since they answer the question "How?"

Perhaps the most perplexing accusative of manner is found in Jude 7 τὸν ὅμοιον τρόπον τούτοις (in like manner to these). The problem is identifying the two things being compared. Some say the similarity is the sexual perversion of the angels and Sodomites. Just as the angels desired sexual relations with women (Gen. 6:1–4), the Sodomites desired sexual relations with angels (Gen. 19:4–11; Bauckham 1983:54). Others say the similarity is the Sodomites being set forth as examples of divine retribution along with the others. The unbelieving Israelites, the angels, and the inhabitants of Sodom and Gomorrah all illustrate that apostates face eternal punishment (Lenski 1966:622–23). The third view is that the similarity could be the common sin of Sodom and Gomorrah and the surrounding cities. For other examples of accusative of manner see Mark 5:26, 43, 6:23, 9:26, 12:27, Luke 11:41, and 16:19.

Reference—An adverbial accusative of reference limits a verb or adjective to a particular frame of reference. In Hebrews 2:17 Christ was made like his brothers that he might become a merciful and faithful high priest *in reference to the things which pertain to God* (τὰ πρὸς τὸν θεόν). Other examples include John 6:10, where about five thousand *in number* (τὸν ἀριθμόν) sat down; 1 Corinthians 9:25, where Paul said that everyone who competes exercises control *in all things* (πάντα); and Ephesians 4:15, where Paul exhorted the Ephesians to grow up *in reference to all things* (τὰ πάντα) (cf. Rom. 12:18).

Perhaps Paul's use of λοιπόν could be an accusative of reference when it introduces his closing remarks "as far as the rest is concerned" (Phil. 4:8). Sometimes, however, it appears as a transitional connective (e.g., Phil. 3:1) or a temporal adverb (e.g., 1 Cor. 7:29) rather than as a concluding epistolary formula (cf. Moule 1968:161–62; O'Brien 1991:348; Thrall 1962:25–30). For the problematic λοιπόν in Mark 14:41, see Turner (1963:336).

Space—An adverbial accusative of space indicates the spacial extension of the verbal action. Luke 2:44 ἦλθον ἡμέρας ὁδόν (They went a day's journey [about 20–25 miles]) (cf. Luke 22:41; John 6:19; Acts 22:21).

Time—Adverbial accusatives of time usually indicate the duration of the verbal action but may also express other temporal relations:

(1) The duration of the verbal idea: Mark 1:13 ἦν ἐν τῇ ἐρήμῳ τεσσεράκοντα ἡμέρας πειραζόμενος (He was tempted in the desert for forty days) (cf. Matt. 20:6; John 1:39; 2:12; Heb. 3:9–10).

(2) The point of time in which the action takes place. In John 4:52 when the nobleman asked his servants the time when his son began improving, they replied Ἐχθὲς ὥραν ἑβδόμην (Yesterday, at the seventh hour). In Acts 20:16 Paul desired to be in Jerusalem τὴν ἡμέραν τῆς πεντηκοστῆς (by the day of Pentecost; cf. Rev. 3:3).

(3) The time from which the action takes place. In response to the question "Who are you?" Jesus responds in John 8:25, Τὴν ἀρχὴν ὅ τι καὶ λαλῶ ὑμῖν (That which I have been telling you from the beginning). Another way in which the accusative of time "from which" is expressed is with λοιπόν (with or without the article; cf. 1 Cor. 7:29 [from now on]; 2 Tim. 4:8 [henceforth]; Heb. 10:13 [since that time]).

(4) The distribution of the action over various segments of time: Luke 21:37 Ἦν δὲ τὰς ἡμέρας ἐν τῷ ἱερῷ διδάσκων, τὰς δὲ νύκτας ἐξερχόμενος ηὐλίζετο εἰς τὸ ὄρος (Every day he was teaching in the temple, but every evening he would go out and lodge on the mountain). In Luke 2:37 the accusative phrase νύκτα καὶ ἡμέραν means that Anna regularly partook of the daily rituals (Fitzmyer 1970:431) rather than praying and fasting continuously day and night. If it is to be considered as durative rather than distributive, then it would be a hyperbole, as our idiom "He played basketball all the time" (cf. Matt. 20:2; Mark 4:27; 1 Cor. 15:30).

Accusative of Apposition

There are two accusatives of apposition in 1 John 2:1 παράκλητον ἔχομεν πρὸς τὸν πατέρα Ἰησοῦν Χριστὸν δίκαιον (we have an advocate with the Father, Jesus Christ the righteous). "Jesus Christ" is in apposition to "advocate," and "righteous" (used as a noun, "the righteous one") is in apposition to "Jesus Christ." Elements in apposition do not have to be adjoining, as illustrated by the first pair (παράκλητον is placed before the verb for emphasis).

Accusative Absolutes

The accusative absolute is a rare and debated category. It is similar in construction to the genitive absolute. The accusative noun or pronoun functions semantically as the subject of an accusative participle to form an adverbial clause. The accusative nominal is not coreferential with any other element in the sentence. The most plausible New Testament example is Acts

26:3 γνώστην ὄντα σε, in which there is a causal force. Paul told Agrippa that he was glad to present his case to him, "because you are especially knowledgeable of Jewish customs." The example sometimes cited in Ephesians 1:17–18 should probably be understood as indirect discourse after an implicit verb of praying. Another possible example is Ephesians 2:1 (ὑμᾶς ὄντας νεκρούς), but this could be interpreted as an anacoluthon that is resumed in 2:4–5 in a slightly different form.

Exercises

Cite the best case function for the following examples and, if appropriate, give alternate possibilities. Translate the passage in such a way as to bring out the force of the function(s) you have chosen.

1.	Matt. 10:8	δωρεάν (both occurrences)
2.	Matt. 26:39	μικρόν
3.	Matt. 28:20	ἡμέρας
4.	Mark 3:12	πολλά
5.	Luke 2:9	φόβον
6.	Luke 12:14	Ἄνθρωπε, με, κριτήν
7.	John 6:71	Ἰούδαν
8.	John 12:16	πρῶτον
9.	John 19:26	Γύναι, υἱός
10.	2 Cor. 1:1–2	Παῦλος, ἀπόστολος, χάρις
11.	2 Cor. 2:13	με, Τίτον
12.	Gal. 4:6	Αββα ὁ πατήρ (two possible options)
13.	1 Thess 5:27	ὑμᾶς, κύριον
14.	1 John 1:10	ψεύστην, αὐτόν
15.	1 John 4:15	Ἰησοῦς, ὁ υἱός
16.	Rev. 3:12	ὁ νικῶν, στῦλον

2 | The Genitive

The genitive case form is often said to display two separate functions: description and separation. In an eight-case system these functions are designated by the terms *genitive* and *ablative*. The semantic functions of nominals with a genitive form, however, cannot all be subsumed under these two categories. This is especially obvious in constructions containing verbal nouns. At the deep structure level they represent a kernel clause containing a subject and verb. For example, when "love" (a verbal noun) is followed by the genitive "of God," the genitive would represent either the subject of the verbal idea (God loves us) or the object (We love God). Such usage conveys neither description nor separation. Thus it seems best to categorize the genitive by its syntactic and semantic functions as evidenced in usage rather than by the form's historical meaning.

Genitives Functioning as Adjectival Phrases

Genitive of Description

The genitive of description is a catch-all category for adjectival genitives that do not easily fit into other categories. All adjectival genitives define, limit, identify, or specify in one way or another. The genitives that are classified as "description" could be analyzed in more detail and placed in newly created categories, but this would only multiply the groups to an unmanageable number.

For example, the genitive in Matthew 24:37 (the days of Noah) does not fit the other adjectival functions (e.g., possession, content). On closer examination, we find that the genitive "of Noah" functions as the subject of an implicit verb "the days in which Noah lived." Because such analysis is not exegetically productive, we will be content with classifying it as description. In John 10:7 the genitive specifies which door is meant ἡ θύρα τῶν προβάτων (the door of the sheep). Further analysis and categorization are again possible (the door through which the sheep enter), but not necessary.

Attributive Genitive

thus the
dfl. act.

The attributive genitive modifies the head noun by naming one of its attributes. It functions as a simple adjective and can be so translated. Thus "their deeds of ungodliness" means "their ungodly deeds" (Jude 15); "the body of sin" means "the sinful body" (Rom. 6:6); and "the riches of glory" means the "glorious riches" (Col. 1:27). The equivalency of the attributive genitive to an adjective is illustrated by comparing the expression "unrighteous mammon" in Luke 16:9 (genitive) with 16:11 (adjective). The attributive genitive is sometimes called *genitive of quality* and is partially due to Hebraic influence (BDF 1961:91).

looks!
possibility
3 possibilities

Luke 18:6 ὁ κριτὴς τῆς ἀδικίας could be interpreted several ways. It is possible to regard κριτής as a verbal noun and to take ἀδικίας as an objective genitive (the one who judges unrighteous acts). Another possibility is to interpret ἀδικίας as a genitive of manner (the one who judges unrighteously). The context, however, clearly supports the attributive idea (the unrighteous judge), for this judge neither feared God nor cared about people; he was an unrighteous person. The genitives "God of peace" (Rom. 15:33; 16:20; Phil. 4:9; 1 Thess. 5:23; Heb. 13:20) and "God of love and peace" (2 Cor. 13:11) seem to imply not only the character of God (His attributes) but also the activity of God (that He is the source and provider of these qualities) (cf. Barrett [1973] 1987:343; O'Brien 1991:512).

The chain of genitives in 2 Corinthians 4:4 τὸν φωτισμὸν τοῦ εὐαγγελίου τῆς δόξης τοῦ Χριστοῦ (the light of the gospel of the glory of Christ) has been interpreted in various ways: "the *glorious light* of the good news of Christ" (Williams), "the light of the *glorious gospel* of Christ" (AV), or "the light that comes from the Good News about the *glorious Christ*" (cf. TEV, Furnish 1984:221–22, Barrett [1973] 1987:131–32). Since the divine glory of Christ is the subject of the following verse, it seems best to interpret τῆς δόξης as an attributive genitive modifying Christ rather than light or gospel and to interpret τοῦ εὐαγγελίου as a genitive of origin. Spiritual illumination comes from the good news about the glorious Christ. Genitive chains sometimes are difficult to interpret. Beekman and Callow (1974:359) suggest that the best way to unravel them is to work backward, determining each relation in reverse order (cf. Rom. 8:21; 2 Cor. 4:6).

Genitive of Possession

The genitive of possession modifies the head noun by identifying the person who owns it: Matthew 26:51 τὴν μάχαιραν αὐτοῦ (his sword). The genitive ὑμῶν in 1 Corinthians 3:21 πάντα ὑμῶν ἐστιν (all things are yours) identifies the owner of πάντα, and the ἡμῶν in Mark 12:7 ἡμῶν ἔσται ἡ κληρονομία (the inheritance shall be ours) identifies the would-be owners of the inheritance. When a genitive relative pronoun functions as a genitive of possession, it is translated "whose" (cf. Mark 1:7; Rom. 9:4). It is best to restrict the idea of ownership to personal property (which in that day included persons) rather than to ideas, names, abstract qualities, or parts of a person.

The genitive in Romans 1:1 could convey either possession or relationship: Παῦλος δοῦλος Χριστοῦ Ἰησοῦ (Paul, a servant of Christ Jesus). The genitive Χριστοῦ Ἰησοῦ could mean that Paul is a bond slave belonging to Christ (genitive of possession) or that Paul has a servant-master relationship with Christ (genitive of relationship). Most favor possession because of the connotations of δοῦλος in the ancient world. Although some (e.g., BW 1979:9) take the genitive in Galatians 5:24 οἱ τοῦ Χριστοῦ as a genitive of relationship (the followers of Christ), most regard it as a genitive of possession (those belonging to Christ) after the analogy of Καίσαρος (belonging to the Emperor) as suggested by Deissmann (1965:377; cf. 1 Cor. 15:23).

Certain types of genitives are mistaken for possession, such as in John 1:19 ἡ μαρτυρία τοῦ Ἰωάννου (the testimony of John). John does not own his testimony in the strict sense of the term. It is best to regard Ἰωάννου as a subjective genitive following the verbal noun μαρτυρία; thus "John testifies" or in context "This is what John testifies."

Genitive of Relationship

The genitive of relationship names a person with whom another person is associated. The association is indicated by a kinship or social role term to which the genitive is adjunctive. The full expression would be after the pattern of "John the son of Zebedee." The genitive (of Zebedee) modifies the kinship term (son) which stands in apposition to the other person (John). Often the kinship or social role term is absent, leaving only an article in the appropriate gender and case.

Kinship—Mark 3:17 Ἰάκωβον τὸν τοῦ Ζεβεδαίου καὶ Ἰωάννην τὸν ἀδελφὸν τοῦ Ἰακώβου (James the son of Zebedee and John the brother of James). The first kinship term (son) is omitted and must be supplied from information elsewhere (e.g., Mark 10:35), whereas the second kinship term ἀδελφόν is present. Both the article and kinship term are absent in Luke 6:15 Ἰάκωβον Ἀλφαίου (James the son of Alphaeus). It is assumed that James is the son of Alphaeus (cf. Mark 3:18, where the articles are present). There is a string of seventy-six genitives of relationship in Luke's genealogy (3:23–38), all omitting the kinship term. See also John 1:12 τέκνα θεοῦ (children of God).

Social—There is a chain of social relationships in 1 Corinthians 1:12 Ἐγὼ μέν εἰμι Παύλου, Ἐγὼ δὲ Ἀπολλῶ, Ἐγὼ δὲ Κηφᾶ, Ἐγὼ δὲ Χριστοῦ (I am the follower of Paul, I am the follower of Apollos, I am the follower of Cephas, I am the follower of Christ). It is obvious that each person represents a group that follows the teachings of its namesake, with the assumption that the teachings differ. The social relation can be expressed in various ways in English, such as "I follow Paul" or "I am with Paul." The genitives could be taken as partitive, meaning that each Corinthian is a member of a particular party. This is conveyed in the NRSV rendering "I belong to Paul," meaning "I belong to the Pauline sect."

Other examples of non-kinship relationships include Matthew 26:51, where Malchus is identified as "the servant of the high priest"; 1 Corinthians 10:20, where idol worshipers are called "partners of demons"; and Philemon 1, where Philemon is identified as "the fellow worker of us." The latter is an example of a mutual role. A genitive of relationship in a slightly altered format occurs in Romans 1:8, where Paul expresses a close personal relationship with God εὐχαριστῶ τῷ θεῷ μου (I give thanks to my God; cf. 2 Cor. 12:21; Phil. 1:3; 4:19; Phlm. 4). In Romans 8:9, Paul says that the one who does not have the Spirit οὐκ ἔστιν αὐτοῦ. This could be either possession (the person does not belong to Christ) or relationship (the person does not have a relationship with Christ).

Genitive of Content

The genitive of content modifies the head noun by denoting its contents. There are two subtypes: spacial content and communicative content.

Spacial content—The genitive of spacial content denotes that which is contained in some type of vessel. For example, to clarify which jar you want passed to you at dinner, you would specify "Please pass the jar of honey." The head noun is usually a container (e.g., a flask, net, basket), and the genitive indicates its contents: Mark 14:13 κεράμιον ὕδατος (a clay jar of water); John 21:8 τὸ δίκτυον τῶν ἰχθύων (the net of fish); and perhaps Mark 5:11 ἀγέλη χοίρων (herd of swine).

The expression "filled with the Spirit" is a figurative way of describing a person in whom the Spirit is permitted to have free control of the thoughts and actions (Luke 1:15, Acts 2:4). The genitive πνεύματος is often interpreted as content. Figurative expressions, however, must be unraveled before the genitive is analyzed. "Filled" is probably a metonymy for "being controlled by." Thus the genitive becomes the agent of the verbal idea (controlled by the Spirit).

Communicative content—The genitive of communicative content denotes that which is contained in some type of discourse (i.e., the topic of a written or verbal communication). Examples include Matthew 13:18 τὴν παραβολὴν τοῦ σπείραντος (the parable which is about the sower); Matthew 24:14 κηρυχθήσεται τοῦτο τὸ εὐαγγέλιον τῆς βασιλείας (this good news which is about the kingdom shall be preached); 1 Corinthians 1:18 Ὁ λόγος ὁ τοῦ σταυροῦ (the message which is about the cross); and Galatians 3:10 ἐν τῷ βιβλίῳ τοῦ νόμου (in the book which contains the law).

The genitive Ἰησοῦ Χριστοῦ in Mark 1:1 Ἀρχὴ τοῦ εὐαγγελίου Ἰησοῦ Χριστοῦ (The beginning of the gospel of Jesus Christ) is normally interpreted as an objective genitive (The beginning of the gospel that *we preach* about Jesus Christ). Problems arise in trying to call it a subjective genitive (The beginning of the gospel *Jesus Christ preaches*), since Mark's Gospel spans the entire ministry of Christ and focuses more on what Christ did rather than on what He preached. Treating εὐαγγελίου as a verbal noun, however, shifts the focus away from the message to the proclamation of the message. Hence it is better classified as a genitive of content (The beginning of the gospel about Jesus Christ).

Genitive of Material

The genitive of material modifies the head noun by identifying the material from which it is made. Thus "the patch of unshrunk cloth" means "the patch made out of unshrunk cloth" (Mark 2:21), and "the ointment of spikenard" means "the ointment made of spikenard" (John 12:3; cf. John 19:39). The genitive σαρκός in Colossians 1:22 ἐν τῷ σώματι τῆς σαρκὸς αὐτοῦ (by the body of his flesh) identifies the substance of which the body was made. Thus Christ was truly incarnate and achieved reconciliation by the death of His physical body. This is a polemical phrase to counter a Docetic understanding of the Person of Christ.

Partitive Genitive

The partitive genitive modifies the head noun by indicating the whole of which it is a part; e.g., "a piece of pie," "one of the group," "a corner of the desk." Perhaps the partitive genitive would be better called "genitive of the whole." It can be categorized into several subtypes:

The part is a personal being(s)—A common type of partitive genitive is where the genitive refers to a group of people of which the head noun (or pronoun) is a member: Mark 2:6 τινες τῶν γραμματέων (certain ones of the scribes).

The part is a bodily member—When the part refers to a bodily member, as in Matthew 5:2 τὸ στόμα αὐτοῦ (his mouth), one might think that the genitive conveys possession. Yet to say the genitive in Matthew 5:2 means that Jesus owns His mouth is a bit odd. It is rather a partitive genitive where the genitive denotes the whole of which the head noun is a part. Mark 1:2 πρὸ προσώπου σου (before your face), however, is best regarded as an idiomatic expression meaning "ahead of you."

The part is geographical—Luke 1:26 πόλιν τῆς Γαλιλαίας (a city of Galilee; i.e., a city which is in Galilee). The genitive Γαλιλαίας is the whole of which πόλιν is a part: Matthew 2:1 Βηθλέεμ τῆς Ἰουδαίας (Bethlehem of Judea; i.e., Bethlehem which is in Judea). Perhaps Matthew 6:5 fits into this category: ἐν ταῖς γωνίαις τῶν πλατειῶν (in the corners of the streets).

The part is a quantity—When the whole is divided quantitatively by such words as "one," "half," "third," or "measure," the genitive is partitive:

Revelation 9:15 τὸ τρίτον τῶν ἀνθρώπων (a third of all humankind). The genitive in Revelation 6:6, "a measure of wheat," could be a partitive genitive or genitive of content.

The part is a quality—When the whole is divided qualitatively into various attributes, the genitive could be considered partitive. The attributes, however, are not strictly parts: Revelation 21:16 τὸ μῆκος καὶ τὸ πλάτος καὶ τὸ ὕψος αὐτῆς ἴσα ἐστίν (the length and breadth and height of it are equal). This may also apply to attributes of persons, as in Romans 2:4 τὸ χρηστὸν τοῦ θεοῦ (the goodness of God; cf. TEV). It cannot be an attributive genitive, since the genitive is not the attribute. Nor can it be possession, since God does not own His goodness; it is part of Him. It could be taken as a subjective genitive, with the adjective χρηστόν being understood in a verbal sense (God does good). It is best, however, to interpret the genitive adjectivally as a partitive genitive, noting that the goodness of God cannot exist without good deeds. Hence it is both that God is good and that God displays His goodness that leads men and women to repentance.

Genitives Functioning in Deep Structure Event Clauses

As noted in the introductory paragraph of this chapter, genitive constructions containing a verbal noun can be considered as the surface manifestation of an underlying kernel clause with a subject and verb. Discerning what should be considered verbal nouns in a particular text is not simple. Nouns with endings that name actions (-σις, -μος) or agents (-της, -τηρ, -τωρ, -ευς) are usually verbal nouns. Those which are built of verb stems (e.g., ἀγάπη, ἀποκάλυψις, ἐλπίς, εὐαγγέλιον, and ὀργή) are often verbal nouns, but in some contexts they may denote an abstraction rather than an event. For example, εὐαγγέλιον is a verbal noun in Romans 16:25 (according to the gospel I preach), but it does not appear to be a verbal noun in Mark 1:1 (the gospel about Jesus Christ). Mark's intent is to explain how the good news about Christ began.

If the noun to which the genitive is joined (e.g., "love" in "the love of God") is a verbal noun, then the genitive functions as a deep structure subject (God loves us), object (we love God), or adverbial modifier (love in a God-like way). If the genitive is the verbal noun, then it functions as the deep structure verb. If both are verbal nouns, then there are two deep structure verbs. These ideas will be developed in the following sections.

Subjective Genitive

In a subjective genitive the genitive represents a deep structure subject, and the verbal noun represents a deep structure verb. For example, "the prayers of me" means "I pray" (Rom. 1:10); "the judgment of God" means "God judges" (Rom. 2:3); "the revelation of Jesus Christ" means "Jesus Christ reveals the gospel" (Gal. 1:12); "the will of God" means "God wills" (Eph. 6:6); "the peace of God" means "God gives peace" (Phil. 4:7); and "the witness of us" means "we bear testimony" (3 John 12).

The construction in 2 Corinthians 5:14 ἡ γὰρ ἀγάπη τοῦ Χριστοῦ συνέχει ἡμᾶς (For the love of Christ controls us) should be interpreted as the love Christ has for us rather than our love for Christ; Christ is the subject of love, not the object. This is discerned from the context that discusses Christ's dying on our behalf (Barrett [1973] 1987:167). Plummer notes that when ἀγάπη is followed either by Christ or God in the Pauline Epistles, it "seems never to be used of man's love to Christ or to God" (Plummer 1915:173; cf. Rom. 5:5; 8:35, 39; 2 Cor. 13:13; 2 Thess. 3:5). Such expressions are frequently objective genitives outside of Paul (Luke 11:42; John 5:42; and perhaps 1 John 2:5; 3:17; 5:3).

Another example of a subjective genitive is Romans 16:25 κατὰ τὸ εὐαγγέλιόν μου (according to the gospel that I preach). The translation "according to my gospel" is somewhat misleading, as if the gospel belonged to Paul or that it was different from what Peter and the other apostles preached. Instead, the genitive μου is the subject of the verbal idea in εὐαγγέλιον (I preach the gospel; cf. Rom. 2:16; 2 Tim. 2:8).

The subjective genitive includes genitives that are joined to passive verbs, passive participles, or verbal adjectives. A verbal adjective is an adjective built with a verb stem and a -τος ending, such as ἀγαπητός (loved), ἐκλεκτός (chosen), and κλητός (called). In Romans 1:7 τοῖς . . . ἀγαπητοῖς θεοῦ (to the ones loved by God) the genitive appears to denote agency. At the deep structure, however, the agent is the subject (to the ones God loves). The same is true for Matthew 25:34 οἱ εὐλογημένοι τοῦ πατρός (the ones the Father blesses). It is conceivable to interpret the genitive in Romans 1:6 κλητοὶ Ἰησοῦ Χριστοῦ as a subjective genitive, "called by Jesus Christ" or "the ones Jesus Christ calls" (Cranfield 1975:67–68). The genitive Ἰησοῦ Χριστοῦ, however, is probably a genitive of possession, "whom God has called to belong to Jesus Christ" (Barrett [1957] 1987:22,

NIV, TEV), with the subject of κλητοί being supplied. It is argued that God is the one who calls people and that the simple genitive often conveys possession.

Objective Genitive

In an objective genitive, the genitive represents a deep structure object and the verbal noun once again represents a deep structure verb. For example, "the blasphemy of the Spirit" means "they blasphemed the Spirit" (Matt. 12:31); "have faith of God" means "believe in God" (Mark 11:22); "the breaking of bread" means "they broke bread" (Acts 2:42); "the knowledge of God" means "you know God" (Col. 1:10); and "the obedience of truth" means "you obey the truth" (1 Pet. 1:22). The subjects of the verbs in these deep structure clauses must be discerned from the context, since they are not usually retained when transformed into the surface structure.

The expression ἡ ἀγάπη τοῦ πατρός (the love of the Father) in 1 John 2:15 could express either the Father's love for us (subjective genitive) or our love for the Father (objective genitive). It appears that John had in mind one's love for the Father because of the parallelism with one's love for the world. The two are mutually exclusive; one cannot love both God and the anti-God world establishment (Marshall 1978a:143–44). Others argue that it is a subjective genitive, while some see both subjective and objective ideas in the passage. Smalley (1984:82–83) says that one's love for the world both inhibits our love for the Father and suggests that the Father's love has not come to fully dwell in us.

There are two objective genitives in Galatians 2:16: οὐ δικαιοῦται ἄνθρωπος ἐξ ἔργων νόμου ἐὰν μὴ διὰ πίστεως Ἰησοῦ Χριστοῦ. Both νόμου and Ἰησοῦ Χριστοῦ are objective genitives following the verbal nouns ἔργων and πίστεως. The kernel clauses would be "A person does the law" and "A person believes in Jesus Christ." In translation we have "a person is not justified by doing what the law requires but by believing in Jesus Christ." Retaining the "of" for the genitive, "by faith of Jesus Christ," gives the impression that a person is justified by the faithfulness of Christ.

Verbal Genitive

When the genitive is a verbal noun, it represents a deep structure verb. The adjoining noun is then either the subject or object (cf. Waterman

1975:289–93). In English translation the deep structure clause could be transformed into a relative clause that modifies the joining noun. Thus verbal genitives function like the genitives of description or attribute and are so classified by some grammars.

One example is Mark 2:26 τοὺς ἄρτους τῆς προθέσεως (the loaves of presentation), which the AV renders "shewbread." The genitive προθέσεως is a verbal noun denoting the action of offering or presenting something to God. Thus the deep structure clause would be "we offer bread to God." The English translation would transform the deep structure clause into a relative clause, "They ate the bread which we offered to God." In the same way "men of good pleasure" means "men with whom God is pleased" (Luke 2:14); "the body of death" means "the body which will die" (Rom. 7:24); "the sons of disobedience" means "the people who disobey God" (Eph. 2:2); "children of wrath" means "those with whom God is angry" (Eph. 2:3); "the day of redemption" means "the day in which God redeems his people" (Eph. 4:30); "the word of hearing" means "the word which they heard" (Heb. 4:2); and "the law of liberty" means "the law which sets people free" (Jas. 2:12).

Compound Verbal Genitive

When a genitive verbal noun is joined to another verbal noun, the construction represents two kernel clauses at the deep structure level. In English translation they may be rendered as two finite verbs linked with "and" or "because." For example, "resurrection of life" means "they will rise and live" (John 5:29) and "hearer of forgetfulness" means "he hears and forgets" (Jas. 1:25).

The problematic construction in Galatians 3:2 ἐξ ἀκοῆς πίστεως (by the hearing of faith) is best understood as forming two propositions which in translation become "by hearing and believing the gospel" (cf. TEV, Barclay, Weymouth). Several other options are also possible. If πίστεως is not a verbal noun, then it could be: (1) an objective genitive, "by hearing the doctrines of the faith"; (2) a subjective genitive, "by the hearing that faith produces" (Lightfoot 1957:135); or (3) manner, "by hearing in a believing way" (cf. RSV, NASB). Another interpretation based on two deep structure clauses is "by believing what you heard" (Longenecker 1990:103, NRSV, NIV). The second clause is transformed into a complement.

Many interpret μετανοίας in Mark 1:4 κηρύσσων βάπτισμα μετανοίας (preaching a baptism of repentance) as a genitive of description. It would then qualify the kind of baptism John was preaching, distinguishing it from other kinds of baptisms of the day, such as Jewish proselyte baptism, the daily washings of the Essenes, and heathen baptisms. This interpretation would attach ethical significance to the baptism. Both βάπτισμα and μετανοίας, however, are verbal nouns and convey two verbal ideas. At the deep structure level there are two kernel clauses: "The people are to repent" and "The people are to be baptized." Thus John preached that people should repent and be baptized (cf. TEV).

Another possible example is Romans 1:5 εἰς ὑπακοὴν πίστεως (unto obedience of faith), where each noun expresses a verbal idea: to obey and to believe. The genitive πίστεως has been interpreted as (1) objective, "obey the faith" (cf. Moffatt); (2) source, "the obedience that comes from faith" (NIV); and (3) apposition, "obedience which consists of faith" (Cranfield 1975:66). The first view is questionable because πίστεως lacks an article. The phrase could be understood to express two verbal ideas: Paul was commissioned to lead men of all nations "to believe and obey" (TEV, REB; cf. Rom. 16:26).

The genitives in 1 Thessalonians 1:3 could be taken in a similar way: "your work of faith, and labor of love, and perseverance of hope." Beekman and Callow (1974:264) suggest the deep structure clauses are "you work because you believe in God, you labor because you love God, and you persevere because you hope for glory" (cf. genitive of reason). Many commentators interpret the genitives as subjective, "the work which faith produces, the labor that love produces, and the perseverance that hope produces."

Genitives Functioning as Adverbial Phrases

Genitive of Time

The genitive of time is a noun (or noun phrase) that modifies a verbal expression by answering the question "When?" It can convey the following different notions of time:

Time during which something happens — Matthew 2:14 παρέλαβεν τὸ παιδίον καὶ τὴν μητέρα αὐτοῦ νυκτὸς καὶ ἀνεχώρησεν εἰς Αἴγυπτον

(He took the child and his mother during the night and fled to Egypt). This notion of time sometimes lends itself to a focus on the "kind of time," as in John 3:2 ἦλθεν πρὸς αὐτὸν νυκτός (He came to him sometime during the night). The broader context implies that Nicodemus came to Jesus at night because the cloak of darkness would conceal him from his peers. The expression could be rendered "He came to Jesus after dark." The same force may be seen in Matthew 24:20 προσεύχεσθε ἵνα μὴ γένηται ἡ φυγὴ ὑμῶν χειμῶνος (pray that you do not have to flee when it is winter).

Time at which something happens—John 11:49 ἀρχιερεὺς ὢν τοῦ ἐνιαυτοῦ ἐκείνου (being high priest that year) and Matthew 25:6 μέσης νυκτὸς κραυγὴ γέγονεν (at midnight a cry was heard). In Jude 6 the expression μεγάλης ἡμέρας (of the great day) is an adverbial genitive of time that modifies the verbal idea in the action noun κρίσιν (judgment). Thus "judgment of the great day" means "God will judge people on that great day" (Beekman and Callow 1974:260). See also Revelation 16:14.

Distributive time—Luke 18:12 νηστεύω δὶς τοῦ σαββάτου (I fast two days each week).

Genitive of Space

The category *space* in the discussions on cases and prepositions (chapters 1–3, 6) refers to both position in space (i.e., in, at, on, under) and extension through space (i.e., toward, from). The first is called *spacial position*, and the second is called *spacial extension*. Spacial extension includes the ideas of "source" and "separation." A genitive noun can modify a verbal expression by answering the questions "Where?", "From where?", and occasionally "To where?" Sometimes the verb is implicit and must be supplied, as with genitives of source and separation.

Locus where—Luke 16:24 ἵνα βάψῃ τὸ ἄκρον τοῦ δακτύλου αὐτοῦ ὕδατος (that he might dip the tip of his finger in water). The genitive ὕδατος modifies the verb by telling where the dipping is to occur (cf. Ἐφέσου and Ἀσίας in Acts 19:26).

Locus to where—Matthew 1:12 Μετὰ τὴν μετοικεσίαν Βαβυλῶνος (after the deportation to Babylon). The genitive Βαβυλῶνος modifies the verbal idea in the noun of action μετοικεσίαν by telling where the Jews were deported. See also τῶν ἁγίων in Hebrews 10:19.

Locus from where—This category includes two subtypes: genitive of separation and genitive of source. Separation is inherent in Mark 2:21 τὸ καινὸν τοῦ παλαιοῦ (the new [is being torn] from the old) and Acts 13:51 οἱ δὲ ἐκτιναξάμενοι τὸν κονιορτὸν τῶν ποδῶν (They shook the dust from their feet). The idea of origin or source is seen in 2 Corinthians 4:7 ἵνα ἡ ὑπερβολὴ τῆς δυνάμεως ᾖ τοῦ θεοῦ καὶ μὴ ἐξ ἡμῶν (that the excellency of the power might be from God and not from us). The genitives θεοῦ and ἡμῶν function adverbially, answering the question "From where?" See also θεοῦ in Romans 1:1.

Romans 1:17 δικαιοσύνη γὰρ θεοῦ ἐν αὐτῷ ἀποκαλύπτεται (for in it the righteousness of God is revealed). The genitive θεοῦ is variously interpreted. Käsemann (1980:24–30) takes it as a subjective genitive, meaning that God exercises righteousness (or covenant faithfulness) in redeeming His people. Murray (1959:30–31) takes it as a genitive of possession, meaning something God has that He gives to those who believe. Cranfield (1975:98) takes it as a genitive of origin, meaning that the state of being righteous comes from God rather than from one's own efforts. The genitive θεοῦ would then function adverbially, modifying an understood verb of motion, "the righteousness that comes from God." The suffix -συνη on δικαιοσύνη, which designates a state or quality, supports the latter two views. The first view is questionable, since one would expect the suffix to be -σις or -μος (indicating a name of an action), if δικαιοσύνη was a verbal noun. The second option is also questionable in that people do not *own* their attributes. The third option seems preferable.

Genitive of Disassociation

The genitive of disassociation is similar to the genitive of separation (a subtype of genitive of space), but there is no spacial dimension or movement involved. For example, Ephesians 2:12 ἀπηλλοτριωμένοι τῆς πολιτείας (alienated from the commonwealth); 1 Timothy 4:1 ἀποστήσονταί τινες τῆς πίστεως (some shall depart from the faith); 1 Timothy 6:5 ἀπεστερημένων τῆς ἀληθείας (deprived of the truth); 1 Peter 2:11 ἀπέχεσθαι τῶν σαρκικῶν ἐπιθυμιῶν (to abstain from fleshly desires); and 1 Peter 4:1 πέπαυται ἁμαρτίας (ceased from sin).

Genitive of Manner

The genitive of manner modifies a verb by answering the question "How?"
John 2:7 Γεμίσατε τὰς ὑδρίας ὕδατος (Fill the jars with water). The genitive ὕδατος modifies the verb γεμίσατε by telling how the water jars are to
be filled (i.e., Filled how? Filled with water; cf. John 6:13).

It is easy to confuse three similar expressions: (a) Give him a glass of water; (b) Fill the glass with water; and (c) The glass is full of water. The
phrase "of water" in (a) functions as an adjectival phrase modifying "glass"
and answers the question "Give him what?" (genitive of content). The
phrase "with water" in (b) is a prepositional phrase that functions as an adverb phrase and answers the question "Fill how?" It modifies the verb "fill"
(genitive of manner). The phrase "of water" in (c) is also a prepositional
phrase that functions as an adverb phrase, but it modifies the adjective "full"
by answering the question "In reference to what?" (genitive of reference).

Genitive of Comparison

The genitive of comparison names that with which something else is compared. It will follow a verb of comparison (e.g., διαφέρω) or a comparative
adjective (e.g., ἰσχυρότερος, κρείττων, μείζων, πλείων) and is translated
with the word "than": Mark 1:7 Ἔρχεται ὁ ἰσχυρότερός μου ὀπίσω μου
(the one who is stronger than I is coming after me). The first μου is the genitive of comparison and is translated "than I." See also Matthew 5:20 and 1
Peter 1:7.

Genitive of Price

The genitive of price specifies the value or price of what is being bought or
sold and in so doing modifies a verb (or adjective) by answering the question "How much?" Verbs include those of buying, such as ἀγοράζω (Mark
6:37; 1 Cor. 6:20; 7:23); acquiring, such as κτάομαι (Acts 22:28); or selling,
such as πωλέω (Matt. 10:29) and πιπράσκω (Matt. 26:9; John 12:5). The
genitives are translated with "for" or "worth": Matthew 10:29 οὐχὶ δύο
στρουθία ἀσσαρίου πωλεῖται (Are not two sparrows sold for a penny?).
Mark 6:37 ἀγοράσωμεν δηναρίων διακοσίων ἄρτους can be variously rendered: "should we buy bread worth two hundred denarii," "should we spend

two hundred denarii on bread," or "should we buy two hundred denarii of bread." For other verbs with the genitive of price, see Matthew 20:13 and Jude 11.

Genitive of Reason

On occasion a genitive noun expresses the unintentional cause or reason why something happened. In Philemon 13 Paul says he was in bonds because of preaching the gospel: ἐν τοῖς δεσμοῖς τοῦ εὐαγγελίου (Vincent 1979:187). The problematic phrase in James 1:17 τροπῆς ἀποσκίασμα is best interpreted as "shadow caused by turning" (cf. Davids 1982:87–88 for various interpretations). Many interpret the genitive in Philemon 1 Παῦλος δέσμιος Χριστοῦ Ἰησοῦ as cause. Paul was a prisoner for the sake of Christ or because of preaching the gospel of Christ (O'Brien 1982:271).

A more complex example is Romans 4:11 τῆς δικαιοσύνης τῆς πίστεως (the righteousness of faith). The two nouns of action may represent two deep structure clauses: "God justified Abraham" and "Abraham believed God." The two kernel clauses are linked by a causal relationship. After the transformations into English we have, "Abraham was made righteous because he believed God."

Genitive of Purpose

The genitive of purpose modifies a verb or the verbal idea in a noun of action by denoting the intent or goal of the action. After the figurative expression is unraveled in Colossians 4:3, the genitive modifies a verb: ἵνα ὁ θεὸς ἀνοίξῃ ἡμῖν θύραν τοῦ λόγου (that God would open to us a door for the word; i.e., that God would provide us opportunity in order that we might preach the gospel). A more involved example with two verbal nouns is 2 Corinthians 1:24 συνεργοί ἐσμεν τῆς χαρᾶς ὑμῶν (literally: We are fellow workers of your joy). There are two clauses at the deep structure: "We work together with you" and "You have joy." The two clauses are linked with a means-purpose relationship (cf. chapter 17). After the transformations into English we have, "We work together with you in order that you might have joy."

Genitive of Means

A genitive noun can modify the verbal idea in a noun of action by denoting means, as in Acts 1:18 "the wages of iniquity." This means "the money Judas received by means of his wicked act."

Genitive of Reference

The genitive of reference is a noun (or noun phrase) that acts as an adverb modifying an adjective, limiting its descriptive force to a particular frame of reference. The translations "with respect to" or "in reference to" bring out this idea. The genitive of reference is common with adjectives conveying (1) fullness, such as μεστός and πλήρης; (2) worthiness or unworthiness, such as ἄξιος and ἔνοχος; or (3) sharing or lacking, such as κοινωνός and μέτοχος. One example is Matthew 3:8 ἄξιον τῆς μετανοίας (worthy of repentance). The construction in Hebrews 3:12 καρδία πονηρὰ ἀπιστίας (an evil heart of unbelief) means a heart that is evil in reference to unbelief rather than to some other kind of sin. A genitive of reference can also modify adverbs, as in Colossians 1:10 περιπατῆσαι ἀξίως τοῦ κυρίου (walk worthily of the Lord). The expression "full of" in Matthew 23:28 ἐστε μεστοὶ ὑποκρίσεως καὶ ἀνομίας (you are full of hypocrisy and iniquity) is a figurative way of saying "very." The scribes and Pharisees were very hypocritical and wicked (Beekman and Callow 1974:254).

Genitives Functioning as Noun Phrases

Genitive Subject

A genitive noun or pronoun in a genitive absolute construction functions semantically as the subject of the verbal idea. The construction is to be translated as an adverbial clause with the participle as the verb and the genitive noun or pronoun as the subject. Mark 5:2 ἐξελθόντος αὐτοῦ ἐκ τοῦ πλοίου (when he came out of the boat). The genitive pronoun αὐτοῦ is the subject of the genitive participle ἐξελθόντος.

Genitive of Apposition

The genitive of apposition explains or identifies the head noun, giving more specific information. The genitive of apposition is unusual in that the head noun does not have to be in the genitive case. Apposition can be made clear in English by using "namely," "that is," or "which is." This is sometimes called the epexegetic genitive.

Adjunctive to a genitive case noun—John 2:21 ἔλεγεν περὶ τοῦ ναοῦ τοῦ σώματος αὐτοῦ (he was speaking concerning the temple, that is, his body).

Adjunctive to a noun in another case—Acts 2:38 λήμψεσθε τὴν δωρεὰν τοῦ ἁγίου πνεύματος (You will receive the gift, namely the Holy Spirit). The gift is the Spirit Himself, the one who administers God's saving grace to the repenting individual. Although outward manifestations may follow, the phrase itself does not refer to a particular gift given by the Holy Spirit (subjective genitive). It is analogous to 2 Corinthians 1:22 and 5:5, where the earnest is the Spirit.

Although the "crown of life" in James 1:12 could be taken as description, it seems best to interpret it as apposition. When a person endures temptation he or she will receive the crown (or reward) which is a joyous, victorious life (cf. Rev. 2:10). Similarly, the "crown of glory" in 1 Peter 5:4 means that the reward is to share Christ's glory. The same is true for "crown of righteousness" (2 Tim. 4:8) and "crown of rejoicing" (1 Thess. 2:19). The laying of the crowns before God's throne (Rev. 4:10) is a literary symbol depicting worship. The worshipers recognize that the rewards were achieved through divine enablement and thus rightfully belong to God.

Most interpret the genitives in Ephesians 2:20 as apposition: τῷ θεμελίῳ τῶν ἀποστόλων καὶ προφητῶν (the foundation of the apostles and prophets). This would mean that the foundation consists of the apostles and prophets, either their office or activity (e.g., Bruce 1984:304). Others attempt to harmonize the passage with 1 Corinthians 3:11 and interpret the genitives as subjective, "the foundation that is laid by the apostles and prophets" (TEV, NEB). However this makes Christ both the foundation and the cornerstone (cf. Eph. 2:20b).

Another problematic verse that is best explained as appositional is Ephesians 4:9 τὰ κατώτερα μέρη τῆς γῆς (the lower parts of the earth). Although some take the genitive γῆς as partitive (referring to Christ's descent into Hades), most take it as appositional (referring to the incarnation).

The contrast seems to be between Christ's ascent to heaven and His descent to earth. Thus the lower regions refers to the earth itself, not to some subterranean cavity (NIV, REB). For discussion, see Lincoln (1990:244–47).

Genitive Direct Object

Certain kinds of verbs take their direct objects in the genitive case. The following list categorizes such verbs and gives examples of each type:

Verbs of ruling or surpassing—Mark 10:42 ἄρχω (I rule); Luke 22:25 κυριεύω (I lord it over); and Matthew 2:22 βασιλεύω (I reign).

Verbs of perception—Although some differentiate between the genitive and accusative objects of ἀκούω, the distinction is not consistently maintained in the New Testament (Moule 1968:36; Zerwick 1963:24). The genitive is said to indicate the kind or source of the sound, and the accusative is said to indicate the intelligibility of the sound. This distinction is used to resolve the problem between Acts 9:7 (those with Paul heard a voice) and 22:9 (those with Paul did not hear a voice). Because of the irregularity in usage, one cannot automatically say that the genitive object in 9:7 means they heard a speaking voice and that the accusative object in 22:9 (along with a negative particle) means they did not understand it. In Acts 22:7 a genitive object is used after ἀκούω, and Paul fully understood what was said. Whether the distinction is valid must be decided on an individual basis and on the sense of the context. It does seem to be valid for Acts 9:7 and 22:9.

Verbs of desiring, lacking, or obtaining—Acts 20:33 and 1 Timothy 3:1 ἐπιθυμέω (I desire) and Hebrews 11:35 τυγχάνω (I attain).

Verbs of remembering or forgetting—John 15:20 μνημονεύω (I remember); Hebrews 6:10 ἐπιλανθάνομαι (I forget); and Luke 24:8 μιμνῄσκομαι (I remind).

Verbs of caring or neglecting—1 Timothy 4:14 ἀμελέω (I neglect) and Matthew 17:17 ἀνέχομαι (I put up with).

Verbs of accusing—Mark 3:2 and 15:4 κατηγορέω (I accuse). The genitive object names the person being charged, and the accusative object names the charge.

Verbs of separation—Luke 2:37 ἀφίστημι (I leave); Luke 22:35 ὑστερέω (I lack); and Romans 8:32 φείδομαι (I spare).

Verbs conveying a partitive idea—Hebrews 2:14 κοινωνέω and μετέχω (I share) and Hebrews 2:9 γεύομαι (I taste).

Verbs of touching—Mark 1:41 ἅπτομαι (I touch). With a genitive object κρατέω means to take hold of part of the body, but with an accusative object it means to seize the entire body or to arrest (Mark 3:21).

Exercises

The interpretation of genitives is not easy, but it is important. Cite the best genitive function and give alternate options where appropriate. Translate the passage in such a way as to bring out the force of the use(s) you have chosen.

1.	Matt. 6:14	αὐτῶν, ὑμῶν
2.	Matt. 11:11	γυναικῶν, Ἰωάννου, βαπτιστοῦ, οὐρανῶν, αὐτοῦ
3.	Matt. 15:26	τέκνων (several options possible)
4.	Mark 9:41	ὕδατος, Χριστοῦ
5.	Mark 14:3	αὐτοῦ, Σίμωνος, λεπροῦ, αὐτοῦ, μύρου, νάρδου, αὐτοῦ, κεφαλῆς
6.	Luke 5:3	πλοίων, Σίμωνος
7.	Luke 6:12	θεοῦ
8.	Luke 17:32	γυναικός
9.	John 7:13	Ἰουδαίων
10.	Acts 1:13	Ἰακώβου
11.	Acts 2:33	πνεύματος
12.	Acts 9:15	ἐκλογῆς
13.	Acts 15:29	εἰδωλοθύτων, αἵματος, πνικτῶν, πορνείας
14.	Rom. 3:22–23	θεοῦ, Ἰησοῦ Χριστοῦ, δόξης, θεοῦ
15.	1 Cor. 1:6	Χριστοῦ
16.	1 Cor. 6:19	ἑαυτῶν
17.	Gal. 5:22	πνεύματος (several options possible); cf. TEV, JB, Williams
18.	Gal. 6:1	πραΰτητος
19.	Col. 3:14	τελειότητος; cf. NIV, TEV.
20.	Titus 2:13	δόξης

3 | The Dative

The dative case form is traditionally perceived as representing three separate functions: interest, location, and means. In an eight-case system these functions are designated by the terms dative, locative, and instrumental, respectively. It is doubtful whether these divisions are exegetically useful to explain the diverse nuances of the dative. As with the genitive, the dative form will be categorized by its syntactic and semantic functions found in the New Testament rather than by what the form historically signified.

Datives Functioning as Noun Phrases

Dative of Indirect Object

An indirect object is a noun or noun phrase that names the person (usually) or thing indirectly affected by the action of the verb. It is common with verbs of giving and speaking and usually occurs along with a direct object. For example, in the sentence "John gave a book to Jane," the direct object is "book" and the indirect object is "Jane." Indirect objects, such as in John 5:27 ἐξουσίαν ἔδωκεν αὐτῷ, may be translated with a simple noun or pronoun (He gave *him* authority) or with a prepositional phrase (He gave authority *to him*). If the simple noun is used, it must conform to English word order (subject, verb, indirect object, direct object). In a passive construction the indirect object receives the subject rather than the direct object: Revelation 13:5 ἐδόθη αὐτῷ ἐξουσία (Authority was given to him). An indirect object can have one of three semantic roles.

Experiencer—The role of experiencer is common with verbs of speaking. The direct object is what is being said (i.e., the complement clause), and the indirect object is the person spoken to: John 1:43 λέγει αὐτῷ ὁ Ἰησοῦς,

Ἀκολούθει μοι (Jesus said to him, "Follow me"). An example with a verb of giving is Matthew 7:6 Μὴ δῶτε τὸ ἅγιον τοῖς κυσίν (Do not give what is holy to the dogs). When the ideas of advantage or disadvantage are not prominent, the semantic role of the indirect object will simply be "experiencer."

Benefaction—This is commonly called dative of advantage *(dativus commodi)*. The dative noun or pronoun identifies the person in whose interest or for whose benefit the action of the verb was performed. The dative of advantage can be expressed in English with the word "for," as in John 16:7 συμφέρει ὑμῖν ἵνα ἐγὼ ἀπέλθω (It is profitable *for you* that I go away). Other examples include Matthew 6:19 (Do not lay up treasures *for yourselves*), Mark 10:51 (What do you wish that I do *for you?*), and Romans 14:7–8 (No one lives or dies *for himself*, but whether we live or die, we do so *for the Lord's sake*).

Opposition—This is commonly called dative of disadvantage *(dativus incommodi)*. The dative noun or pronoun identifies the person adversely affected by the action of the verb. It is often expressed in English with the word "against," as with the ὑμῖν in Luke 10:11 (Even the dust from your town that sticks to our feet we wipe off *against you)*, and the ἑαυτοῖς in Matthew 23:31 (Therefore you are testifying *against yourselves)*.

Dative of Direct Object

Certain kinds of verbs take their direct objects in the dative case. The following list categorizes such verbs and gives examples of each type:

Verbs of worship—Matthew 2:2 and 4:9 προσκυνέω (I worship).

Verbs of service—Matthew 4:11 διακονέω (I serve); Luke 15:29 δουλεύω (I am enslaved to); and Matthew 4:10 λατρεύω (I serve).

Verbs of thanksgiving—Colossians 1:3 εὐχαριστέω (I give thanks).

Verbs of obedience and disobedience—John 3:36 ἀπειθέω (I disobey). Often the ideas of disobedience and disbelief coalesce. Thus to disobey may imply not to believe (cf. Heb. 3:18–19).

Verbs of belief and unbelief—Luke 24:11 ἀπιστέω (I disbelieve) and Galatians 3:6 πιστεύω (I believe). In Galatians 3:6 Abraham believed God (θεῷ), meaning that he believed what God said (i.e., the promise). Most distinguish πιστεύω with a dative (intellectual assent) from πιστεύω followed by εἰς and the accusative (trust, commitment, and allegiance). The latter normally presupposes intellectual assent; but perhaps the lines of distinction should not be sharply drawn as to which constitutes saving belief. Although John uses πιστεύω followed by εἰς and the accusative for salvific faith most of the time (e.g., John 3:16), there are cases where it is used for unsatisfactory faith (John 2:23–24; 12:42–43). Also πιστεύω with a dative is used for both salvific faith (Acts 16:34; Gal. 3:6) and unsatisfactory faith (John 8:31). Brown (1966:512–13) suggests that the difference is merely one of focus (intellectual credence or active commitment). Belief in the existence of God, however, is expressed differently (Heb. 11:6).

Verbs of rebuking—Mark 1:25 ἐπιτιμάω (I rebuke).

Verbs of helping—Mark 9:24 βοηθέω (I help).

Verbs of pleasing—Romans 8:8 ἀρέσκω (I please).

Verbs of following or meeting—Mark 1:18 ἀκολουθέω (I follow); Mark 5:2 ὑπαντάω (I meet); and Mark 14:13 ἀπαντάω (I meet). Datives that follow verbal nouns formed from verbs of meeting function as direct objects of deep structure verbs. The direct object was retained as the verb was transformed into a verbal noun. For example, the dative in John 12:13 ἐξῆλθον εἰς ὑπάντησιν αὐτῷ should be considered as a direct object even though it follows a noun (they went out to meet him). Other examples include Matthew 8:34 πᾶσα ἡ πόλις ἐξῆλθεν εἰς ὑπάντησιν τῷ Ἰησοῦ (the whole city went out to meet Jesus) and Acts 28:15 ἦλθαν εἰς ἀπάντησιν ἡμῖν (they came to meet us).

Dative Subject

A dative noun or pronoun can function semantically as the subject of a dative participle. The dative nominal will be coreferential with another dative construction in the sentence. The participial construction is to be translated as an adverbial clause, changing the participle into its corresponding verb with the dative nominal as its subject; Matthew 8:23 ἐμβάντι αὐτῷ εἰς τὸ πλοῖον ἠκολούθησαν αὐτῷ. The first αὐτῷ is the subject of the participle, and the second is the direct object of ἠκολούθησαν (When he embarked in the boat, they followed him).

Dative of Apposition

The dative of apposition identifies or further defines another dative noun. Luke 1:47 ἠγαλλίασεν τὸ πνεῦμά μου ἐπὶ τῷ θεῷ τῷ σωτῆρί μου (my spirit rejoices in God my Savior).

Datives Functioning as Adverbial Phrases

Dative of Reference

The adverbial dative of reference is a nominal that functions adverbially to limit a verb or adjective to a particular frame of reference. This idea can be conveyed in English with such expressions as "with reference to," "concerning," or "about."

Limiting a verb—In Romans 6:2 Paul says ἀπεθάνομεν τῇ ἁμαρτίᾳ (we have died in reference to sin). The dative limits the scope of the death that Paul is discussing. Other examples include Matthew 18:12 Τί ὑμῖν δοκεῖ (What does it seem from your point of view?); Luke 18:31 τελεσθήσεται πάντα τὰ γεγραμμένα διὰ τῶν προφητῶν τῷ υἱῷ τοῦ ἀνθρώπου (all things which have been written by the prophets about the Son of Man will be fulfilled); Romans 4:20 ἐνεδυναμώθη τῇ πίστει (he was strengthened in reference to faith); and Romans 6:10 ζῇ τῷ θεῷ (he lives in reference to God).

Datives of reference can also modify a linking verb, as in 1 Corinthians 2:14 μωρία γὰρ αὐτῷ ἐστιν (for they are, as far as he is concerned, foolishness) and Ephesians 6:12 οὐκ ἔστιν ἡμῖν ἡ πάλη πρὸς αἷμα καὶ σάρκα (the battle is not, as far as Christians are concerned, against blood and flesh). Sometimes the dative will limit the verbal idea in a verbal noun, as in 2 Corinthians 11:6 ἰδιώτης τῷ λόγῳ (unskilled in the word). Paul is saying that he is an amateur when it comes to public speaking.

Limiting an adjective—Matthew 5:3 Μακάριοι οἱ πτωχοὶ τῷ πνεύματι (Blessed are the poor in reference to their spirit; or better, Blessed are those who are spiritually poor). Compare with Matthew 5:8 (pure in heart), Acts 7:20 (beautiful to God), Acts 26:19 (I was not disobedient in reference to the vision God gave me), Romans 4:19 (weak in faith), Hebrews 5:11 (dull in hearing), and James 2:5 (poor in reference to worldly goods).

The problematic datives in 1 Peter 3:18 θανατωθεὶς μὲν σαρκὶ ζωοποιηθεὶς δὲ πνεύματι (having been put to death in the flesh but made alive in the spirit) are best viewed as reference (Kelly [1969] 1988:151; Selwyn [1947] 1981:196). Christ was put to death in reference to His physical mode of existence and made alive in reference to His spiritual mode of existence (cf. TEV, put to death physically, but made alive spiritually). Although this seems to be required by the parallelism, it might suggest that the spiritual aspect of Christ (His divine soul) died also. Perhaps this is why some interpret πνεύματι as a dative of agency (made alive by the Spirit; cf. NIV). Being made alive in reference to the spirit could be taken in two ways: (1) His death included His soul (not annihilation but alienation from the Father) which at the resurrection was reconciled to the Father, or (2) He was brought back to life in a spiritual (glorified) mode of existence. The second is preferable (cf. Davids 1990:137).

The idiomatic questions Τί ἡμῖν καὶ σοί (Matt. 8:29; Mark 1:24) and Τί ἐμοὶ καὶ σοί (Mark 5:7; John 2:4) may be viewed as containing double datives of reference with elided verbs. Mark 1:24 could be variously rendered: (1) "What reference do we have with you?" (2) "What do we have to do with you?" (3) "What do we have in common?" or perhaps (4) "Why are you bothering us?" The problematic statement in John 2:4 becomes clearer when the datives are recognized as reference: Τί ἐμοὶ καὶ σοί, γύναι. The idea is that what was on Mary's mind (σοί), the fact that they are out of wine, was not Jesus' responsibility (ἐμοί). The problem should have been taken to the governor of the feast. In addition, the word γύναι carries a different connotative value than its English gloss (woman) when used as a vocative. The Greek γύναι can be used as a term of endearment (cf. John 19:26), whereas the English term would have a derogatory connotation. The expression could be rendered "Dear mother, what you have just said does not pertain to me" or as the NEB "Your concern, mother, is not mine."

Perhaps the dative in Philippians 1:21 could be understood as reference: ἐμοὶ γὰρ τὸ ζῆν Χριστὸς καὶ τὸ ἀποθανεῖν κέρδος (for to me to live is Christ and to die is gain). Paul is making a personal confession: as far as he is concerned, existence on earth means living a Christ-centered life, but dying means dwelling in the very presence of Christ.

Dative of Space

The dative of space indicates the place where the action of the verb occurs. There are two subtypes: literal and metaphorical.

Literal—The literal dative of space denotes an actual physical location. Blass and Debrunner (1961:107) claim that the dative of place is absent in the New Testament except for a few stereotyped expressions, such as "at the right hand of God" (cf. Acts 2:33; 5:31). However, there are many clear examples: Matthew 27:48 περιθεὶς καλάμῳ ἐπότιζεν αὐτόν (having placed it on a reed, he gave it to him to drink); Luke 10:30 λῃσταῖς περιέπεσεν (he fell in the midst of thieves); John 19:2 ἐπέθηκαν αὐτοῦ τῇ κεφαλῇ (they put it on his head); Acts 9:3 ἐγένετο αὐτὸν ἐγγίζειν τῇ Δαμασκῷ (he came near Damascus); 1 Corinthians 9:13 οἱ τῷ θυσιαστηρίῳ παρεδρεύοντες (the ones serving at the altar); 2 Corinthians 3:7 ἡ διακονία τοῦ θανάτου ἐν γράμμασιν ἐντετυπωμένη λίθοις (the ministry of death engraved in letters on stones); Colossians 2:14 προσηλώσας αὐτὸ τῷ σταυρῷ (having nailed it on a cross); Hebrews 9:24 νῦν ἐμφανισθῆναι τῷ προσώπῳ τοῦ θεοῦ ὑπὲρ ἡμῶν (now to appear in the presence of God for us); and Hebrews 12:22 προσεληλύθατε Σιὼν ὄρει (you have come to Mount Zion). The latter is an example of spacial extension rather than spacial position.

Metaphorical—The dative of space is metaphorically extended to include what is commonly called the *dative of sphere*. It denotes not a literal, physical location, but rather the sphere in which an action occurs or in which something exists. Examples include Mark 8:12 ἀναστενάξας τῷ πνεύματι αὐτοῦ λέγει (having groaned in his spirit, he said) and Hebrews 3:10 Ἀεὶ πλανῶνται τῇ καρδίᾳ (They always err in their hearts). Most examples normally cited as datives of sphere are better understood as datives of reference.

The problematic dative τῇ ἐλπίδι in Romans 8:24 has been variously interpreted. Some take it as means, "we have been saved by hope" (AV, TEV), but this seems to be contrary to Pauline thought of being saved by faith, unless "faith" and "hope" are regarded as synonymous (as Westcott suggests 1974:323). Others take it as sphere "we have been saved and now live in the realm of the hope of its consummation" (Käsemann 1980:238; Morris 1988:324–25).

Dative of Time

A dative of time can express (a) the time at which something happens (it happens at midnight), (b) the time during which something happens (it happens sometime during a certain night), (c) an expanse of time (it happens for a long time), or (d) distributive time (it happens daily).

The translation will vary according to the context. An example of (a) is Luke 2:38 αὐτῇ τῇ ὥρᾳ (at that very moment). Examples of (b) include Matthew 17:23 τῇ τρίτῃ ἡμέρᾳ ἐγερθήσεται (he will arise the third day) and Mark 1:21 καὶ εὐθὺς τοῖς σάββασιν εἰσελθὼν εἰς τὴν συναγωγὴν ἐδίδασκεν (and on the Sabbath he entered into the synagogue and began to teach). An example of (c) is John 2:20 Τεσσεράκοντα καὶ ἓξ ἔτεσιν οἰκοδομήθη ὁ ναὸς οὗτος (This temple has taken us forty-six years to build; cf. Luke 1:75; 8:27; John 14:9; Acts 8:11; Rom. 16:25). An example of (d) is 2 Corinthians 4:16 (day by day). On occasion the dative of time modifies an underlying verb, as in 1 Timothy 2:6 τὸ μαρτύριον καιροῖς ἰδίοις (to give testimony at the proper time).

Dative of Means

A common function of dative nominals is to specify the means a person intentionally uses to achieve a particular end. It often refers to an implement (John writes a letter with a pen), but may refer to other types of means, such as actions. The dative of means can be translated into English as "by," "with," or "by means of": Mark 5:5 ἦν κράζων καὶ κατακόπτων ἑαυτὸν λίθοις (he was crying out and cutting himself with stones). The λίθοις is a dative of means and identifies the instrument used. Other examples include Matthew 7:22 τῷ σῷ ὀνόματι δαιμόνια ἐξεβάλομεν (by means of your name we exorcised demons); Luke 6:38 ᾧ γὰρ μέτρῳ μετρεῖτε ἀντιμετρηθήσεται ὑμῖν (for God will measure you by means of the measure which you use to measure others); Romans 1:20 τοῖς ποιήμασιν νοούμενα (being understood by the things which have been made); 2 Corinthians 3:3 ἐγγεγραμμένη οὐ μέλανι (not written with ink); and 1 Peter 1:18–19 οὐ φθαρτοῖς, ἀργυρίῳ ἢ χρυσίῳ, ἐλυτρώθητε . . . ἀλλὰ τιμίῳ αἵματι . . . Χριστοῦ (You were not redeemed . . . with corruptible things, such as silver or gold, but with the precious blood of Christ).

Most take the dative in John 21:8 as location (in the boat), but Brown (1970:1072) rightly contends that it should be means (by boat): οἱ δὲ ἄλλοι μαθηταὶ τῷ πλοιαρίῳ ἦλθον (The other disciples came by boat). This is contrasted with Peter's coming by swimming through the water.

When the dative is a verbal noun, it often represents a deep structure verb. For example, in Acts 8:11 Simon astounded the people *by performing feats of magic* (ταῖς μαγείαις). The clause represents two propositions at the deep level, joined in a means-result relationship: "Simon performs feats of magic" and "Simon astounds the people." The same analysis can be applied to Ephesians 2:8 χάριτί ἐστε σεσῳσμένοι (you are saved by grace). The two propositions are "God shows grace" and "God saves you." The first proposition conveys means; the second is the result (cf. Nida and Taber 1974:53–54). See also Luke 22:48 and Galatians 2:13.

Dative of Agency

The dative of agency denotes the personal agent who performs the action of the verb. Since the verbs involved are in the passive voice, the dative could be considered semantically to be the subject of a deep structure clause. Normally the agent of a passive verb is conveyed by ὑπό and the genitive. Examples include Matthew 6:1 πρὸς τὸ θεαθῆναι αὐτοῖς (to be seen by them); Luke 23:15 οὐδὲν ἄξιον θανάτου ἐστὶν πεπραγμένον αὐτῷ (nothing worthy of death was done by him); Romans 8:14 ὅσοι γὰρ πνεύματι θεοῦ ἄγονται (for as many as are led by the Spirit of God); 1 Timothy 3:16 ὤφθη ἀγγέλοις (he was seen by angels); and James 3:7 δεδάμασται τῇ φύσει τῇ ἀνθρωπίνῃ (tamed by humankind).

Dative of Manner

The dative of manner expresses the way in which the verbal action is performed. It may be translated either as a prepositional phrase, using such words as "with" or "in," or as a simple adverb. For example, Mark 8:32 παρρησίᾳ τὸν λόγον ἐλάλει could be translated either "he was speaking the word with boldness" or "he was boldly speaking the word." The dative of manner answers the question "How?" In Acts 16:37 Paul and Silas were beaten and imprisoned publicly (δημοσίᾳ) but were released privately (λάθρᾳ). Other examples include Matthew 2:7 (Herod called the Magi se-

cretly), Matthew 3:12 (burn with unquenchable fire), Mark 5:7 (having cried
with a loud voice), Acts 9:31 (living in the fear of the Lord), 1 Corinthians
10:30 (partake with thanksgiving), 1 Corinthians 11:5 (praying or prophesy-
ing with her head uncovered), and Hebrews 2:7 (crowned with glory and
honor).

Sometimes a cognate of the verb is used as a dative of manner. The action
of the verb is intensified by restating it in its noun form: Luke 22:15
Ἐπιθυμίᾳ ἐπεθύμησα (I earnestly desired); James 5:17 προσευχῇ
προσηύξατο (he earnestly prayed) (cf. John 3:29).

Dative of Degree

A dative of degree is often called a dative of measure. It modifies a comparative adjective rather than a verb by indicating the degree of difference: Mark
10:48 ὁ δὲ πολλῷ μᾶλλον ἔκραζεν (but he was crying out much more).
The same phrase πολλῷ μᾶλλον occurs twice in Romans 5:9–10 comparing
the past and future redemptive acts of God toward believers. Since God has
already justified and reconciled them, they have *much more* certainty that
His future redemptive acts will also come to pass. Another example is
Hebrews 1:4, where Christ is said to be so much (τοσούτῳ) better
(κρείττων) than the angels.

Dative of Association

The dative of association denotes the person (or thing) with whom (or
which) something is done. This often occurs with verbs with a συν- prefix,
as in Luke 15:2 συνεσθίει αὐτοῖς (he eats with them), Luke 15:6 Συγχάρ-
ητέ μοι (rejoice with me); and 1 Corinthians 4:8 ὑμῖν συμβασιλεύσωμεν
(we might reign with you). Datives of association also occur with other
verbs that convey a joint venture, as in Mark 8:2 ἤδη ἡμέραι τρεῖς
προσμένουσίν μοι (already three days they have remained with me) and
Acts 24:26 ὡμίλει αὐτῷ (he talked with him). In English "with" can be used
for both association and means.

Dative of Reason

The dative of reason expresses the unintended cause for something that happened. The designation "reason" is preferred over "cause" because there are

several different cause/effect relations (cf. logical relations in chapter 17). For example, "reason" is the unintentional cause, whereas "means" is the intentional cause. The dative of reason can be translated with such words as "for," "because of," or "on account of." Examples include Luke 15:17 ἐγὼ λιμῷ ὧδε ἀπόλλυμαι (I am perishing here because of famine); Romans 4:20 οὐ διεκρίθη τῇ ἀπιστίᾳ (he did not waver because of unbelief); Romans 11:20 τῇ ἀπιστίᾳ ἐξεκλάσθησαν (because of unbelief they were broken off); 2 Corinthians 2:7 τῇ περισσοτέρᾳ λύπῃ καταποθῇ (he might be overwhelmed because of excessive sorrow); Galatians 6:12 ἵνα τῷ σταυρῷ τοῦ Χριστοῦ μὴ διώκωνται (that they might not be persecuted because of the cross of Christ); and Ephesians 2:1 ὄντας νεκροὺς τοῖς παραπτώμασιν καὶ ταῖς ἁμαρτίαις (being dead because of trespasses and sins). Lincoln (1990:93) comments that the dative in Ephesians 2:1 expresses both the cause and the manifestation of death.

The problematic dative in Colossians 2:14 χειρόγραφον τοῖς δόγμασιν (translated by the AV as "handwriting of ordinances") should probably be taken as reason. The χειρόγραφον is a verbal noun, meaning a document of indebtedness that we write (i.e., an IOU) or someone else writes against us. Lightfoot ([1879] 1959:187) correctly observes that the dative τοῖς δόγμασιν modifies the verbal idea behind χειρόγραφον. O'Brien (1982:125) adds that the dative states the reason the document of indebtedness was written. The idea would be that "God canceled the record of debts that had been written against us because we failed to live up to the ordinances." Others take the dative as association, meaning that God canceled our debt along with the binding rules of the law (TEV, NRSV, NIV). However, this might suggest that the law was also nailed to the cross (cf. Rom. 7:12).

Datives Functioning as Adjectival Phrases

Dative of Possession

A dative of possession modifies another noun by indicating the person who owns it. For example, Luke 21:4 ἐκ τοῦ περισσεύοντος αὐτοῖς (out of their excess) and Acts 10:6 ᾧ ἐστιν οἰκία παρὰ θάλασσαν (whose house is alongside the sea). The dative of possession may be in the predicate, as in Matthew 19:27 τί ἄρα ἔσται ἡμῖν (what then shall we have?), rather than as an adjunct to another noun. A more complex example is Matthew 18:12

ἐὰν γένηταί τινι ἀνθρώπῳ ἑκατὸν πρόβατα. This could be rendered "if there were a hundred sheep belonging to a man" or better "if someone had a hundred sheep."

Dative of Relationship

A dative of relationship modifies another noun by specifying a related person. The construction is similar in form to the genitive of relationship. The kinship or social role term linking the related persons, however, is usually mentioned. One example is John 13:35 ἐμοὶ μαθηταί ἐστε (you are my disciples). In English we use possessive pronouns to convey relationship (e.g., her grandfather, my boss). Yet, these possessive pronouns do not function to convey possession (e.g., we do not own our grandfathers or employers). Greek possessive pronouns also display the same mismatch between form and function (cf. Mark 2:18). Other examples include Luke 9:38 (he is my only son) and Acts 19:31 (being his friends). In Matthew 27:57 ἐμαθητεύθη τῷ Ἰησοῦ (he became a disciple of Jesus) the dative modifies the nominal idea in the verb ἐμαθητεύθη (become a disciple). Luke 5:10 ἦσαν κοινωνοὶ τῷ Σίμωνι (they were partners of Simon) could be relationship or association.

Dative of Identification

Genitives and datives after ὄνομα are often considered possession. This is perhaps due to English usage (his name is John) or due to the analogy with possessive pronouns (cf. Matt. 7:22). Names, however, are not pieces of property that are owned. The following genitive or dative semantically qualifies ὄνομα by specifying the person or place that is identified by that name. Thus ὄνομα αὐτοῦ (Matt. 1:21) and ὄνομα αὐτῷ (John 1:6) both mean "the name by which this person is identified is. . . ." It is obvious that the dative cannot be possession when geographical placenames are used in the same construction. For example, in Luke 1:26–27 it would be rather odd to say that Nazareth owns its name. The same analysis would be valid for possessive pronouns used in a similar way. Just because they are called "possessive pronouns" does not mean that they always convey possession.

When the word ὄνομα itself is in the dative, it functions to qualify an adjacent nominal. Thus the dative ὀνόματι in Mark 5:22 modifies εἷς τῶν ἀρχισυναγώγων (one of the synagogue officials, who is named Jairus); compare with Acts 18:24 (a certain Jew, who is named Apollos). In Acts 9:11 the noun being modified by ὀνόματι must be supplied (look for a man from Tarsus who is named Saul). In Luke 1:61, however, ὀνόματι modifies the verb (no one is called by this name).

Exercises

Cite the best dative function for the following passages and give alternate options where appropriate. Translate the passage in such a way as to bring out the force of the use(s) you have chosen.

   1. Matt. 6:25   ὑμῖν, ψυχῇ, σώματι
   2. Matt. 11:29   καρδίᾳ, ψυχαῖς
   3. Matt. 15:25   αὐτῷ, μοι
   4. Matt. 27:46   φωνῇ, μεγάλῃ
   5. Mark 2:8   πνεύματι
   6. Mark 5:9   σοι, μοι
   7. Mark 6:19   αὐτῷ
   8. Luke 3:16   ὕδατι [different options possible]
   9. Luke 6:1–2   χερσίν, σάββασιν
  10. Luke 6:31   ὑμῖν, αὐτοῖς
  11. Luke 8:29   πνεύματι, χρόνοις, ἀλύσεσιν, πέδαις
  12. Luke 12:20   νυκτί, τίνι
  13. John 16:25   παρρησίᾳ
  14. John 18:15   Ἰησοῦ, ἀρχιερεῖ, Ἰησοῦ
  15. Acts 12:2   μαχαίρῃ
  16. Rom. 11:30   θεῷ, ἀπειθείᾳ
  17. 1 Cor. 5:12   μοι
  18. 1 Cor. 14:20   φρεσίν, κακίᾳ, φρεσίν
  19. 2 Cor. 5:13   θεῷ, ὑμῖν
  20. Eph. 2:5   παραπτώμασιν, Χριστῷ, χάριτι

4   The Article

In English there are two kinds of articles, the definite article (the) and the indefinite article (a, an). Greek, however, has only the definite article (ὁ, ἡ, τό); Latin has no article. Many European languages developed an indefinite article from the number "one," as English did. There are also traces of this in koine Greek. Occasionally εἷς (one) and τις (someone) are used in place of an indefinite article (Matt. 8:19, Luke 10:25).

Because the Greek article is often difficult to carry over into English, one might erroneously conclude that the Greek article was used somewhat arbitrarily. A.T. Robertson remarks, "The article is never meaningless in Greek, though it often fails to correspond with the English idiom" (1934:756). The Greek article will usually serve some kind of function, whether syntactical (e.g., to indicate case relations) or semantic (e.g., to particularize some noun). Nevertheless, the reason for its use or nonuse in many cases remains an enigma, especially with proper names and words like νόμος and πνεῦμα. It is very difficult to set forth exact rules that will cover every case. Sometimes, as Moule (1968:113) says, "the context is a surer guide to the meaning than is the use of the article."

Functions of the Article

The Article Used to Make a Noun Definite

The basic function of the article is to make a noun definite. The word *definite* refers to an expression that is specific rather than to something that is general or vague. When an article is said to make a noun definite, it can mean either to specify one of many (the door rather than any door) or to particularize a general quality (the faith rather than faith in general). In either case the article's limiting or specifying function is to mark clear boundaries for the sake of identification. It is often said that the presence of the article identifies, and the absence of the article qualifies. There are, however, many exceptions. Perhaps this general rule should be restated: when the article is present the noun is definite; when it is absent the noun may or may not be definite.

Distinguishing persons or things—The article is often used to distinguish one person or thing from other persons or things; that is, to individualize something, setting it apart from others of the same class. This is sometimes called the *deictic use.* The word "deictic" means to point out. Robertson says, "The article is associated with gesture and aids in pointing out like an index finger" (1934:756).

The article in Luke 18:13 distinguishes one person from all other persons: Ὁ θεός, ἱλάσθητί μοι τῷ ἁμαρτωλῷ (God be merciful to me the sinner). The NRSV, NIV, and AV read "a sinner." The use of the article, however, is significant. The tax collector realized that he as an individual was a sinner before God. He singled himself out from all others, acknowledged his personal sins, and pleaded for mercy. This must be done before receiving the saving grace of God; salvation is not bestowed corporately as the Jews had thought.

The article is used in Matthew 5:1 to distinguish one particular mountain from other mountains: ἀνέβη εἰς τὸ ὄρος (he went up into the mountain). The NIV, AV, and REB read "he went up into a mountain." The article, however, may point out a specific mountain, perhaps one often used by Jesus when He lectured, and one well known by the people. The NRSV, Phillips, NEB, NJB all retain the definite article. Nine times in the New Testament it is said that Jesus went up into "the" mountain. It is possible that the article points to the hilly region that surrounds the Sea of Galilee rather than to a specific mountain (cf. Zerwick 1963:54).

Distinguishing classes—Instead of distinguishing one object from many similar objects, the article is often used to distinguish one particular class from other classes. The class is viewed as a whole and is characterized by common traits. This is often called the *generic use.* English translations will make the noun plural or indefinite (using an indefinite article or no article). One example is John 10:10 ὁ κλέπτης οὐκ ἔρχεται εἰ μὴ ἵνα κλέψῃ (thieves do not enter, except to steal). Jesus is referring not to a particular thief, but to thieves as a class of people as distinguished from other classes of people, a group bent on enriching self at the expense of others. Also in John 2:25 ἵνα τις μαρτυρήσῃ περὶ τοῦ ἀνθρώπου (that any should testify concerning man) Jesus was not speaking about a particular man, but about humankind as a generic class (as opposed to other classes of beings, such as angels). Jesus does not need evidence concerning the depravity of humanity because He knows the human heart.

Particularizing an abstract quality—Another use of the article is to call attention to a particular aspect of abstract qualities, such as ἀγάπη, ἐλπίς, νόμος, πίστις, or χάρις. The article is present about seventy-five percent of the time with the nouns listed. It is not always easy to determine the exact intent of the author in the use or nonuse of the article with abstract nouns. It is commonly held that νόμος with the article refers to the Mosaic Law. In Romans νόμος is used forty-three times in reference to the Mosaic Law, twenty-one times with the article and twenty-two times without. It is the context rather than the article that indicates νόμος refers to the Mosaic legislation. Blackwelder ([1958] 1976:148) suggests that its absence when clearly referring to the Mosaic Law indicates the nature of that law. Νόμος is also used with the article to refer to something other than the Mosaic Law (e.g., Rom. 7:21).

Since English does not normally tolerate articles before abstract nouns, they are usually omitted in translations. For example, in Matthew 12:41 the AV reads "The men of Nineveh shall rise in judgment (ἐν τῇ κρίσει) with this generation, and shall condemn it." The article before κρίσει, however, refers to a specific judgment, not to the general concept (cf. NRSV, NIV). In 1 John 4:18 the articles particularize a certain kind of love and fear: ἡ τελεία ἀγάπη ἔξω βάλλει τὸν φόβον. The NIV reads "perfect love drives out fear." Yet this might imply that any kind of love brought to maturity can cast out fear. The article points to a certain kind of love, a genuine love toward God and humankind engendered by Christ's sacrificial love toward us. The word "fear" also has an article. It probably does not refer to the general state of being afraid, but to a specific fear, perhaps that of eternal judgment. See also John 1:17 and 2 Thessalonians 2:10.

The Article Used to Refer to a Previous Reference

The article can function to direct the reader's attention to a previous mention of the noun. This is sometimes called the *anaphoric article*. The initial occurrence of a noun is often anarthrous (does not have an article), and subsequent occurrences that refer to the same thing are articular (have an article). This is often exegetically significant. The article in James 2:14 μὴ δύναται ἡ πίστις σῶσαι αὐτόν points to the previous mention of "faith," where it was qualified as being without works. "What does it profit, my brothers, if a man claims to have faith but does not have works? Can *that kind of faith* save him?" If the force of the article is not brought out, it could give the impression that James is saying faith cannot save a person (cf. Barclay, AV).

In Ephesians 2:8 τῇ γὰρ χάριτί ἐστε σεσῳσμένοι (For by grace you are saved) the article points back to the mention of "the grace of his goodness" in the previous verse. Perhaps an adequate rendering would be, "for by that grace." The article of previous reference also helps clarify Galatians 3:23: Πρὸ τοῦ δὲ ἐλθεῖν τὴν πίστιν ὑπὸ νόμον ἐφρουρούμεθα. The NRSV reads "Now before faith came, we were imprisoned and guarded under the law." The implication is that faith was absent under the Old Testament dispensation. This is hardly the case. Abraham is the prime example of one who had saving faith. The article before "faith" refers back to the previous verse in which "faith" has "Jesus Christ" for its object. What is meant is that people were kept under the tutelage of the law with its typology embedded in the sacrificial system until its fulfillment in Christ. This was all they had to believe in. Now we can believe in the finished work of Christ. "Before faith came" then means "before the faith made possible by the coming of Christ" (cf. Gal. 3:25, 26).

The Article Used as a Pronoun

The Greek article can be used as a shorthand device to take the place of a pronoun. It may take the place of a possessive pronoun, alternative pronoun, personal pronoun, demonstrative pronoun, or relative pronoun.

Possessive pronoun — The article often serves as a possessive pronoun. If something is possessed, then it is distinguished from other objects of the same class not possessed. "Our house" is not any house in general, but a specific house. The functions of the article and possessive pronoun therefore on occasion coalesce. Possession, however, must often be understood in a loose sense. In Mark 1:41 ἐκτείνας τὴν χεῖρα αὐτοῦ ἥψατο (he stretched out his hand and touched him) the article functions as a possessive pronoun "his."

The αὐτοῦ is the genitive object of "touch" (cf. Matt. 8:3, where αὐτοῦ follows the word "touch"). Another example is Ephesians 5:25 Οἱ ἄνδρες, ἀγαπᾶτε τὰς γυναῖκας (Men, love your wives), where the article must take the sense of a personal pronoun; otherwise, Paul would be saying, "Men, love the women." See also John 3:17.

Alternative pronoun—An alternative construction, in which various nouns are contrasted or at least set apart from each other, can be formed with articles preceding both μέν and δέ. The translation for the singular would be "one . . . another." The translation for the plural would be "some . . . others." There are four different groups set apart in Ephesians 4:11 αὐτὸς ἔδωκεν τοὺς μὲν ἀποστόλους, τοὺς δὲ προφήτας, τοὺς δὲ εὐαγγελιστάς, τοὺς δὲ ποιμένας καὶ διδασκάλους (he gave some apostles, some prophets, some evangelists, and some pastors and teachers).

Personal pronoun—The article is often used for a personal pronoun. One particular construction, common in narrative literature, is the article followed by δέ (also by μέν or μὲν οὖν in Acts) and then by a finite verb or adverbial participle. The article refers back to a previous mention of the current subject or speaker, and the δέ functions as a switch-reference device; that is, it indicates a change of subject or speaker from the preceding sentence. The switch-reference function of δέ will often hold true apart from this particular construction and is an important syntactical observation.

For example, in Matthew 4:3 Satan is the speaker, and Jesus is mentioned in an oblique case. The ὁ δέ in Matthew 4:4 ὁ δὲ ἀποκριθεὶς εἶπεν (And he [Jesus] answering said) indicates a switch back to Jesus as the speaker. The article in such cases is usually translated as a personal pronoun (he, they), but sometimes as a demonstrative (that one, those). There is a potential ambiguity when this construction is followed by a participle. Matthew 4:20 οἱ δὲ εὐθέως ἀφέντες τὰ δίκτυα ἠκολούθησαν αὐτῷ could mean either "they, having immediately left their nets, followed him" or less likely "the ones who immediately left their nets followed him." The latter implies that some did not make an immediate response. See also Matthew 8:32 and 26:57.

Demonstrative pronoun—Matthew 14:2 διὰ τοῦτο αἱ δυνάμεις ἐνεργοῦσιν ἐν αὐτῷ (on account of this, *these* miracles are being done by him). In Matthew 14:33 οἱ δὲ ἐν τῷ πλοίῳ προσεκύνησαν αὐτῷ (But *those* in the boat worshiped him) the οἱ δέ also functions as a switch-reference device.

Relative pronoun—Examples include Matthew 5:16 δοξάσωσιν τὸν πατέρα ὑμῶν τὸν ἐν τοῖς οὐρανοῖς (They might glorify your father who is in heaven) and 1 Timothy 3:13: ἐν πίστει τῇ ἐν Χριστῷ Ἰησοῦ (in the faith which is in Christ Jesus) (cf. Matt. 26:28). Turner (1963:165) argues that the article is never used for a relative pronoun in the New Testament, because examples like those above could be treated as a noun phrase in apposition. Semantically, there is little difference.

The Article Used to Construct a Noun Phrase

The article may precede various words (such as adverbs, adjectives, participles, infinitives), phrases (such as prepositional phrases), and clauses, turning them into noun phrases which then function syntactically in accord with the case of the article (Moule 1968:106, contra DM 1955:146). The article may at the same time function at the semantic level by denoting previous reference, by distinguishing persons, or the like.

Preceding an adverb—Mark 11:12 τῇ ἐπαύριον (The next [day]). The word ἡμέρα "day" is understood. In Luke 5:10 ἀπὸ τοῦ νῦν (From the present time) the article constructs a noun phrase out of the adverb which then functions as the object of the preposition. In addition, the article distinguishes this beginning as unique from all others.

Preceding a genitive—In Galatians 5:24 οἱ δὲ τοῦ Χριστοῦ (Those who belong to Christ) the nominative case article turns the entire expression into a noun phrase which functions as the subject. Semantically, the article also distinguishes this particular group from any other group. In 1 Corinthians 1:18 Ὁ λόγος ὁ τοῦ σταυροῦ (the word, namely, the one concerning the cross) the article turns the following genitive construction into a noun phrase which functions in apposition to λόγος. The article also has semantic value in raising the phrase to prominence, marking a contrast with the words of men.

Preceding a prepositional phrase—In Hebrews 13:24 οἱ ἀπὸ τῆς Ἰταλίας (they of Italy) the article turns the entire expression into a noun phrase which syntactically functions as the subject. Another example is 1 John 2:15 τὰ ἐν τῷ κόσμῳ (the things in the world), where the noun phrase functions as the object.

Preceding a clause—The difficult construction in Mark 9:23 Τὸ Εἰ δύνῃ can be readily understood in light of this use of the article. Jesus is commenting on one particular phrase spoken by the boy's father. "Jesus said to him, 'Let me comment on that which you have just said, namely, "if you are able." All things are possible to the one who believes.'" The article not only refers back to what the man had just said, but it also turns the clause into a noun phrase (Moule 1968:110) which probably functions as the object of an understood verb. The article can also precede quotations or proverbial expressions. See Matthew 19:18 and Romans 13:9.

Preceding other elements—The article can also precede adjectives (Matt. 7:6), participles (Matt. 7:8), and infinitives (Phil. 2:6, 13), turning them into noun phrases.

The Article Used with Monadic Nouns and Proper Names

Monadic nouns—A monadic noun refers to something of which there is thought to be only one (e.g., γῆ, ἥλιος, θεός, οὐρανός, σελήνη). The article is present about eighty percent of the time with the nouns listed, even though it is not needed to distinguish them from others since they are one of a kind. Dana and Mantey (1955:139–40) suggest that the article with θεός usually signifies divine personality, either God the Father or the Triune Godhead, whereas its absence focuses on the essence or attributes of divinity.

Proper nouns—The article is not normally needed with proper nouns, since the name already tends to individualize the person, country, nationality, city, or the like. Perhaps the article was used to call attention to a particular person (this John, not that John), to a person mentioned previously (the John I mentioned before), or to a person known by the readers (the John who ministered to you). Turner (1963:165–66) suggests that the classical and Hellenistic practice of omitting the article at the first mention of a person and inserting the article on subsequent references may be observed in the New Testament. However, it is not consistently practiced. Some of the variation may be due to an author's preference and style, especially in John.

Examples include Acts 19:13 τὸν Ἰησοῦν ὃν Παῦλος κηρύσσει (the particular Jesus whom Paul preaches) and Acts 19:1 (the Apollos whom we have just been discussing). The name *Jesus* usually has the article in the Gospels, pointing to the Jesus the readers know and have believed in. The article is also usually found before Χριστός in the Gospels, meaning "the Messiah";

whereas in the Epistles it is generally absent, perhaps because of its being considered a proper name. One might expect articles to be used more frequently with indeclinable proper nouns to mark their case, but it seems as if the reverse is more often observed.

The Article with Nouns Connected with καί

When two nouns are separated by καί and each noun has its own article, the author intends a distinction between them. When the two nouns are separated by a καί and only the first has an article, the author intends for the reader to group the two nouns together in some fashion. One application of the latter observation was set forth as a rule by Granville Sharp in 1798. He applied it only to singular nouns with a personal reference to establish that the nouns refer to the same person. His basic principle has been much abused, partly because of misunderstanding the limitations he imposed. He stated:

> When the copulative καί connects two nouns of the same case, [viz. nouns (either substantive or adjective, or participle) of personal description respecting office, dignity, affinity, or connection, and attributes, properties, or qualities, good or ill,] if the article ὀ, or any of its cases, precedes the first of the said nouns or participles, and is not repeated before the second noun or participle, the latter always relates to the same person that is expressed or described by the first noun or participle: i.e. it denotes a farther description of the first named person.

The rule contains three disqualifications: (1) Plural elements disqualify the construction as being an example of the Granville Sharp rule (cf. Ephesians 4:11, pastors and teachers). (2) Non-personal nouns disqualify the construction (cf. Acts 2:23, the counsel and foreknowledge of God, and Titus 2:13, the blessed hope and glorious appearing). Posttribulationists interpret Titus 2:13 as a legitimate example of the Granville Sharp rule. If this is a correct application of the rule, then the glorious appearing (Christ's return at the end of the tribulation) and the blessed hope (the rapture) would refer to the same event. Another passage that seemingly falls into this category is 2 Thessalonians 2:1, "concerning the coming of our Lord and our gathering together unto him." Sharp, however, clearly rejects these applications in his fourth rule. (3) Proper names disqualify the construction. Sharp considered Ἰησοῦς to be a proper name, but θεός, κύριος, σωτήρ, and Χριστός to be nouns of personal description, denoting office, rank, title, or the like.

Some of the legitimate examples are quite significant. In Titus 2:13 the construction τοῦ μεγάλου θεοῦ καὶ σωτῆρος ἡμῶν (our great God and Savior) means that our savior, Jesus Christ, is God. Since both nouns refer to the same person, the pronoun "our" modifies both nouns. To make it modify only the second tends to separate the nouns, "the great God and our Savior" (AV, Phillips). The NWT separates the two nouns even more, "of the great God and of our Savior Christ Jesus." This removes any thought of Christ being God. For other examples, see 2 Peter 1:1, 2:20 (cf. Robertson 1977:61–8; Kuehne 1973–1974).

When two plural nouns are preceded by a single article and linked with καί, they should still be grouped together in some way, even though they are not always identical. Wallace (1983:59–84) has identified five categories that apply to plural nouns.

(1) Distinct groups that are united for some reason. Although historically the Pharisees and Sadducees were opposed to each other, the construction in Matthew 3:7 links them together in their opposition to Christ.

(2) Overlapping groups. In Revelation 21:8 seven substantives are joined together referring to individuals who will be condemned in the lake of fire (the cowardly, unbelieving, vile, murderers, perverts, sorcerers, and idolaters). It is obvious that those who are both murderers and perverts will also be included.

(3) First group subset of second. In Matthew 5:20 the phrase "the scribes and Pharisees" probably means "the scribes and other Pharisees." In Matthew 9:11 the phrase "the tax-collectors and sinners" means "the tax-collectors and other sinners."

(4) Second group subset of first. All examples of this type have textual variants, but if original they would be translated as type 3 but in reversed order (cf. Mark 2:16; 1 Cor. 5:10).

(5) Identical groups. In Revelation 1:3 a blessing is promised to the ones hearing and keeping the words of the prophecy. The participles refer to the same group. There are no clear examples of two nouns being linked in type 5; almost all involve participles.

Of the five types, the first and last are the most common. Nevertheless, some passages are still difficult to classify, such as Ephesians 2:20 (apostles and prophets) and 4:11 (pastors and teachers). Wallace (1983:82–83) suggests that both are examples of type 2.

Articles Used in Copulative Sentences

It is often said that the subject of a copulative sentence (i.e., one with εἰμί or γίνομαι) will be indicated by the article and the predicate nominative will be indicated by the absence of the article. For example, the subject of 1 John 4:8 ὁ θεὸς ἀγάπη ἐστίν (God is love) is the nominative θεός, not the nominative ἀγάπη, since θεός has the article. There are, however, many cases that do not fit this generalization (illustrated below). The following rules (adapted from McGaughy 1972:23–65) are much more useful in determining the subject of a copulative sentence. They are ordered so that if Rule 1 does not determine the subject, go on to Rule 2, and so on. The article does not enter the process until Rule 3c.

Rule 1 (Verb Agreement): If one of the elements does not agree in person and number with the verb, then the subject will be either the element that does agree, as in Matthew 5:14 Ὑμεῖς ἐστε τὸ φῶς τοῦ κόσμου (*You* are the light of the world), or the pronominal suffix on the verb, as in 2 Corinthians 3:3 ἐστὲ ἐπιστολὴ Χριστοῦ (*You* are an epistle of Christ).

Rule 2 (Case Agreement): If one of the elements is not in the nominative case, then the subject will be either the element that is in the nominative case, as in 1 Corinthians 11:14 ἀτιμία αὐτῷ ἐστιν (*Dishonor* is to him), or the pronominal suffix, as in 1 Corinthians 6:19 οὐκ ἐστὲ ἑαυτῶν (*You* are not of yourselves).

Rule 3 (Textual Anaphora): If Rules 1 and 2 do not determine the subject, then the subject must be determined contextually by its pointing to an antecedent. There are four subrules that aid in this analysis.

Rule 3a: The subject is indicated by demonstrative or relative pronouns, even if the predicate nominative has the article: Matthew 3:17 Οὗτός ἐστιν ὁ υἱός μου (*This* is my Son; cf. versions on Matt. 10:2). The same is true with personal pronouns, as in Matthew 16:20 αὐτός ἐστιν ὁ Χριστός (*He* is the Christ).

Rule 3b: The subject is that element represented only by the verb ending. John 21:7 Ὁ κύριός ἐστιν (*He* is the Lord). This example, as well as those for Rules 1 and 3a, shows that the article does not always determine the subject.

Rule 3c: The subject is usually that element with the article. There are only five possible exceptions not already covered by the previous rules where the predicate nominative has the article but the subject does not (John 20:31; 1 John 2:22; 4:15; 5:1, 5). In all five the definite predicate nominative follows the verb and thus can be explained by the Colwell rule (see below). All five are also examples of early Christian confessions, which tend toward stereotyped forms (e.g., John 20:31 ἵνα πιστεύσητε ὅτι Ἰησοῦς ἐστιν ὁ Χριστὸς ὁ υἱὸς τοῦ θεοῦ). The attempt to eliminate the exceptions by reversing the subjects could possibly work with John 20:31, 1 John 2:22, and 5:1, "the Messiah is Jesus" rather than "Jesus is the Christ" (cf. Acts 18:5, 28, NRSV), but it does not seem to work with 1 John 4:15 and 5:5, "Whoever confesses that the Son of God is Jesus." The main problem is that the switch ignores the topicalization in each passage. This is especially noticeable in John 20:31, where Jesus was the subject of the previous sentence.

Rule 3d: If both elements have the article (e.g., John 8:54c; 15:1; 1 John 2:7) or both do not have the article (e.g., Luke 1:63; 1 Cor. 5:11; Eph. 5:23; 1 Tim. 3:12; Heb. 11:1; Jas. 5:17; 1 John 5:17), then the first one is normally the subject. Saying the two nouns are interchangeable when both have or do not have articles also ignores the topicalization of themes through a discourse unit. That is, the topic the author is discussing in a discourse unit will normally be the subject to which something else is predicated, not vice versa.

Although there are exceptions, the Colwell rule does seem to be correct for the majority of cases. Colwell (1933:13) states, "A definite predicate nominative has the article when it follows the verb; it does not have the article when it precedes the verb." For example, a definite predicate nominative with the article follows the linking verb in John 8:12 Ἐγώ εἰμι τὸ φῶς τοῦ κόσμου, whereas the same predicate nominative without the article precedes the verb in John 9:5 φῶς εἰμι τοῦ κόσμου. The problem in applying the Colwell rule is to determine when the predicate nominative is definite. The rule itself does not establish the definiteness of a noun, an observation sometimes ignored when applying it to John 1:1. We have already mentioned that monadic and proper nouns are definite. The same applies to nouns qualified with a genitive. Colwell notes that proper names in the predicate regularly do not have the article. Other examples of the Colwell rule include Matthew 13:37 (cf. John 5:27), 27:42, John 1:49, and 19:21.

This is often applied (as Colwell himself did) to John 1:1: καὶ θεὸς ἦν ὁ λόγος (and the Word was God). The NWT reads, "and the Word was a god," meaning one of many and in essence removing Christ as the supreme God. There are two ways to respond. First, applying the Colwell rule, it seems as if John placed θεός (obviously the predicate nominative) before the verb for emphasis. The reason the article is absent is not because it is indefinite (one of several divine beings as in Arianism), but because it is definite in its own right, and a definite predicate nominative does not have an article when it comes before the verb. With the Jewish cultural setting, one could easily argue that θεός was considered monadic and therefore definite without the article (cf. Deut. 6:4). The NWT's rendering "a god" would then be incorrect. Second, many argue that the absence of the article before θεός directs attention to the quality or essence of godhood (Westcott 1975:3; Harner 1973:75–87). Thus it does not mean that Christ was a god, but that Christ fully possessed the qualities of God. It seems best, however, to adopt the first view and say the absence of the article pertains to the word order chosen by John to emphasize Christ's deity (Kuehne 1975:8–22).

Reasons for Anarthrous Constructions

A construction is anarthrous when it does not have an article. Sometimes the absence of the article is more or less expected. Other times it deviates from the expected and is therefore exegetically significant.

Abstract Nouns

An article is not required with abstract nouns because they are inherently qualitative (cf. 1 Cor. 13:13). Nevertheless, they are often definite in the New Testament because of the wider theological context, regardless of whether or not they have an article (e.g., "faith" normally refers to one's faith in Christ or God rather than faith in general). The absence of the article in such cases would still tend to focus on quality, such as the nature of one's faith in Christ. The main exegetical problem with abstract nouns is to account for the presence of the article rather than its absence.

Monadic and Proper Nouns

Nouns that are definite on their own do not require articles. For example, monadic nouns (one of a kind) are definite on their own and do not require an article. Also proper nouns are distinctive by being a name of something specific and again do not require articles. Both monadic and proper nouns, however, often have articles.

Nouns in Genitive Constructions

A genitive qualifier tends to make the head noun definite even though it might not have the article. Thus in Romans 1:16 Paul writes δύναμις θεοῦ, but he has in mind a specific activity of God, that of saving fallen humanity. Also δικαιοσύνη θεοῦ and ὀργὴ θεοῦ in Romans 1:17–18 are made definite by the genitive construction. The genitives specify which righteousness and wrath are being discussed and thus tend to make the nouns definite.

In connection with this, Apollonius' canon states that in general two nouns in regimen (a noun qualified by a genitive noun) will both have articles or both be without them; thus τῷ λόγῳ τῆς ἀληθείας (Col. 1:5) and λόγῳ ἀληθείας (2 Cor. 6:7) are both expected. This rule holds true more than eighty percent of the time. There are two basic modifications that will explain most exceptions: (1) the head noun may be anarthrous while the genitive qualifier is articular, especially if the head noun is the object of a preposition, a predicate nominative, or vocative; (2) either may be anarthrous if it is a proper name (including κύριος) even though the other may be articular (cf. Hull 1986:3–16, Moule 1968:115, Turner 1963:180).

Objects of Prepositions

Certain words when used as objects of prepositions can be definite without an article. This is similar to our expressions "He is in bed" or "She has gone to town." The words "bed" and "town" are definite without articles. The words are usually geographical or temporal, such as Matthew 17:27 (to the lake), Matthew 24:27 (from the east), Mark 2:1 (at home), Mark 15:21 (from the country), Luke 7:32 (in the marketplace), Luke 17:29 (from heaven), John 1:1 (in the beginning), and Acts 16:13 (to the river). The Greek article is absent in each of the above phrases.

Technical Expressions

Technical expressions will not have articles, such as titles of books and names in opening salutations (DM 1955:149). Dana and Mantey also suggest that stereotyped expressions, such as ἐν λόγῳ κυρίου (by the word of the Lord) in 1 Thessalonians 4:15, although quite definite, will not have articles. They note that "this is due to the tendency toward abbreviation of frequent or customary phraseology."

To Make a Noun Non-differentiated

When the noun is not intended to be differentiated from others of the same class, it will not have an article. In John 4:27 the disciples returned from the city and were surprised that Jesus was talking with a woman (μετὰ γυναικός). To insert an article "with the woman" misses the force of the anarthrous construction (cf. AV). It was not considered proper for a Jewish man to speak with women in public; this is what surprised the disciples, not that Jesus was speaking with a particular woman.

In Hebrews 4:15 the author says that Christ was tempted in all points like as we are, yet He was without sin (χωρὶς ἁμαρτίας). Westcott (1974:107) suggests that the expression means that Christ was not tempted from a sinful nature. The absence of the article would then focus on the quality of sin or the propensity to sin. Others say the anarthrous construction refers to sin in general. Although He was tempted, He did not commit any kind of sin at all. The latter appears to be more in keeping with the context of the book.

To Focus on the Quality of the Noun

When the author wants to focus on the quality, character, nature, or class of the noun, he will omit the article. In Hebrews 1:2 the author writes ἐλάλησεν ἡμῖν ἐν υἱῷ (literally, "He [God] spoke to us in Son"). Westcott (1974:7) says the absence of the article focuses attention on the nature rather than the personality of the Son. Thus the character of the Son is contrasted with that of the prophets. In Hebrews 5:8 the author repeats the anarthrous υἱός, "although being Son, he learned obedience from what he suffered." The focus is again on the character of the Son rather than on His specific identity.

In 1 Peter 3:1 the second occurrence of λόγος does not have an article. The AV inserts an article, "Likewise, ye wives, be in subjection to your own husbands; that, if any obey not the word, they also may without the word be won by the conversation [conduct] of the wives." No one can be won to the Lord without the Word of God. The husband must have received the Word either before or after the winsome conduct of his Christian wife. What is meant is that the husband's disbelief can be softened by the conduct of the wife without her having to say anything.

Exercises

In the following examples, cite the best article function and give alternate options where appropriate. Whenever possible, translate the passage in such a way as to bring out the force of the use(s) you have chosen.

1. Matt. 2:7   τοὺς μάγους
2. Matt. 8:20   Αἱ, τά, τήν
3. Matt. 15:24–27   ὁ δέ, ἡ δέ, ὁ δέ, ἡ δέ
4. Matt. 16:23   τά, τά
5. Matt. 27:24   τὰς χεῖρας
6. Mark 6:3   ὁ, ὁ
7. Luke 10:7   τά, ὁ ἐργάτης
8. Luke 11:46   ὁ δέ, τοῖς, τούς, τοῖς
9. Luke 14:3   τούς; cf. Luke 7:30
10. John 1:4   ἡ, τό (Which one precedes the subject? Are the terms interchangeable?)
11. John 4:24   absence of article before πνεῦμα
12. John 6:11   τούς, τῶν
13. John 13:9   τάς, τήν
14. John 16:21   ἡ, ἡ, τό, τῆς, τήν
15. Rom. 3:21   absence of article before νόμου, τοῦ, τῶν
16. 1 Cor. 13:4   ἡ, ἡ, ἡ
17. Gal. 5:14   ὁ, τῷ, τόν
18. Eph. 5:5   τοῦ; cf. commentaries
19. Phil. 2:9   τό, τό
20. Heb. 3:1   τόν

5 Pronouns and Adjectives

Pronouns

Pronouns are words that take the place of nouns while pointing to a place in the text where the noun occurs. Most of the nominal case functions studied in chapters 1–3 also apply to pronouns. The use of pronouns avoids the repetition of the noun and gives variety and flexibility to the language. The noun that the pronoun takes the place of is called the *antecedent*. In addition to being substitutes for nouns, pronouns serve another important function. They point to other locutions where the antecedent is identified. That is, they are used as cohesive devices to tie a discourse unit together. Words, such as pronouns, that provide cohesion to a discourse by referring to other words are called *pro-forms*.

The distinctions between different kinds of pronouns and even between pronouns and adjectives are often blurred (Zerwick 1963:67–71; Moule 1968:93–95). Pronouns that function as pronouns agree with their antecedent in gender and number. Those that function as adjectives agree with the noun they modify in gender, number, and case.

Personal Pronouns

The personal pronouns are ἐγώ (I), ἡμεῖς (we), σύ (you, sg.), ὑμεῖς (you, pl.), αὐτός (he), and αὐτοί (they). When used as personal pronouns, they are usually in oblique cases (gen., dat., acc.), as in Matthew 13:54 ἐδίδασκεν αὐτούς (he was teaching them). Quite often the gender and number are exegetically significant. In John 3:7 Jesus told Nicodemus μὴ θαυμάσῃς ὅτι εἶπόν σοι, Δεῖ ὑμᾶς γεννηθῆναι ἄνωθεν (Do not be surprised because I told you [sg.], "You [pl.] must be born again"). By using the plural, Jesus is making a universal statement that applies to everyone, including Nicodemus and the rest of the Sanhedrin. Personal pronouns can function in various ways:

Emphasis—Nominative case personal pronouns are often used to emphasize or give prominence to the subject. Since the subject is already indicated by the pronominal suffix on the verb, the nominative case personal pronoun is redundant. When present it usually conveys some kind of emphasis (e.g., importance, gravity, surprise, anger, contrast, comparison, or identity).

The pronoun highlights a thematically important statement in Matthew 16:16 Σὺ εἶ ὁ Χριστὸς ὁ υἱὸς τοῦ θεοῦ τοῦ ζῶντος (*You* are the Christ, the Son of the living God). The third person pronoun is used in Luke 8:42 to intensify a grave situation: αὐτὴ ἀπέθνῃσκεν (*she* was dying). Perhaps the pronoun in John 3:10 conveys surprise: Σὺ εἶ ὁ διδάσκαλος τοῦ Ἰσραὴλ καὶ ταῦτα οὐ γινώσκεις (*You* are a teacher of Israel, and you do not know these things?). The question in Acts 4:7 conveys anger: ἐποιήσατε τοῦτο ὑμεῖς (Why have *you* done this?).

Contrast is a common form of emphasis. After the two disciples on the road to Emmaus mentioned that the religious leaders had handed Jesus over to be crucified, they said (Luke 24:21) ἡμεῖς δὲ ἠλπίζομεν (but *we* were hoping). The ἡμεῖς marks a contrast between their expectations and what took place. Both the first person and third person pronouns are used in Mark 1:8 to mark a contrast: ἐγὼ ἐβάπτισα ὑμᾶς ὕδατι, αὐτὸς δὲ βαπτίσει ὑμᾶς ἐν πνεύματι ἁγίῳ (*I* baptize you with water, but *he* will baptize you with the Holy Spirit). For a series of contrasts, see the ἐγὼ δὲ λέγω ὑμῖν phrases in the Sermon on the Mount (Matt. 5:22, 28, 32, 34, 39, 44).

Pronouns are used in Luke 11:48 to help draw a comparison: αὐτοὶ μὲν ἀπέκτειναν αὐτούς, ὑμεῖς δὲ οἰκοδομεῖτε (*they* killed the prophets, and *you* build their tombs). In John 4:26 Jesus uses a pronoun to emphasize His identity: Ἐγώ εἰμι, ὁ λαλῶν σοι (*I* am he, the one talking with you).

Identical Adjective—When the third person personal pronoun αὐτός follows an article, it means "the same." It is found either with a noun, as in Matthew 26:44 τὸν αὐτὸν λόγον (the same word), or without, as in Romans 2:1 τὰ γὰρ αὐτὰ πράσσεις (for you do the same things).

Intensive pronoun—The nominative form of the third person personal pronoun αὐτός can be used as an intensive pronoun with nouns, verbs, or other pronouns to emphasize identity (The president himself came to our house).

With nouns αὐτός will be in the predicate position (i.e., not preceded by an article), thus Romans 8:16 αὐτὸ τὸ πνεῦμα συμμαρτυρεῖ τῷ πνεύματι ἡμῶν (the Spirit himself bears witness with our spirit). The neuter pronoun αὐτό (itself) agrees with the grammatical gender of πνεῦμα rather than the natural gender (cf. AV). With proper names the article before the noun may be absent: Mark 12:37 αὐτὸς Δαυὶδ λέγει αὐτὸν κύριον (David himself called him Lord). Sometimes it has a demonstrative force as well: Luke 12:12 διδάξει ὑμᾶς ἐν αὐτῇ τῇ ὥρᾳ (he will teach you at that very hour; cf. Luke 10:7, 21; 20:19). This dual function seems to be equivalent to the intensive and demonstrative pronouns used separately, as in Philippians 1:6 αὐτὸ τοῦτο (this very thing). The word "very" reflects the intensive idea.

With verbs the intensive αὐτός can be used with any person and number pronominal suffix; thus βλέπω αὐτός (I myself see); βλέπεις αὐτός (you yourself see); βλέπει αὐτός (he himself sees); βλέπομεν αὐτοί (we ourselves see); βλέπετε αὐτοί (you yourselves see); and βλέπουσι αὐτοί (they themselves see). For examples with first person verb, see Luke 11:4, 22:71, 1 Corinthians 9:27, and Philippians 2:24; with second person, see Luke 11:52, Acts 2:22, Romans 15:14, and 1 Thessalonians 2:1; for third person, see Matthew 27:57, Luke 7:5, 24:36, and John 5:20.

With emphatic personal pronouns αὐτός increases the degree of emphasis. For example, Acts 10:26 καὶ ἐγὼ αὐτὸς ἄνθρωπός εἰμι (I myself am also a man); Romans 8:23 ἡμεῖς καὶ αὐτοὶ ἐν ἑαυτοῖς στενάζομεν (even we ourselves groan within ourselves); and 1 Thessalonians 4:9 αὐτοὶ γὰρ ὑμεῖς θεοδίδακτοί ἐστε (for you yourselves are taught by God) (cf. Rom. 7:25).

The epistolary plural—The epistolary plural (or literary plural) is a debatable category. Does "we" ever mean "I"? Some on the basis of findings in the papyri argue that the usage is koine and should be expected in the New Testament (Robertson 1934:406; Zerwick 1963:4; cf. Moulton 1978:86). Blass and Debrunner (1961:146–47) allow the construction in the New Testament, but only outside of Paul. Lofthouse (1955) also argues that Paul does not confuse "I" and "we," contending that when Paul refers to himself alone he uses "I" and when he includes himself in a larger circle he uses "we."

The proposed epistolary plurals may use either personal pronouns or the pronominal suffix on a verb. It is obvious in 1 John 1:4 that John alone is the author, yet he writes καὶ ταῦτα γράφομεν ἡμεῖς (and we are writing these things). The singular form of the verb occurs in the rest of the epistle (e.g.,

2:1, 7). Smalley (1984:14) interprets the plural as "we (the writer, in solidarity with all the representatives of orthodoxy in the church) are writing this." Brown (1982:172) mentions that in this passage John "does not wish to speak simply in his own name, as he normally does. Physically, he and he alone is going to write; but at the start he wants to make it clear that what he writes bears more than personal authorization—it is Community tradition from the Community tradition-bearers." Accordingly, the "we" in 1 John 1:4 is not a literary plural.

The first person plural, however, is interpreted as epistolary in other passages. In Romans 1:5 Paul writes, "we have received grace and apostleship." Cranfield (1975:65), Käsemann (1980:14), and Morris (1988:48) argue that Paul is referring only to himself and not including the other apostles (cf. commentaries for reasons given). Other possible cases include 1 Thessalonians 2:18, 3:1, 2 (cf. 3:5).

Inclusive and exclusive—Many languages have two different forms of the first person plural pronouns (we, us) to indicate whether the speaker includes himself with the people spoken to (inclusive) or simply refers to himself and his associates (exclusive). Neither Greek nor English has forms that distinguish the inclusive and exclusive use of pronouns. This ambiguity must be resolved before translations into some languages are possible. It is also important for the exegesis of some passages.

In Matthew 3:15 Jesus says, "It is proper for us ($\dot{\eta}\mu\hat{\iota}\nu$) to fulfill all righteousness." Was Jesus including the person He was speaking to (John the Baptist) or excluding him? If the plural is inclusive, it would include John; if not, it would refer to Jesus and the other members of the Godhead. In Mark 9:5 Peter says, "It is good for us ($\dot{\eta}\mu\hat{\alpha}s$) to be here, let us build ($\pi o\iota\dot{\eta}\sigma\omega\mu\epsilon\nu$) three tents." Whom does Peter want to help build the tents? Does he include or exclude Jesus, the person spoken to? John writes in 1:14 of his Gospel, "He dwelt among us ($\dot{\eta}\mu\hat{\iota}\nu$), and we beheld ($\dot{\epsilon}\theta\epsilon\alpha\sigma\dot{\alpha}\mu\epsilon\theta\alpha$) his glory." What did John mean? Did Jesus dwell among John and his associates (exclusive), or did Jesus dwell among John and his readers, the people in the world (inclusive)? The pronominal suffix on the verb is most likely exclusive, referring to the transfiguration. If the "we" in Acts 6:3 (whom we may appoint) is taken as exclusive, then only the apostles made the decision regarding the deacons (episcopal church polity). However, if it is interpreted as inclusive, then it includes those being addressed; i.e., the church (congregational church polity). The pronouns in Hebrews 2:3 are clearly inclusive (How shall we escape?).

Switch-reference device—The third person nominative αὐτός is often used as a switch-reference device, signifying a change in subject to someone or something that had been mentioned previously. On occasion it merely serves to resume the previous subject. It is often found in narrative literature with various constructions, such as καὶ αὐτός, αὐτὸς δέ, or αὐτός alone. In Mark 8:29 καὶ αὐτὸς ἐπηρώτα αὐτούς (and he asked them) the construction indicates a change from the speaker of the previous utterance (the disciples) to the speaker of the current utterance (Jesus) (cf. Mark 4:38; 14:15; Luke 1:22; 2:50; 4:15; 5:1, 14, 16; 6:8, 11).

Personal pronouns used for reflexive—In Matthew 6:19 a personal pronoun is used as a reflexive pronoun: Μὴ θησαυρίζετε ὑμῖν θησαυρούς (Do not store up treasures for yourselves; cf. Matt. 6:20). It is common in Hellenistic Greek for personal pronouns to function as reflexives (cf. Metzger 1975:616). This is why the orthography in the UBS² (e.g., αὐτούς) has been changed in the UBS³ (e.g., αὑτούς) (cf. Mark 9:16; Luke 23:12; 20:10; Acts 14:17; Rom. 1:24; Eph. 2:15; Phil. 3:21; Heb. 5:3; Rev. 8:6; 18:7). The versions translate most of these as reflexive. The pronouns in Luke 23:12 and Romans 1:24 seem to be used in a reciprocal sense.

The reflexive use of personal pronouns enters into the exegetical and textual debate on 1 John 5:18. The two interpretations reflect two textual readings: (1) those who interpret ὁ γεννηθείς as Christ (e.g., Smalley 1984:303) prefer αὐτόν (the one derived from God [Christ] keeps him [the believer] safe); and (2) those who interpret ὁ γεννηθείς as the believer prefer ἑαυτόν (the one born of God [the believer] keeps himself). If αὐτόν were adopted, it could still be taken as reflexive. John, however, always uses ὁ γεγεννημένος for the believer, not ὁ γεννηθείς. Thus the first view seems preferable. Brown (1982:620–22) leaves the matter undecided by translating, "the one begotten by God [the Christian] is protected."

Relative Pronouns

The relative pronouns are ὅς (who, which) and ὅστις (who, which, whoever, whichever). A relative pronoun is a word that introduces a dependent clause and at the same time refers to an antecedent (The ball which I hit went into the sand trap). The relative pronoun "which" introduces the clause "I hit" and refers back to its antecedent "ball." Relative clauses usually function adjectivally, modifying the antecedent. Sometimes, however, they function adverbially. The adverbial nuances of relative clauses will be studied in chapter 15.

Relative pronouns normally agree with their antecedent in gender and number. There are exceptions. For example, they may agree with the natural gender of the antecedent rather than the grammatical gender, as in Philemon 10 (τέκνου ὅν) and Revelation 13:14 (θηρίῳ ὅς), where both nouns are neuter but the relative pronouns are masculine, The neuter noun μυστήριον (mystery) in 1 Timothy 3:16 μέγα ἐστὶν τὸ τῆς εὐσεβείας μυστήριον (great is the mystery of godliness) is followed by the masculine relative ὅς. The change in gender indicates that the reference is to a personal being rather than merely to the impersonal "mystery of godliness." It is obvious from the context that Paul is speaking of Christ. Some manuscripts read ὅ, which is probably a scribal modification to bring the relative into agreement with its antecedent. The reading θεός is not supported by any uncial in the first hand earlier than the eighth or nineth century (Metzger 1975:641).

The gender is also exegetically significant in Matthew 1:16. The feminine relative pronoun ἐξ ἧς ἐγεννήθη Ἰησοῦς (from whom was born Jesus) breaks the pattern in Matthew's genealogy by pointing back to Mary rather than to Joseph. This helps underscore the virgin birth by implying that Joseph did not father the Christ child. In 1 Corinthians 15:10 Paul writes εἰμι ὅ εἰμι (I am what I am). One might expect the masculine relative here (I am who I am), but this would change the meaning. Paul is focusing on what he has become by the grace of God rather than on who he is.

Lack of antecedent—Sometimes a relative pronoun is used without an antecedent (e.g., Matt. 10:38, Heb. 5:8). These can be treated two ways, either as a demonstrative (the one whom, that which) or as an indefinite pronoun (whoever, whatever). In the former, the reference is usually made clear from the context, as in 1 John 1:1 Ὅ ἦν ἀπ᾽ ἀρχῆς (That which was from the beginning). An example of the latter is 1 John 4:6 ὅς οὐκ ἔστιν ἐκ τοῦ θεοῦ οὐκ ἀκούει ἡμῶν (whoever is not from God does not listen to us).

Attraction—A relative pronoun will normally agree with its antecedent in gender and number. Its case is determined by how it functions in the relative clause: Matthew 2:9 ὁ ἀστήρ, ὅν εἶδον (the star which they saw). The relative pronoun ὅν agrees in gender and number with ὁ ἀστήρ, but it is accusative because it is the object of εἶδον. Occasionally the relative pronoun will also agree with the case of its antecedent. At times this agreement is coincidental, but other times it occurs when it is not grammatically expected. This happens when either the relative pronoun or antecedent is attracted to the case of the other. *Direct attraction* occurs when the relative pronoun adopts the case of its antecedent. In John 4:14 ἐκ τοῦ ὕδατος οὗ ἐγὼ δώσω αὐτῷ (from the water which I will give him) the relative pronoun οὗ is genitive like its antecedent ὕδατος rather than accusative, as one would expect since it functions as the object of its clause (I will give him water; cf. Acts 3:25). *Indirect attraction* occurs when the antecedent adopts the case of the relative, as in Mark 12:10 Λίθον ὃν ἀπεδοκίμασαν οἱ οἰκοδομοῦντες (The stone which the builders rejected). This does not occur as much as direct attraction.

Confusion of relative and indefinite relative—The classical distinction between ὅς (who, which) and ὅστις (whoever, whichever) was no longer strictly maintained in koine Greek, so that one may be used for the other. The indefinite relative ὅστις is often used in a definite sense (Mark 15:7; Luke 2:4; Gal 4:24). This is frequently observed in Luke's writings. The relative ὅς often becomes indefinite when used with the particle ἄν or ἐάν, as in Matthew 5:22 ὃς δ' ἂν εἴπῃ (whoever should say), and sometimes when used alone, as in Mark 9:40 ὃς οὐκ ἔστιν καθ' ἡμῶν, ὑπὲρ ἡμῶν ἐστιν (whoever is not against us is for us). When there is a clear antecedent, neither ὅς or ὅστις will be used as an indefinite relative.

Relative as correlative—With μέν . . . δέ the relative can function as a correlative (see definition below); thus Matthew 21:35 ὃν μὲν ἔδειραν, ὃν δὲ ἀπέκτειναν, ὃν δὲ ἐλιθοβόλησαν (they beat one fellow, killed another, and stoned yet another; cf. Matt. 22:5; Luke 23:33; 2 Tim. 2:20).

Correlative Pronouns

A correlative is a word that expresses mutual relations. There are correlative pronouns, correlative adjectives, and correlative conjunctions. Correlative conjunctions are used in parallel structure (Neither John nor Bill can go). The primary correlative pronouns are the quantitative ὅσος (as much as, as great as, as many as), the qualitative οἷος (such as, as, of what kind), and the qualitative ὁποῖος (of what sort, as, such as). Both οἷος (2 Cor. 10:11; Phil. 1:30) and ὁποῖος (Gal. 2:6) may at times approach the force of a relative. Other correlatives include the qualitative τοιοῦτος (of such a kind) and the quantitative τοσοῦτος (so great, so large, so far). These are often used as correlative adjectives.

Demonstrative Pronouns

The demonstrative pronouns are οὗτος (this), ἐκεῖνος (that), and ὅδε (this). The latter occurs mostly in Revelation. A demonstrative is a word that points out or specifies something. Οὗτος points out something nearby and ἐκεῖνος something remote. The proximity or remoteness may pertain to the literary context, the situational context, or the mental context of ideas in the mind of the author or speaker. Thus the antecedent of οὗτος does not necessarily refer "to the noun which is nearest, but to the noun which is most vividly in the writer's mind" (Turner 1963:44); e.g., Matthew 3:17 οὗτός ἐστιν ὁ υἱός μου (This is my Son). Regarding the literary context, the neuter singular τοῦτο usually refers to what follows, whereas the neuter plural ταῦτα seems only to point to what precedes. When referring backward, demonstratives may serve as discourse boundary markers (J. Callow 1978:8).

Demonstrative used as a pronoun—Demonstratives often function as true pronouns, taking the place of and pointing to an antecedent. They may be variously translated in English, sometimes as a personal pronoun (this, this one, that one, he, these, those, they). Some have thought that the demonstrative "this" in Ephesians 2:8 refers to "faith" (For by grace you are saved through faith, and this [τοῦτο] is not your own doing, but is the gift of God). While it is true that faith is a gift of God, the neuter demonstrative τοῦτο cannot refer to faith, since πίστεως is feminine. It most likely refers to the entire gift of salvation, which would certainly include faith. Sometimes the demonstrative pronoun will agree with the natural gender rather than the grammatical gender. For example, the masculine pronoun ἐκεῖνος is used in John 14:26 and 16:13–14 to refer to the neuter noun πνεῦμα to emphasize the personality of the Holy Spirit.

Demonstrative used as an adjective—Demonstratives may also function as adjectives that point out the noun they are modifying. When the demonstrative is used with a noun it is called a demonstrative adjective. The demonstrative will be in the predicate position (i.e., not preceded by an article), as in Matthew 3:9 ἐκ τῶν λίθων τούτων (from these stones).

Possessive Pronouns

The possessive pronouns are ἐμός (my), ἡμέτερος (our), σός (your, sg.), and ὑμέτερος (your, pl.). The most common way of expressing possession, however, is with the genitive of personal pronouns: Matthew 11:29 τὸν ζυγόν μου (my yoke). The use of possessive pronouns may give some emphasis. They usually stand in the attributive position (i.e., preceded by an article): John 18:36 Ἡ βασιλεία ἡ ἐμή (my kingdom) and Matthew 13:27 ἐν τῷ σῷ ἀγρῷ (in your field). Sometimes they are used as a substantive, as in John 17:10 τὰ ἐμὰ πάντα σά ἐστιν καὶ τὰ σὰ ἐμά (all my things are yours, and your things are mine). Possessive pronouns do not always convey possession in a semantic sense. For example, even though possessive pronouns are used in Mark 2:18 οἱ σοὶ μαθηταί (your disciples), Jesus does not own His disciples. The possessive pronoun functions as the equivalent to a genitive of relationship (cf. Matthew 7:3, 22).

Reflexive Pronouns

The reflexive pronouns are ἐμαυτοῦ (of myself), σεαυτοῦ (of yourself), ἑαυτοῦ (of himself), and ἑαυτῶν (of themselves). A reflexive means that the subject and object of a sentence refer to the same person or thing; the action of the verb is directed back to the subject (I hit myself). One example is Matthew 16:24 ἀπαρνησάσθω ἑαυτόν (let him deny himself). Middle voice verbs are rarely reflexive (Matt. 27:5). Reflexive pronouns can convey various nuances of the genitive, dative, and accusative cases (they do not occur in the nominative case). For example, a genitive of possession is expressed in Matthew 21:8 ἑαυτῶν τὰ ἱμάτια (their own garments; cf. Matt. 25:1, Luke 11:21). A genitive of relationship is expressed in Matthew 8:22 ἄφες τοὺς νεκροὺς θάψαι τοὺς ἑαυτῶν νεκρούς (let the dead bury their own dead; cf. Luke 2:39). Sometimes a reflexive can be used for a reciprocal pronoun, as in Ephesians 5:19 λαλοῦντες ἑαυτοῖς (speaking with one another; cf. 1 Cor. 6:7; Col. 3:16; 1 Thess. 5:13).

Reciprocal Pronoun

The reciprocal pronoun is ἀλλήλων (of one another). It expresses a mutual action, relationship, or interchange between persons. Usually the interaction includes the subject, as in 1 John 4:7 Ἀγαπητοί, ἀγαπῶμεν ἀλλήλους (Beloved, let us love one another). Sometimes the subject is not included (e.g., Matt. 25:32).

Interrogative Pronouns

The interrogative pronouns are τίς (who?), τί (what? why?), the qualitative
ποῖος (of what kind? which? what?), and the quantitative πόσος (how
great? how much? how many?). The questions will always be content questions, as in John 1:19 Σὺ τίς εἶ (Who are you?). The neuter accusative τί is
often used as an interrogative adverb, meaning "why?" One example is
Matthew 6:28 τί μεριμνᾶτε (Why do you worry?). It is also used as an interrogative adverb with διά or εἰς, as in Matthew 13:10 Διὰ τί ἐν
παραβολαῖς λαλεῖς αὐτοῖς (Why are you speaking to them in parables?).
Sometimes τίς is used as the exclamatory particle "how!" (Luke 12:49) or as
a relative pronoun (Mark 14:36).

Indefinite Pronoun

The word τις can function as an indefinite pronoun (someone, anyone,
something, anything) or as an indefinite adjective (a certain person). As an
indefinite pronoun, it stands in place of an unidentified person or thing, as
in Matthew 12:47 εἶπεν τις αὐτῷ (Someone said to him). As an indefinite
adjective, it modifies common nouns: Luke 1:5 ἱερεύς τις (a certain priest).

Adjectives

An adjective is a word used to modify a noun or other substantive. It will
agree with the noun it modifies in gender, number, and case. This agreement often clarifies misunderstandings. For example, in Matthew 26:27 the
AV reads "Drink ye all of it." One might think that Jesus told His disciples
to down the entire cup. If so, then the next person would not have anything
to drink, since they were sharing the same cup. The adjective "all" is nominative masculine plural and modifies the subject; it cannot modify the cup:
Πίετε ἐξ αὐτοῦ πάντες. Thus the meaning is "All of you drink from it."
As in English, nouns can also function as adjectives: Matthew 3:6 ἐν τῷ
Ἰορδάνῃ ποταμῷ (in the Jordan River).

Adjectives Used Attributively

An attributive adjective ascribes a quality or quantity to the noun with which it agrees. This happens when (1) the adjective is articular and the noun is anarthrous, as in Luke 6:45 (ὁ ἀγαθὸς ἄνθρωπος, the good man), (2) both the adjective and noun are articular (ὁ ἀγαθὸς ὁ ἄνθρωπος, the good man), or (3) both the adjective and noun are anarthrous (ἄνθρωπος ἀγαθός, a good man). There is some emphasis attached to the adjective in the second type, which could be brought out in English by making it a relative clause or an appositive. For example, we could translate 1 John 1:2 τὴν ζωὴν τὴν αἰώνιον as either "the life which is eternal" or "the life, the eternal one." There is also emphasis in the third type when the adjective precedes the noun: Matthew 10:31 πολλῶν στρουθίων διαφέρετε ὑμεῖς (you are worth more than *many* sparrows).

Some adjectives, such as ὅλος and πᾶς, have an attributive meaning even though they are used in the predicate position (i.e., articular noun with anarthrous adjective). Thus Matthew 4:23 ἐν ὅλῃ τῇ Γαλιλαίᾳ means "in all Galilee."

Adjectives Used Predicatively

A predicate adjective makes an assertion about a noun. This happens when (1) it is the predicate of an linking verb, as in John 4:11 τὸ φρέαρ ἐστὶν βαθύ (the well is deep), or (2) if it is the predicate of an elliptical verb. In either case, the adjective is called a *predicate adjective*. The latter is of two subtypes. The first subtype occurs when the noun is articular and the adjective is anarthrous (i.e., both ὁ ἄνθρωπος ἀγαθός and ἀγαθὸς ὁ ἄνθρωπος mean "the man is good"). In Matthew 7:13–14 πλατεῖα ἡ πύλη . . . στενὴ ἡ πύλη (the gate is wide . . . the gate is narrow) the predicate adjectives precede the nouns to emphasize the contrast (cf. Matt. 5:3–11). The second subtype occurs when both the adjective and noun are anarthrous (cf. Wallace 1984:128–67). For example, Mark 6:35 ὥρα πολλή (the hour is late); Romans 7:8 ἁμαρτία νεκρά (sin was dead); and Hebrews 9:17 διαθήκη . . . βεβαία (a will is effective).

Another type of predicate adjective occurs in the accusative case. It is called a predicate accusative or object complement. In John 5:11 the adjective is used as a predicate accusative after an implicit copula: Ὁ ποιήσας με ὑγιῆ ἐκεῖνός μοι εἶπεν (The one who made me [to be] whole said to me).

Adjectives Used as Nouns

Adjectives often function as nouns (e.g., the poor, the rich, the blind). In Matthew 5:3 Μακάριοι οἱ πτωχοὶ τῷ πνεύματι (Blessed are the poor in spirit) the adjective πτωχοί is used as the subject noun, and the adjective μακάριοι is the predicate adjective. The adjective will usually have an article when functioning as a noun, but it is not necessary. For example, in Romans 5:7 Paul says that it would be difficult for one to die for "a righteous person" (δικαίου), whereas one might dare to die for "a good person" (τοῦ ἀγαθοῦ). The article before the second probably means "his benefactor" (Cranfield 1975:264).

The adjective ἅγιος is often used as a noun, meaning "that which is holy." In the singular it can be used for the sanctuary, sacrificial items, and Christ. In the plural it is used for angels, believers, and other devout persons. In reference to believers it is usually translated "saints." Paul often uses the articular neuter adjective as an abstract noun, as the adjective μωρὸν (foolish) in 1 Corinthians 1:25 τὸ μωρὸν τοῦ θεοῦ σοφώτερον τῶν ἀνθρώπων ἐστίν (the foolishness of God is wiser than men).

The adjective can display the same syntactic functions as a noun. For example, it is used as a direct object in Matthew 7:11 δώσει ἀγαθὰ τοῖς αἰτοῦσιν αὐτόν (he will give good things to those who ask him) and as an object of a preposition in Matthew 6:13 ῥῦσαι ἡμᾶς ἀπὸ τοῦ πονηροῦ (deliver us from the evil one). In the latter example it is uncertain whether τοῦ πονηροῦ is neuter and refers to evil in general (as in Luke 6:45; Rom. 12:9) or masculine and refers to Satan (as in Eph. 6:16; 1 John 2:13–14). Jesus, however, equates τοῦ πονηροῦ with ὁ διάβολος in Matthew 13:38–39.

Adjectives Used as Adverbs

Some adjectives, such as ἴδιον, λοιπόν, μικρόν, μόνον, ὀλίγον, πολύ, πρῶτον, can be used adverbially to modify the verb. In Matthew 5:24 ὕπαγε πρῶτον διαλλάγηθι τῷ ἀδελφῷ σου (go first and be reconciled to your brother) the adjective πρῶτον functions adverbially modifying the verb ὕπαγε. Mark 1:19 προβὰς ὀλίγον εἶδεν Ἰάκωβον (having gone ahead a little way, he saw James). The adjectives will usually have neuter gender and function as adverbial accusatives or adverbial datives.

Irregularities in Comparative Adjectives

There are three degrees of adjectives: positive, comparative, and superlative. For the English adjective "good" the degrees would be expressed "good," "better," and "best." Adjectives ending in -τερος or -ιων are comparative, and those ending in -τατος or -ιστος are superlative. One would expect the comparative adjectives to be used to compare two items (this tastes better than that) and the superlative to be used to compare more than two (this tastes best of all), but this is not always the case in the New Testament:

Positive for comparative—In Matthew 18:8 Jesus says, "It is better for you (καλόν σοί ἐστιν) to enter into life crippled or lame than to have two hands or two feet and be thrown into eternal fire." The positive degree adjective καλόν (good) is used for a comparative (better).

Positive for superlative—Matthew 22:38 αὕτη ἐστὶν ἡ μεγάλη καὶ πρώτη ἐντολή (this is the greatest and most important commandment). The adjectives μεγάλη and πρώτη are in the positive degree (great, first) but are to be understood in the superlative degree (greatest, most important).

Comparative for superlative—Matthew 18:1 Τίς ἄρα μείζων ἐστὶν ἐν τῆ βασιλεία τῶν οὐρανῶν (Who then is the greatest in the kingdom of heaven?). It is obvious that the comparative adjective μείζων cannot be rendered "greater," for then there would only be two persons in heaven. See also 1 Corinthians 13:13 where Paul uses the comparative μείζων (greater) in reference to three things (faith, hope, and love).

Comparative for elative—Acts 17:22 κατὰ πάντα ὡς δεισιδαιμονεστέρους ὑμᾶς θεωρῶ (in every way I perceive that you are very religious). The adjective δεισιδαιμονεστέρους is comparative in form (more religious) but is translated as elative (very religious).

Superlative for elative—Most adjectives with a superlative form are used in the elative degree. They are the equivalent of an emphatic adjective, using "very," "most," or "exceedingly." The superlative in Mark 4:1 ὄχλος πλεῖστος (greatest crowd) should be rendered as an elative (a very great crowd).

Exercises

In the following examples, cite the best use for the pronoun or adjective and give alternate uses where appropriate. Translate the passage in such a way as to bring out the force of the use(s) you have chosen.

1. Matt. 11:5   τυφλοί, χωλοί, λεπροί, κωφοί, νεκροί, πτωχοί
2. Matt. 11:11   μικρότερος
3. Mark 4:25   ὅς, ὅς, ὅ (cf. NIV)
4. Mark 9:43   καλόν
5. Luke 8:26–27   ἥτις, τις
6. Luke 16:7   Σύ
7. John 1:50–51   σοι, ὑμῖν (explain the switch in number)
8. John 2:24   αὐτός, αὐτόν, αὐτοῖς, αὐτόν
9. John 4:22   ὑμεῖς, ὅ, ἡμεῖς (inclusive or exclusive)
10. John 4:42   σήν, αὐτοί
11. 1 Cor. 1:10   αὐτό, αὐτῷ, αὐτῇ
12. 1 Cor. 11:21   ὅς, ὅς
13. 1 Cor. 15:30   ἡμεῖς (inclusive, exclusive, or epistolary plural)
14. Col 3:13   ἀλλήλων, ἑαυτοῖς
15. 2 Tim. 3:16   θεόπνευστος
16. 1 John 3:3   ταύτην, ἐκεῖνος

6 Prepositional Phrases

A preposition is a word used before substantives to form phrases which modify verbs, nouns, or adjectives. For example, in Ephesians 5:2 the prepositional phrase ἐν ἀγάπῃ (in love) modifies the verb περιπατεῖτε (walk). The preposition, the case ending of the noun, the word modified, and the context all supply information regarding the meaning of the phrase. Some grammarians treat prepositions as a separate entity, as if their meaning dominated the meaning of the phrase. Others treat prepositions under the noun case system, as if the reverse were true.

Those who regard prepositions as a subset of the noun case system echo the historical school of linguistics, for in classical Greek the noun was the dominant element. The preposition was used simply to help clarify the case meaning of the noun. For example, the expression ἡ φωνὴ τοῦ ἀνθρώπου could be "the voice of the man" or "the voice from the man." The addition of ἀπό would clarify the relation intended by the case, "the voice from the man." In koine Greek the preposition gained more independent force, while the case lost some of its significance. It is best to consider the prepositional phrase as a syntactical unit that must be analyzed as a whole in light of various factors: (a) the possible nuances of the preposition with objects in certain cases, (b) the possible case functions, (c) the relative frequencies of the uses, (d) the influence of the literary and situational contexts, especially the force of the verb and the object of the preposition, (e) whether the object noun is an event word, and (f) the distinctive prepositional usage of New Testament and Hellenistic Greek in general (cf. Harris 1978:1173).

Several features of New Testament usage should be kept in mind. Some reflect changes from classical to Hellenistic Greek, and some reflect Semitic influence (cf. Harris 1978:1173–75). Perhaps most important for exegesis is the tendency of Hellenistic Greek toward laxity in usage; that is, prepositions tend to overlap into the semantic domain of other prepositions. For example, in Mark 13:3 Jesus sat εἰς the Mount of Olives. *Εἰς* here overlaps with a common meaning of ἐπί (Jesus sat *on* the mountain). In Mark 13:9 Jesus says that His followers will be flogged εἰς the synagogues. *Εἰς* now overlaps with a common meaning of ἐν, denoting location (believers will be flogged *in* the synagogues). For other examples along with discussion, see Zerwick (1963:28–37) and Turner (1963:254–57).

Prepositions have often been enlisted as proof for certain doctrines, such as the εἰς in Mark 1:9 ἐβαπτίσθη εἰς τὸν Ἰορδάνην (he was baptized into the Jordan) to support baptism by immersion. In view of the overlap between εἰς and ἐν, it would be precarious to base doctrine solely on prepositions (cf. Mark 1:5, where ἐν is used). The following caveats in the exegetical use of prepositions have been adapted from Harris (1978:1175–78):

Do not insist on classical distinctions—As noted above, Hellenistic Greek is not characterized by the strict usage of classical Greek. The preposition ἐν, for example, displays a wide variety of meanings beyond its root idea, much of which comes from Semitic influence. One of the major shortcomings of Lenski's commentaries is his tendency to insist on the classical meaning of ἐν. Moule (1968:49) states, "It is a mistake to build exegetical conclusions on the notion that Classical accuracy in the use of prepositions was maintained in the κοινή period." In connection with this, it might be misleading to say any preposition (especially ἐν) has a literal or proper meaning. Rather prepositions have a range of possible meanings with some more common than others.

Do not neglect stylistic variation—Harris notes that a change of prepositions (Rom. 3:30), a change of case with repeated prepositions (Matt. 19:28), or the use and nonuse of prepositions in the same context (1 John 3:18) does not always signal a change of meaning.

Do not disregard probable distinctions—Although there is a general laxity in usage, sometimes an author will use a particular preposition because of its traditional distinctiveness. Zerwick (1963:35) notes that εἰς does not take on the local meaning of ἐν in Matthew and the Epistles. Thus Philippians 1:5 κοινωνίᾳ ὑμῶν εἰς τὸ εὐαγγέλιον should be understood as "you cooperate to spread the gospel" rather than "your fellowship in the gospel" (cf. O'Brien 1991:61–62).

Be cautious about seeking double meanings—The notion of *sensus plenior* (two or more meanings of a word or phrase in a single occurrence) is a debatable issue. Harris states, "It seems illegitimate, simply on *a priori* hermeneutical principles, to exclude the possibility that *on occasion* an author may use a single preposition in a dual sense." He cites the δι᾽ ὕδατος in 1 Peter 3:20 as an example. Some say the preposition διά could be used in both (1) a local sense, to be brought safely through the water, and (2) an instrumental sense, to be preserved by means of the water. Selwyn and Kelly are cited in support. Harris also refers to 1 Timothy 2:15, where the διά could mean that the woman is delivered through the ordeal of childbirth and that she is saved by means of bearing children. Regarding Colossians 1:17 he cites F. F. Bruce who says the πρό means both time and rank; Christ has both temporal priority to the universe and primacy over it.

Do not neglect the significance of not repeating the preposition before the second object—Not repeating the preposition may indicate that the author considered both objects as an undivided unit. Thus the water and Spirit in John 3:5 ἐὰν μή τις γεννηθῇ ἐξ ὕδατος καὶ πνεύματος (except one is born by water and Spirit) should be thought of as a unit, rather than as two separate steps in the regenerative process. It could refer to the inward cleansing effected by the Spirit (cf. Matt. 3:11). This also has significance in Paul's usual opening benedictions in which he invokes divine blessings from both the Father and the Son: χάρις ὑμῖν καὶ εἰρήνη ἀπὸ θεοῦ πατρὸς ἡμῶν καὶ κυρίου Ἰησοῦ Χριστοῦ (Grace to you and peace from God our Father and Lord Jesus Christ).

Grammatical Functions

Prepositional Phrases Used Adverbially

Prepositions are almost always found in prepositional phrases that function as adverb phrases. As adverb phrases they modify verbs, participles, infinitives, or adjectives. For example, Paul writes in Galatians 1:18 μετὰ ἔτη τρία ἀνῆλθον εἰς Ἱεροσόλυμα (after three years I went up to Jerusalem). Both prepositional phrases μετὰ ἔτη τρία and εἰς Ἱεροσόλυμα function as adverb phrases modifying the verb, the first telling when and the second telling where Paul went.

Prepositional Phrases Used Adjectivally

Prepositional phrases can also modify nouns or pronouns (The people in the church were singing) rather than verbs (The people were singing in the church). The prepositional phrase is usually in the attributive position (i.e., preceded by an article). Thus Romans 11:21 τῶν κατὰ φύσιν κλάδων (the according to nature branches) means "the natural branches," and 1 Timothy 6:3 τῇ κατ᾽ εὐσέβειαν διδασκαλίᾳ (the according to godliness instruction) means "the godly instruction." Sometimes the prepositional phrase is best rendered as a relative clause: 1 Peter 1:10 περὶ τῆς εἰς ὑμᾶς χάριτος (concerning the grace which would be extended to you; cf. 1:11) and Matthew 3:17 φωνὴ ἐκ τῶν οὐρανῶν (a voice which came from heaven).

Prepositional Phrases Used as Nouns

When an article precedes a prepositional phrase and there is no head noun to modify, the article and prepositional phrase function as a noun phrase: Romans 4:14 οἱ ἐκ νόμου (those who follow the law); Romans 9:6 οἱ ἐξ Ἰσραήλ (those from Israel; i.e., Israelites); and Galatians 3:7, 9 οἱ ἐκ πίστεως (those who believe; i.e., believers). In Acts 1:3 Jesus was teaching τὰ περὶ τῆς βασιλείας (the things pertaining to the kingdom). In 1 Corinthians 9:20 Paul became as a Jew so that he might gain τοῖς ὑπὸ νόμον (the ones under the law).

Κατά with the accusative can function as a periphrasis for a genitive noun. It is said to be equivalent to a genitive of possession, but other functions are possible. In Ephesians 1:15 Paul writes ἀκούσας τὴν καθ᾽ ὑμᾶς πίστιν (having heard of your faith). Actually the κατά phrase functions here as a subjective genitive, not possession. It thus represents a deep structure subject (having heard that you believe). The same is true in Romans 1:15 τὸ κατ᾽ ἐμὲ πρόθυμον, where "the willingness of me" becomes "I am willing" (cf. NIV, TEV). In Acts 17:28 the κατά phrase functions as a genitive of relationship (your poets). The titles of the Gospels (e.g., *KATA IΩANNHN*) could also be considered periphrasis for genitive nouns. Thus we have "The Gospel of John" rather than "The Gospel According to John" (implying four conflicting accounts; cf. Zerwick 1963:44).

In addition, prepositional phrases with εἰς can function as a predicate nominative, as in Matthew 19:5 ἔσονται οἱ δύο εἰς σάρκα μίαν (the two shall be one flesh) and Matthew 21:42 οὖτος ἐγενήθη εἰς κεφαλὴν γωνίας (This one has become the head of the corner).

Prepositional Phrases Used with Indirect Objects

As in English, Greek indirect objects may be preceded by prepositions. They will have the same semantic roles as dative indirect objects (experiencer, benefaction, opposition). For example, Matthew 18:26 Μακροθύμησον ἐπ' ἐμοί (Show mercy to me); Luke 1:13 εἶπεν πρὸς αὐτόν (he spoke to him); and 1 Corinthians 2:6 Σοφίαν λαλοῦμεν ἐν τοῖς τελείοις (We speak wisdom to the ones who are mature).

Prepositions Used as Independent Adverbs

On rare occasions in the New Testament the lone preposition may serve as an adverb. One example is in 2 Corinthians 11:23 ὑπὲρ ἐγώ (I more). Sometimes prepositions are combined with temporal or local adverbs (cf. 2 Cor. 8:10, 9:2). The use of prepositions as adverbs is more common with improper prepositions than with regular prepositions.

Semantic Functions

The following discussions are based on the semantic function of the entire phrase in context. Much has been adapted from Louw and Nida (1988). Since most prepositions have a rather large number of nuances, the discussions might be best used as a reference guide when working with actual text.

ἀνά

Location—The preposition ἀνά conveys "up" only in compound words. In phrases with μέσος it expresses spacial position, as in Matthew 13:25 (*among* the wheat) and Revelation 7:17 (*at* the center of the throne area).

Distribution—In 1 Corinthians 14:27 Paul instructs those with the gift of tongues to speak "one at a time" (ἀνὰ μέρος). In Luke 10:1 the Lord sent out the disciples "in pairs" (ἀνὰ δύο). In Matthew 20:9 the workers received "a denarius apiece" (ἀνὰ δηνάριον). The distributive ἀνά in the above examples functions in a manner relation, telling how the people are to speak in tongues, how the Lord sent the disciples out, and how the workers were paid.

ἀντί

Substitution—When Joseph and Mary returned from Egypt with Jesus, they learned that Archelaus reigned *in place of* his father Herod (Matt. 2:22). In Mark 10:45 Jesus gave His life as a ransom ἀντί for many, not simply for their benefit, but in their stead, for they could not effect the ransom themselves (Taylor 1952:444).

Exchange—Paul admonishes us not to repay evil *in return for* evil (Rom. 12:17).

Reason—Paul, quoting from Genesis 2:24, says "Because of this (ἀντὶ τούτου) a man will leave his father and mother to unite with his wife, so that the two become as one" (Eph. 5:31). The LXX reads ἕνεκεν τούτου instead of ἀντὶ τούτου. See also Luke 1:20.

Contrast—James writes, "Instead (ἀντί), you should say, 'if the Lord wills'" (Jas. 4:15).

The difficult phrase "grace for (ἀντί) grace" in John 1:16 could mean (a) substitution, that the greater grace through the New Covenant has replaced the earlier grace through the Old Covenant; (b) accumulation, that grace is realized throughout a believer's life as grace gives way to more grace (Barrett 1978:168); or (c) correspondence, that the grace given to us corresponds to the grace of the Word. Although the second is favored by the NIV and TEV, Brown (1966:16) notes that accumulation is normally expressed by ἐπί, not ἀντί. The third option is not a normal usage of ἀντί.

ἀπό

Space—The people begged Jesus to depart *from* their region (Mark 5:17). The idea of source is a subset of spacial extension: Paul said he passed along to the Corinthians the teachings he received *from* the Lord (1 Cor. 11:23).

Disassociation—Paul says that for the sake of his people he could wish to be accursed and *separated from* Christ (Rom. 9:3).

Time—Ἀπό expresses the extent of time from a previous point. Satan was a murderer *from the beginning* (John 8:44). The ἀπό phrase in Romans 1:20

ἀπὸ κτίσεως κόσμου (from the creation of the world) could be interpreted as source or time. If κτίσις refers to what was created, then the phrase would denote the source of knowledge about God. If κτίσις refers to the act of creating, then the phrase would denote the time from which knowledge about God was evident to humans. Most interpret the phrase temporally, since the next expression τοῖς ποιήμασιν (by the things made) adequately expresses the source of the knowledge (Cranfield 1975:114). "People have understood about the invisible things of God *ever since the creation* by means of what God made." Paul's intent is to show that all who have ever lived are without excuse.

Reason—Jesus said it was terrible for this world *because of* its temptations (Matt. 18:7). Also Jesus was heard *because of* His godly reverence (Heb. 5:7). When the object is a verbal noun, the phrase can be transformed into an adverbial clause: Acts 12:14 ἀπὸ τῆς χαρᾶς (because she was glad; cf. Matt. 13:44; 14:26).

Agency—When we are tempted, we should not say that we are tempted *by* God (Jas. 1:13); the woman fled to a place prepared *by* God (Rev. 12:6).

Means—Jesus said we would know false prophets *by* their fruit (Matt. 7:16).

Partitive—Prepositional phrases with ἀπό can function as partitive genitives. Luke 9:38 (a man from the crowd) and Matthew 27:21 (one of the two).

διά

Space—The spacial area through which movement occurs often employs διά with the genitive; for example, "*through* the roof" (Luke 5:19) and "*through* Samaria" (John 4:4).

Time—Although διά with the genitive can denote the time "after" which something happens (Mark 2:1), it more commonly expresses the time "during" which something happens (Acts 5:19) or the entire extent of the time that something occurs; i.e., "throughout" (Mark 5:5).

Reason—Reason can be expressed by διά with the accusative. Herod had John put in jail *because* of Herodias (Mark 6:17; cf. Matt. 9:11; Luke 23:25).

Agency—Intermediate agency is normally conveyed by διά with the genitive. For example, God delivered the law to Moses *by* angels (Gal. 3:19) and John sent a message to Christ *through* His disciples (Matt. 11:2; cf. John 1:3;

3:17). Sometimes it can express direct agency (1 Cor. 1:9). In Galatians 1:1 Paul uses διά twice, stating that his apostleship was by divine agency, not by human agency.

Means—Means can be expressed with διά with the genitive. John said he would rather not communicate *with* paper and ink (2 John 12). Means is also expressed in such phrases as "*through* his blood" (Acts 20:28), "through the cross" (Eph. 2:16), and "through the offering" (Heb. 10:10), all of which refer to an action: the sacrificial death of Christ.

Manner—How something is done can be expressed by διά with the genitive, as in Luke 8:4 (Jesus spoke in a figurative way) and Hebrews 13:22 (the author writes briefly).

Benefaction—The person benefited by an event can be indicated using διά with the accusative. Jesus remarked that the Sabbath was made *for the benefit of* humankind and that humankind was not made *for the benefit of* the Sabbath (Mark 2:27).

Attendant circumstance—An event that accompanies the main event can be expressed using διά with the genitive. This function may help explain two problematic texts. First Timothy 2:15 σωθήσεται διὰ τῆς τεκνογονίας has been explained as (1) time (physically delivered through the time of child bearing), (2) means (spiritually saved by means of child bearing and raising, rather than engaging in adultery), (3) means (spiritually saved by means of the incarnation of Christ), or (4) attendant circumstance (spiritually saved in connection with fulfilling their God-given roles). The latter two seem the most plausible.

The passage in 1 John 5:6 presents us with two difficulties: the meaning of the water and blood and the meaning of διά and ἐν· Οὗτός ἐστιν ὁ ἐλθὼν δι᾽ ὕδατος καὶ αἵματος, Ἰησοῦς Χριστός, οὐκ ἐν τῷ ὕδατι μόνον ἀλλ᾽ ἐν τῷ ὕδατι καὶ ἐν τῷ αἵματι (This is the one who came by water and blood, Jesus Christ; not in water only but also in the water and in the blood). First, some interpret the water and blood as Christian baptism and the Eucharist, ways by which Christ comes to the believer. Others view both as pertaining to Christ's death (cf. John 19:34). Most view the terms as referring to the baptism and death of Christ. Second, it is probably best to view the switch from διά to ἐν as a stylistic variation with the same meaning. The διά phrase could be interpreted as (1) metaphorical location, the baptismal waters and death on the cross together constitute the path through which Jesus came to save (BAG 1957:178c); (2) means, Jesus came as Savior by means of His baptism and death; or (3) attendant circumstance, the waters of baptism and the blood of redemption accompanied His salvific mission and were a necessary part of it (Moule 1968:57; cf. Brown 1982:572–78, Smalley 1984:277–80).

εἰς

Space—*Eis* normally conveys spacial extension, as when Jesus told His disciples to go *into* the city (Matt. 26:18) and when Peter and John went *to* the tomb (John 20:3), but it can also convey spacial position, as when the soldiers beat Jesus *on* His head (Matt. 27:30), a would-be disciple wanted to say goodbye to those *in* his house (Luke 9:61), and the Jewish authorities did not want the gospel to spread *among* the people (Acts 4:17). Perhaps the problematic εἰς in Romans 11:32 could be understood as a metaphorical extension of spacial position. God imprisoned people *in* their own disobedience, meaning that He gave them over to their disobedient ways from which they could not escape apart from divine grace. To argue for a causal use of εἰς here would yield a different meaning: God imprisoned them *because of* their disobedience.

Time—*Eis* can express the time something will continue: "until the end" (Matt. 10:22). It can also express a period through which something occurs or the extent of time (Luke 12:19).

Reason—The causal use of εἰς is controversial. Some argue that εἰς in Matthew 12:41 is causal: the people of Nineveh repented *because of* the preaching of Jonah. However, it could be temporal (when Jonah preached; cf. NJB, TEV). The possible occurrence in Romans 4:20 is probably reference rather than cause: Abraham did not doubt *in reference to* the promise of God (cf. NIV). The same could be said of Matthew 3:11, where John said that he baptized people *in connection with* their repentance. With such support the causal use of εἰς is called on to solve the *crux interpretum* in Acts 2:38. It is argued that Peter admonished the people to repent and be baptized in the name of Jesus Christ *because of* the remission of sins. However, the more common nuances of purpose or reference make good sense. Purpose need not imply that baptism is a requirement for forgiveness. Baptism was considered a natural corollary of repentance and forgiveness, and thus was often conceptually linked with these terms (contra Mantey 1951:45–48).

Purpose—Purpose often occurs with verbs of motion, sending, and choosing. The idea of purpose includes aspirations toward a goal. Paul was alarmed that the people were turning away from Christ *in order to* accept another gospel (Gal. 1:6). When the object of the preposition is an event word, the prepositional phrase may need to be transformed into an adverbial purpose clause. Examples include Matthew 25:6 εἰς ἀπάντησιν αὐτοῦ (in order that we might meet him; cf. Acts 28:15); Luke 5:32 εἰς μετάνοιαν (in order that they might repent; cf. Rom. 2:4); Romans 1:1 εἰς εὐαγγέλιον θεοῦ (in order that I might proclaim the good news that God has given; cf. 2 Cor. 2:12); Romans 1:5 εἰς ὑπακοήν (in order that the Gentiles might obey; cf. Rom. 6:16; 15:18; 16:26; 2 Cor. 10:5; 1 Pet. 1:2); and 2 Thessalonians 2:13 εἰς σωτηρίαν (in order that you might be saved).

Result—In Romans 5:18 the sin of Adam *resulted in* condemnation, while the righteousness of Christ *resulted in* acquittal. In Romans 10:10 people are to confess with the mouth εἰς σωτηρίαν (so as to receive salvation). See also 2 Corinthians 7:9.

Reference—Reference is conveyed in English with the words "concerning," "about," "in reference to," or "with respect to." Sometimes εἰς is used in this sense. In Acts 2:25 David spoke *concerning* Christ. This use is common in baptismal formulas. To be baptized into (εἰς) the name of the Lord Jesus (Acts 19:5; cf. Matt. 28:19) means to be baptized with respect to the Lord Jesus Himself. It is abbreviated in Galatians 3:27 to εἰς Χριστόν (with respect to Christ; cf. Rom. 6:3). It probably does not have any mystical connotations, since Paul uses the same expression in reference to himself (1 Cor. 1:13, 15). To be baptized in reference to another person is to be identified with that person. It is a public testimony that a close personal relationship or union exists between the two parties. A similar idea is probably intended in the parallel formula using ἐπί. In Acts 2:38 Peter exhorts the people to be baptized in (ἐπί) the name of Jesus Christ. This could also mean "with respect to" (cf. Matt. 18:5; Acts 4:18).

Means—In Acts 7:53 the law was delivered *by* the direction of angels.

Manner—Manner tells the way in which something is done, such as "in vain" (Phil. 2:16) and "in peace" or "peaceably" (Luke 8:48).

Benefaction—Εἰς can express something done for another, as when the disciples asked if they were to buy food *for* all these people (Luke 9:13).

Opposition—Hostility "against" another is often expressed by εἰς (Luke 12:10; 15:18). The hostility could involve actions, speech, or frame of mind depending on the verb and general context.

ἐκ

Space—Ἐκ often conveys spacial extension "out of" or "from." For example, the prophet said that God would call His Son *out of* Egypt (Matt. 2:15). Source, as mentioned earlier, is a subset of spacial extension: Paul did not seek glory *from* men (1 Thess. 2:6). With words meaning "right" or "left" ἐκ means "at" (sit at your right hand; cf. Matt. 20:21, 23).

Disassociation—Christ redeemed us *from* the curse of the law (Gal. 3:13); no one can snatch believers *from* God's hand or power (John 10:28; cf. Acts 15:29).

Derivation—Derivation indicates that from which someone or something is descended or made. Those who are *from* God listen to God's words (John 8:47); the soldiers wove a crown made *from* thorns (Matt. 27:29; cf. Rom. 1:3).

Time—Although not as common, ἐκ can express the time when something began, as in John 9:1 (blind since birth), or the length of time that something happens, as in Acts 9:33 (bed-ridden for eight years).

Reason—In John 6:66 many of Jesus' followers left Him *because of* His teaching about the bread of life (cf. Rev. 9:2; 16:10–11).

Means—Means is often expressed by ἐκ (Luke 16:9; Jas. 2:18). If the object of the preposition is an event word, it could be transformed into a participle. For example, Galatians 2:16: οὐ δικαιοῦται ἄνθρωπος ἐξ ἔργων νόμου ἐὰν μὴ διὰ πίστεως Ἰησοῦ Χριστοῦ (a person is not justified by means of doing what the law requires but by means of believing in Jesus Christ; cf. Rom. 3:20). The difficult expression in Romans 1:17 ἐκ πίστεως εἰς πίστιν is best explained as means that is perhaps intensified by the addition of the second phrase (by faith and faith alone).

Agency—God's children are not born *by* the will of humankind, but *by* God (John 1:13).

Manner—Mark 6:51 (beyond measure) and 2 Corinthians 9:7 (not reluctantly).

Partitive—Matthew 10:29 (one of them).

ἐν

Space—Ἐν commonly expresses spacial position. Jesus said He was *in* His Father's house (Luke 2:49); Bethlehem was not least *among* the rulers of

Judah (Matt. 2:6); God showed Moses the tabernacle design *on* the mountain (Heb. 8:5); and Christ is seated *at* the right hand of God (Heb. 1:3). It might also express spacial extension, as when an angel of the Lord went down *into* the pool (John 5:4, TR).

Time—Ἐν expresses two temporal ideas: the time when something occurs (Matt. 11:22) or the period within which something occurs (Matt. 2:1). The first can be rendered "when" or "at," the second "during" or "while."

Reason—In John 16:30 Jesus' disciples said they believed that He came from God *because of* what He was saying (cf. Gal. 1:24).

Agency—Paul says that we are all baptized into one body *by* one Spirit (1 Cor. 12:13). Jesus asks, "If I *by* Beelzebul cast out demons, then *by* whom do your sons cast them out?" (Matt. 12:27). Oaths could be considered a type of agency that specifies the guarantor. In Matthew 5:34–36 both ἐν and εἰς are used in an oath; Jesus says not to swear by (ἐν) heaven, by (ἐν) earth, by (εἰς) Jerusalem, or by (ἐν) your head. Heaven (God's throne), earth (God's footstool), and Jerusalem (God's city) could be considered circumlocutions for God.

Means—In Revelation 6:8 the rider on the fourth horse was given authority to kill *by* sword, *by* famine, and *by* plague (cf. 1 John 2:3). The translation is altered with a verbal noun as object, as in Romans 1:9 ἐν τῷ εὐαγγελίῳ τοῦ υἱοῦ αὐτοῦ (Paul serves God by preaching the good news about God's Son).

Association—In Jude 14 the Lord will come *with* thousands of His holy ones. Paul often speaks of believers being *in* Christ, and John speaks of Christ being *in* the Father, and the Father *in* Christ (John 10:38). Although expressions such as ἐν Χριστῷ could be understood in a mystical sense as metaphorical extensions of location (Turner 1963:263), it might be better to consider them as denoting a close, personal, life enhancing relationship or union with Christ (BAG 1957:259a; Moule 1968:80; for overview see Harris 1978:1192–93). See also John 15:4.

Reference—In Romans 11:2 Paul rhetorically asks, "Do you not know what the Scripture says *about* Elijah?"

Manner—Paul says he serves God *with* all his heart (Rom. 1:9a). The prepositional phrase with ἐν can be rendered by a simple adverb of manner when the object is a verbal noun. Examples include John 16:29 ἐν παρρησίᾳ (confidently); Acts 16:36 ἐν εἰρήνῃ (peaceably); James 3:13 ἐν πραΰτητι (meekly); and 1 Peter 1:17 ἐν φόβῳ (reverently). Other times it is rendered as a participle, as in Luke 6:12 ἐν τῇ προσευχῇ (he spent the whole night praying).

Experiencer—In Matthew 17:12 Jesus said that Elijah had already come and the Jews did *to* him as they pleased (cf. Gal. 1:16, to reveal his Son to me).

Attendant Circumstance—The Lord *will* return with a shout, *with* the voice of an archangel, and *with* a trumpet call of God (1 Thess. 4:16). These phrases denote actions that accompany the Lord's return rather than describe how He comes (manner).

ἐπί

Space—Ἐπί can convey both spacial position and extension. Jesus walked *on* the water (Mark 6:48 gen.); Jesus stands *at* the door and knocks (Rev. 3:20 acc.); Jesus went in and out *among* us (Acts 1:21 acc.); the women went *to* the tomb (Luke 24:22 acc.); a fig tree was *by* the road (Matt. 21:19 gen.); you will be brought *before* governors and kings (Matt. 10:18 acc.); Jesus made a good profession *before* Pilate (1 Tim. 6:13 gen.); the seed is cast *unto* the ground (Mark 4:26 gen.).

Time—Ἐπί in any of its cases can denote time when something occurs. The disciples returned *at* that moment (John 4:27 dat.; cf. Jude 18 gen.; Heb. 9:26 dat.; Acts 3:1 acc.). It can also signify a period within which something occurs, as when David ate the consecrated bread *during the time of* Abiathar (Mark 2:26 gen.), or a period through which something occurs, as when there was no rain *for a period* of three years (Luke 4:25 acc.).

Reason—Reason may be conveyed by ἐπί with the dative. In Mark 1:22 the people were amazed *because* of His teachings.

Purpose—Believers are called *to* be free (Gal. 5:13 dat.); the Pharisees and Sadducees were coming *to* be baptized by John (Matt. 3:7 acc.).

Reference—Ἐπί with the genitive or dative can express reference. The Scriptures spoke *about* Jesus (John 12:16).

Manner—In 2 Corinthians 9:6 the expression ἐπ᾽ εὐλογίαις means "generously" (he who sows generously will reap generously).

Basis—The idea of "on the basis of" can be expressed with ἐπ᾽ and either the genitive or dative. For example, in Matthew 18:16 church discipline is to be decided *on the basis of* two or three witnesses.

Means—People are not to live *by* bread alone (Matt. 4:4 dat.).

Opposition — With the dative or accusative ἐπί denotes hostility. Children will rise up *against* parents (Matt. 10:21).

Benefaction — The people saw the miracles Jesus performed *for* the sick (John 6:2 gen.).

Experiencer — Gamaliel warned the council to be careful about what they do *to* these men (Acts 5:35 dat.).

Authority — Ἐπί with any of its cases can express the object of one's control, authority, or rule. Jesus gave His disciples authority *over* the power of the enemy (Luke 10:19 acc.).

κατά

Space — Various meanings are again possible. For example, the herd of swine rushed *down* the steep bank (Mark 5:13 gen.); the Levite went *down toward* the place (Luke 10:32 acc.); the disciples were not to greet anyone *on* the road (Luke 10:4 acc.); Paul taught the Jews who lived *among* the Gentiles (Acts 21:21 acc.); and famine spread *throughout* the land (Luke 15:14 acc.).

Time — With the accusative κατά can express time when something occurs, distributive time, or approximate time. For example, the Lord laid the foundation of the world *in* the beginning (Heb. 1:10); Jesus' parents went *yearly* (κατ᾽ ἔτος) to the Passover (Luke 2:41); and Paul and Silas were praying *about* midnight (Acts 16:25).

Correspondence — With the accusative κατά can express correspondence in which two things are compared, one often being a standard. For example, Christ died *according to* the Scriptures (1 Cor. 15:3).

Reference — The idea of "with regard to" is expressed by κατά with the accusative in Romans 1:3–4. With regard to Christ's physical nature (κατὰ σάρκα), He is of the lineage of David, but in regard to His divine nature (κατὰ πνεῦμα ἁγιωσύνης), He is the Son of God.

Guarantor — Κατά with the genitive can be used in oaths, designating the guarantor of the oath. Because God could not swear *by* anyone greater, He swore *by* Himself (Heb. 6:13).

Opposition — Κατά with the genitive can also denote hostility. Tertullus brought accusations *against* Paul (Acts 24:1).

Manner — The word of the Lord spread over a large area *in* a powerful way (Acts 19:20 acc.); church activity should be done *in* an orderly manner

(1 Cor. 14:40 acc.); and those who prophesy are to speak *one at a time (καθ' ἕνα;* 1 Cor. 14:31 acc.).

μετά

Association—The idea of association is commonly expressed with μετά with the genitive. The association can either be a person, as when Jesus departed *with* His disciples (Mark 3:7), or a thing, as a large crowd came *with* clubs and swords (Matt. 26:47). It can also be used when one thing is combined with another, as when wine was mixed *with* gall (Matt. 27:34).

Manner—Manner can be expressed with μετά and the genitive. Paul admonishes women to dress *with* modesty (1 Tim. 2:9; cf. Matt. 24:30, 1 Thess. 1:6). Sometimes it can be translated with an adverb, as in Matthew 13:20 μετὰ χαρᾶς (joyfully; cf. Acts 4:31).

Time—*After* the time of trouble, the sun will be darkened (Mark 13:24 acc.); *after* these things John saw an opened door in heaven (Rev. 4:1 acc.).

Opposition—The Lord will fight *against* them with the sword of His mouth (Rev. 2:16 gen.).

Space—Μετά with the accusative can denote place behind or after. For example, *behind* the second veil (Heb. 9:3).

παρά

Space—Παρά can convey spacial extension (from) or spacial position (among, near). For example, a decree went out *from* Caesar (Luke 2:1 gen.); the story was spread *among* the Jews (Matt. 28:15 dat.); Jesus passed *alongside* the sea (Mark 1:16 acc.); Jesus set the child *beside* Him (Luke 9:47 dat.); and he who does the law is righteous *before* God (Rom. 2:13 dat.).

Association—Two disciples spent the rest of the day *with* Jesus (John 1:39 dat.); Jesus spoke certain things while *with* His disciples (John 14:25 dat.).

Agency—Παρά with the genitive can denote agency. The things told to Mary *by* the Lord will come to pass (Luke 1:45; cf. Matthew 19:26).

Comparison—Paul says that one person thinks one day is more important *than* another (Rom. 14:5 acc.); the Son was made greater *than* the angels (Heb. 1:4 acc.).

Opposition—Paul warns the Galatians to beware of preaching *contrary to* what he taught them (Gal. 1:8–9 acc.; cf. Rom. 16:17 acc.).

Substitution—People worshiped nature *instead of* the Creator (Rom. 1:25 acc.).

περί

Space—John wore a leather belt *around* his waist (Matt. 3:4 acc.).

Time—Approximate time can be expressed with περί and the accusative case. The landowner went out *about* the third hour (Matt. 20:3).

Reference—Περί with the genitive and occasionally the accusative can convey reference. Paul writes *concerning* the things the Corinthians had written (1 Cor. 7:1 gen.). He tells Titus to be a good example *in regard to* all things (Titus 2:7 acc.). Also God sent His Son *in reference* to sin (Rom. 8:3 gen.), that is, to take away sin (cf. NIV, TEV).

Benefaction—With the genitive περί can express "for the benefit of." The blood of the covenant was shed *for* many (Matt. 26:28). Paul encourages believers to pray *for* all the saints (Eph. 6:18).

Association—Paul and those *with* him sailed from Paphos (Acts 13:13 acc.).

πρό

Space—Instead of letting Peter in, Rhoda went and told the others that he was standing *before* the gate (or at the door) (Acts 12:14).

Time—God chose those to be His *before* He made the world (Eph. 1:4).

πρός

Space—Peter stood *by* the gate (John 18:16 dat.); Pilate sent Jesus *to* Herod (Luke 23:7 acc.); God told Paul that he was like an ox kicking *against* its owner's stick (Acts 26:14 acc.); all the people gathered *at* the door (Mark 1:33 acc.); Sapphira fell down *at* Peter's feet and was buried *beside* her husband (Acts 5:10 acc.).

Time—With an accusative object πρός indicates a period of time. Paul was separated from the Thessalonians *for awhile* (1 Thess. 2:17).

Purpose—The Lord gave the apostles, prophets, evangelists, pastors, and teachers to the church *for* the perfecting of the saints (Eph. 4:12 acc.).

Result—Jesus said that Lazarus' sickness was not the kind that would *result in* death (John 11:4 acc.).

Association—John writes that the Word was *with* God (John 1:1 acc.). Harris (1978:1205) suggests that the πρός in John 1:1 refers to active communion rather than passive association. Other examples include Matthew 13:56, where Jesus' sisters were *among* the people, and Acts 3:25, where God made a covenant *with* their ancestors.

Reference—Jesus spoke the parable *with reference* to the Jewish leaders (Mark 12:12 acc.). This could be opposition (against; cf. NIV). Jesus did not answer Pilate one word *in reference to* anything that was said (Matt. 27:14 acc.).

Correspondence—Paul saw that Peter and Barnabas were not conducting themselves *according to* the truth of the gospel (Gal. 2:14 acc.).

Comparison—Paul says his present sufferings were not worthy *to be compared* with the glory that is to come (Rom. 8:18 acc.).

Opposition—Our battle is not *against* blood and flesh (Eph. 6:12 acc.).

Reason—Moses wrote the law about divorce *because* their minds were closed to what God had instructed (Mark 10:5). This is not a common use of πρός.

σύν

Σύν expresses accompaniment or association, as in Luke 1:56 where Mary remained *with* Elizabeth about three months. Although not as common, it can also link things and events, as in Matthew 25:27 and 1 Corinthians 10:13.

ὑπέρ

Benefaction—The idea "for the benefit of" is commonly expressed by ὑπέρ with the genitive. Paul asks that prayer be offered *for* all persons (1 Tim. 2:1; cf. Mark 9:40).

Substitution—Substitution can also be expressed by ὑπέρ with the genitive. Paul wanted to keep Onesimus with him so he could minister to him *in place of* Philemon (Philem. 13). This usage of ὑπέρ is common in the papyri, where one person would sign his name in place of another who was illiterate. In the same way, Christ's vicarious suffering can be conveyed by ὑπέρ, as in John 11:50, 2 Corinthians 5:14–15, and Galatians 3:13 (cf. Robertson 1934:630–32, 1977:35–42).

The problematic phrase in 1 Corinthians 15:29 οἱ βαπτιζόμενοι ὑπὲρ τῶν νεκρῶν (the ones being baptized for the dead) has been interpreted several dozen ways, four of the more common being: (1) substitution, a practice by pagans or misinformed Christians who are baptized *vicariously for* the dead; (2) benefaction, the apostles were giving their lives (a metaphorical baptism) *in behalf of* those who are spiritually dead (i.e., in taking them the gospel); (3) reference, a Christian convert is baptized *in reference to* his or her future resurrection; and (4) space, baptism *over* the graves of the dead. The first is most natural. If so, then Paul's point is to underscore the widespread belief in a bodily resurrection, not to endorse the practice of baptism for the dead (see Fee 1987:763–67 for discussion).

Reason — The nations praised God *because* of His mercy (Rom. 15:9 gen.).

Reference — Paul says *in reference to* Titus that he is his partner (2 Cor. 8:23 gen.); John the Baptist said that this is the one *concerning* whom he spoke (John 1:30 gen.).

Comparison — Comparison in the sense of excelling or surpassing something else is conveyed by ὑπέρ with the accusative. A student is not *greater than* his teacher (Matt. 10:24).

ὑπό

Space — People do not put a lamp *under* a bowl or *under* a bed (Mark 4:21 acc.).

Agency — The usual preposition denoting the agent of passive verbs is ὑπό with the genitive. Jesus was in the wilderness being tempted *by* Satan (Mark 1:13). Both direct and intermediate agency are observed in Matthew 1:22 ἵνα πληρωθῇ τὸ ῥηθὲν ὑπὸ κυρίου διὰ τοῦ προφήτου (that it might be fulfilled which was spoken by the Lord through the prophet). The direct agent (or the one primarily responsible for the action) is expressed by ὑπό and the genitive. The intermediate agent (one who actually carries out the action originated by the direct agent) is expressed by διά and the genitive. This, along with the use of κύριος for Yahweh in the LXX, lends grammatical support for divine inspiration.

Reason — The word is choked in some *because* they worry about the riches and pleasures of this life (Luke 8:14 gen.). Jesus asks the people if they went out to see a reed shaken *by reason of* the wind (Matt. 11:7 gen.). Several grammars cite these examples as means because the English translations use "with" or "by." However, ὑπό is not used to denote an instrument consciously used by a rational being to accomplish an intended task (means). Means employs the simple dative case or some other preposition, such as ἐν, but not ὑπό. The difference is that means is the intentional cause, whereas reason is the unintentional cause.

Authority—Ὑπό denotes the person, institution, or power that exercises control or authority over someone or something. Christ came to redeem those who were *under* the power of the law (Gal. 4:5).

Improper Prepositions

The so-called improper prepositions are those that do not combine with verb roots to form compound words. The designation "improper" is misleading, since they are prepositions in the fullest sense of the word. There are forty-two different improper prepositions in the New Testament. Some of the more common ones are ἄχρι (until), ἔμπροσθεν (before), ἕνεκα (on account of), ἐνώπιον (in the presence of), ἔξω (outside), ἐπάνω (above), ἕως (as far as), ὀπίσω (behind), πέραν (on the other side), and χωρίς (without). All improper prepositions occur with genitive objects except ἅμα (together with) and ἐγγύς (near), which can occur with dative objects. Their usage is much simpler than that of regular prepositions. Besides functioning in prepositional phrases, most also function as adverbs and some as conjunctions. For a complete list and discussion, see Robertson and Davis (1933:249–51).

Prepositions in Composition

Proper prepositions are often prefixed to verbs. The force of the preposition is not always discernible from its independent usage. The various nuances can be classified under three headings: (1) A sense which can be expressed by the separate preposition, whether from New Testament usage (e.g., καταβαίνω "I go down"), derived from New Testament usage (κατακρίνω "I judge"; i.e., "I decide against"), or from usage outside the New Testament (e.g., ἀναβαίνω "I go up"); (2) A perfective sense which intensifies the meaning of the verb (κατέφαγον "I devoured," διαβλέπω "I see clearly"); and (3) A sense that has so coalesced with the verb that it has lost or defies explanation (e.g., ἔξεστιν "it is lawful"). For discussion, see Chamberlain ([1941] 1979:132–48), Moulton and Howard (1979:294–328), Moule (1968:87–92). One should be careful about dissecting compound words and explaining each part in isolation from the rest and from the context (e.g., παρακαλέω: "I exhort" is quite different from "I call alongside").

Exercises

In the following examples, focus on the semantic function of the prepositional phrase. Most will be adverbial. Make special note of those which function adjectivally. Translate the passage in such a way as to convey the use(s) you have chosen.

  1. Matt. 19:8–9   πρός, ἀπό, ἐπί
  2. Matt. 26:55   ἐν, ἐπί, μετά, κατά, ἐν
  3. Mark 3:21–23   παρά, ἀπό, ἐν, ἐν
  4. John 1:7   εἰς, περί, διά
  5. John 1:18   εἰς
  6. John 13:1   πρό, ἐκ, πρός, ἐν, εἰς
  7. John 17:14–15   ἐκ, ἐκ, ἐκ, ἐκ
  8. John 20:4–7   εἰς, εἰς, ἐπί, εἰς
  9. John 21:6   εἰς, ἀπό
 10. Acts 4:27   ἐπί, ἐν, ἐπί, σύν
 11. Rom. 9:5   ἐκ, κατά, ἐπί
 12. Gal. 1:11–12   ὑπό, κατά, παρά, διά
 13. Eph. 2:8–10   διά, ἐκ, ἐκ, ἐν, ἐπί, ἐν
 14. Eph. 6:22   πρός, εἰς, περί
 15. 1 Thess. 4:17–18   σύν, ἐν, εἰς, εἰς, σύν, ἐν
 16. Heb. 12:2   ἀντί

7 Present, Imperfect, and Future

time & kind of motion

Normally the terms present, imperfect, and future are called tenses. The word "tense" comes from the Latin tempus, meaning "time." Most first year Greek students are taught that tense in Greek means not only time of action but also kind of action. Scholars, however, are beginning to question this dual notion of Greek tense. Does the morphology that indicates what we commonly call "tense" (such as the augment and -σα for aorist indicatives) express both time and kind of action? Are we guilty of trying to fit the Greek verbal system into a time-based Latin mold? There is good support for the contention that the morphological features associated with Greek tense indicate only aspect, not time, and that time is established by the context rather than grammatical form (cf. Porter 1989:76–83; McKay 1981:290, 296). If this contention is correct, then it would be misleading to retain the term "tense."

It is crucial for an exegete to know what information comes from the surface structure forms and what information comes from the context. Although the thesis that time is not grammaticalized in Greek may sound extreme, it seems to be the logical conclusion one draws from the study of the nuances of Greek "tenses." In our study of the present indicative, for example, we will find that it can have past, present, future, and even non-temporal reference. The present indicative has a past reference in John 1:29 Τῇ ἐπαύριον βλέπει τὸν Ἰησοῦν ἐρχόμενον πρὸς αὐτόν (On the next day he *saw* Jesus coming to him), a present reference in Acts 16:18 Παραγγέλλω σοι ἐν ὀνόματι Ἰησοῦ Χριστοῦ ἐξελθεῖν ἀπ᾽ αὐτῆς (I *command* you in the name of Jesus Christ to come out of her), a future reference in Luke 19:8 where Zacchaeus told the Lord τοῖς πτωχοῖς δίδωμι (I *will give* to the poor), and a timeless reference in John 3:18 ὁ πιστεύων εἰς αὐτὸν οὐ κρίνεται (the one who believes in him *will never be judged*). The same range of temporal references is found with the aorist. If the present and aorist indicatives can have past, present, future, and non-temporal references, then it might be questionable whether time is a function of morphology.

Objections to this thesis include the distinction between the present and imperfect, the unexpectedness of the present in historical contexts, the purpose of the augment, and the role of the future. The difference between the present and imperfect might be one of function, not time. Both are found in narrative contexts, but the present seems to be used more often to highlight certain features, such as the opening of a scene. Porter contends that augments have lost their significance and persist in the language only as formal features of secondary tenses (Porter 1989:208–9). The imperfect appears to denote past time because it is primarily used in narrative contexts. Yet it can also be found in timeless contexts. The future does not fit easily into the aspectual system. It seems best to view the future as grammaticalizing the speaker's expectation regarding a possible event (almost as a mood to express the speaker's attitude).

According to the proposed thesis, the information that is grammaticalized (i.e., indicated by morphology) is aspect. *Aspect* can be defined as the subjective conception of an action by the speaker or writer, not the objective nature of the event itself (McKay 1972:44, Porter 1989:88, Fanning 1990:85). It is not the same as *Aktionsart,* a term discussed in many grammars. Both pertain to the kind of action, but aspect refers to one's perception of the action, whereas *Aktionsart* refers to the actual, objective nature of that action (Fanning 1990:31). Also some use the term *Aktionsart* for information supplied by the verbal root.

The verb system can be divided into three aspects: (1) perfective (aorist), (2) imperfective (present/imperfect), and (3) stative (perfect/pluperfect). The perfective aspect denotes that the speaker or writer perceives the verbal idea in its entirety as a single, undivided whole, as when a person in a helicopter views an entire parade at once. The imperfective signifies that the speaker perceives the verbal idea as an event in progress, as when a person sits in the grandstand and watches one float at a time pass by. The stative means that the speaker conceives the verbal idea as a condition or state of affairs, as when the parade manager considers all the arrangements, conditions, and accompanying events in existence at the parade (illustration from Porter 1989:91). This would be the information conveyed by the morphological features we normally associate with "tense." Temporal relations and finer nuances of each aspect are conveyed through an interaction of the verbal aspect and the contextual, lexical, and discourse features of the text (cf. Fanning 1990:126–96 for analysis of this process).

Although there are a few problems with the proposed framework, I have adopted it as a working hypothesis for chapters 7 and 8 because it solves more problems than it creates, appears to be heading in the right direction, and is illustrative of the state of grammatical analysis. Further work needs to be done to distinguish members of the same aspect; e.g., the present and imperfect. Nevertheless, there is still merit in the traditional view that temporal distinctions are grammaticalized in the indicative mood, even though it results in a greater number of anomalies. This does not necessarily indicate a flaw in the analysis, since all languages have forms which overlap into the semantic domain of other forms.

The Present Form

Both the present and imperfect, as noted above, are part of the imperfective aspect and grammaticalize the same information. Also both have similar contextual nuances. In the imperfective aspect, the writer or speaker perceives and communicates a progressive notion of an event. The progressive idea should be distinguished from the durative idea (that the action objectively continues for some time). Aspect morphology only grammaticalizes one's perception of the action, and one's perception may not necessarily correspond to objective reality.

Descriptive Present

The descriptive present highlights the progressive nature of an action taking place at the time of speaking. The time frame is determined by the context. The descriptive present is best rendered into English with the present continuous tense (John is riding his horse). The present continuous tense is not often used in modern translations because frequent use would be rather awkward.

One example is Matthew 8:25 Κύριε, σῶσον, ἀπολλύμεθα (Lord, save us, we are drowning). The AV reads, "Lord, save us: we perish." The descriptive present, however, pictures a scene in which the boat is becoming filled with water and sinking lower and lower. It is a scene of increasing panic among the disciples. Another example is Matthew 25:8 αἱ λαμπάδες ἡμῶν σβέννυνται (our lamps are going out). Barclay translates "our lamps have gone out." This again obscures the picture. The descriptive present pictures the flames flickering smaller and smaller, perhaps beginning to smoke some, and the increasing anxiety of the five foolish virgins.

Iterative Present

The iterative idea refers to the repetition of the same action. It may refer to a custom or habitual practice of a certain person or society, such as having a parade once a year. In Matthew 23:23 the Lord tells the scribes and Pharisees ἀποδεκατοῦτε τὸ ἡδύοσμον καὶ τὸ ἄνηθον (You make it a practice to tithe mint and dill; cf. Luke 18:12).

Sometimes it may be helpful to translate using an adverb of frequency, such as "always," "usually," "customarily," "normally," or other expressions, such as "keeps on." In Mark 2:18 the disciples of John and the Pharisees νηστεύουσιν (make it a practice to fast on a regular basis); in Colossians 1:3 Paul says that when he and his associates pray for the Colossians εὐχαριστοῦμεν (we regularly give thanks). Perhaps the iterative idea can help interpret 1 Thessalonians 5:17 ἀδιαλείπτως προσεύχεσθε, which is rendered in the AV "Pray without ceasing." If we understand the verb as an iterative present, then Paul is exhorting us to have a regular prayer life rather than to be continuously in prayer; that is, it refers to an unceasing habit rather than to an unceasing activity (Wanamaker 1990:200). Others interpret it as always being in the attitude of prayer or as maintaining a prayer vigil.

The customary or habitual sense may offer a solution to the exegetical problem in 1 John 3:6 πᾶς ὁ ἐν αὐτῷ μένων οὐχ ἁμαρτάνει· πᾶς ὁ ἁμαρτάνων οὐχ ἑώρακεν αὐτὸν οὐδὲ ἔγνωκεν αὐτόν (No one who remains in him habitually sins; no one who habitually sins has seen him or has known him) and 1 John 3:9 Πᾶς ὁ γεγεννημένος ἐκ τοῦ θεοῦ ἁμαρτίαν οὐ ποιεῖ (No one who is born of God habitually sins). Without the habitual idea, the passages could imply that sinless perfection is the norm for the Christian life (contra 1 John 1:8–2:1). Smalley (1984:158–65, 172) avoids the iterative idea by suggesting that the passages refer to the potential state of sinlessness. Turner (1965:151) goes beyond the idea of habitual acts of sin and says it refers to the condition (or state) of being a sinner. A Christian might take the initial steps but stop short of the state of being dominated by sin. This, however, confuses the imperfective and stative aspects (cf. Marshall 1978a:178–84; Fanning 1990:212–17 for discussion).

Tendential Present

The tendential idea refers to an action which was begun, attempted, or proposed, but not carried out. Some divide this category into conative (action intended but not undertaken) and inchoative (action started but not completed). The tendential idea can be expressed in English with such words as "try," "trying," or "attempting." In John 10:32 Jesus asks διὰ ποῖον αὐτῶν ἔργον ἐμὲ λιθάζετε; (For which of these works are you contemplating stoning me?). The Jews were not actually stoning Jesus as He uttered these words, as is implied in several versions (NIV, NJB, AV). The information grammaticalized by the present form is Jesus' perception of the progressive nature of this contemplation. In John 13:6 Peter asks, Κύριε, σύ μου νίπτεις τοὺς πόδας (Lord, are you going to wash my feet?). The literal translation "Lord, are you washing my feet?" would either convey amazement or ignorance. Also in Galatians 5:4 Paul argues that those who are *trying* to be justified (δικαιοῦσθε) by keeping the law have severed themselves from Christ and the way of grace. It would be contrary to Pauline theology to fail to bring out the tendential force: "You, who are *being* justified by the law, are being severed from Christ" (cf. AV).

The present in Acts 26:28 is variously understood. Agrippa tells Paul Ἐν ὀλίγῳ με πείθεις Χριστιανὸν ποιῆσαι which is rendered in the AV "Almost thou persuadest me to be a Christian." One problem is whether it should be taken as a statement (AV, NJB, REB, RSV) or as a rhetorical question (NIV, TEV, NRSV). Another problem is whether it is a confession or irony. The use of the term Christian may suggest irony, since it was sometimes used in a derogatory way. Taking the utterance as a question that conveys irony and interpreting the present as tendential yields "Are you really trying to persuade me to become a Christian in such a short time?" It is an action attempted but not accomplished because of Agrippa's resistance.

Historical Present

The historical present is normally interpreted rhetorically, that is, to vividly bring a past event before the reader. Although there is some merit in the traditional understanding, historical presents (non-λέγω) are better understood as having a discourse function of giving prominence to the beginning of a paragraph, to the introduction of new participants, or to a change in setting (cf. Buth 1977:7–13; Fanning 1990:232). Since the aorist is the normal tense form in narrative, the historical present is striking and lends prominence to the opening of a scene or to other places where the author wishes to draw the attention of the reader (Porter 1989:196; J. Callow 1984:17). English versions normally translate the historical present with a simple past. The historical present occurs most often in Mark and John and least often in Luke and Acts. Kilpatrick (1977:258–62) suggests that the use or nonuse of the historical present is a matter of style, with the more literary writers, such as Luke, using it only when it is in his sources.

A historical present is used in Mark 1:21 to highlight the arrival of Jesus and His disciples in Capernaum: Καὶ εἰσπορεύονται εἰς Καφαρναούμ (And they arrived at Capernaum); in Mark 1:40 to highlight the opening of a new scene: Καὶ ἔρχεται πρὸς αὐτὸν λεπρός (and a leper came to him); and in Mark 2:3 to highlight new participants within an episode: καὶ ἔρχονται φέροντες πρὸς αὐτὸν παραλυτικόν (and they came bringing to him a paralytic).

Some historical presents seem to have lost their vividness and are used as an ordinary narrative tense form (Fanning 1990:234). This is especially true of verbs of speaking, such as λέγω. There are several strings of these non-vivid historical presents in John (e.g., 1:29–51; 2:1–10; 4:1–38).

Gnomic Present

The gnomic idea conveys either actions that are omnitemporal (always happens) or concepts that are timeless (lie outside the limitations of time). The latter refers to ideas that are universally accepted as true. The gnomic idea can sometimes be expressed in English by using "always," "ever," or "never."

A present is used in Matthew 7:17 to express something that always happens: πᾶν δένδρον ἀγαθὸν καρποὺς καλοὺς ποιεῖ, τὸ δὲ σαπρὸν δένδρον καρποὺς πονηροὺς ποιεῖ (a healthy tree produces good fruit, but a diseased tree produces bad fruit). Jesus is using a well-known observation from human experience to teach a spiritual lesson. Other gnomic presents include Luke 6:39 Μήτι δύναται τυφλὸς τυφλὸν ὁδηγεῖν (Can a blind person ever lead another blind person?) and 2 Corinthians 9:7 ἱλαρὸν γὰρ δότην ἀγαπᾷ ὁ θεός (God always loves a joyful giver) (cf. Matthew 6:26, Mark 2:22, Jas. 3:3–12).

Futuristic Present

The present is often used with a future reference. It is as if the future event is regarded by the speaker as so certain to take place that he or she expresses it as being in progress. English has a similar idiom. For example, the statement "I am going to the store this afternoon" is expressed with much more certainty of fulfillment than the regular future, "I'll go to the store this afternoon." Translation of the futuristic present into English can either use the future tense or a phrase such as "going to." It is the context that supplies the future connotation; the present form supplies the speaker's perception of a process.

In John 14:3 Jesus says πάλιν ἔρχομαι καὶ παραλήμψομαι ὑμᾶς πρὸς ἐμαυτόν (I will come back and receive you to myself). The certainty of this future expectation in the mind of Jesus causes Him to express it with the present. Theologically it reflects a divine resolve that cannot fail to come to pass without impinging the character of God. See also Matthew 6:1, 17:11, 26:2, 27:63, Mark 10:33, John 4:21, and 14:28.

Durative Present

A present tense form is called durative when the context conveys an action that began in the past and continues into the present. The time element is often explicit in the context, as illustrated by 1 John 3:8: ἀπ᾽ ἀρχῆς ὁ διάβολος ἁμαρτάνει (the devil has been sinning from the beginning). To say the devil is sinning from the beginning does not make sense in English. English translations will therefore employ the present perfect. Other examples include Luke 15:29, where the brother of the prodigal son tells his father that he has been serving (δουλεύω) him for many years; John 14:9, where Jesus tells Philip that He has been (εἰμί) with them for a long time; and

John 15:27, where Jesus tells the disciples that they must testify of Him, since they have been (ἐστε) with Him from the beginning.

Present of Existing Results

The present of existing results focuses on the enduring consequence of a past act, as if the act continued through its results. Again it is the context that makes it clear that the act is past. The present grammaticalizes the perceived progressive nature of the results. In 1 Corinthians 11:18 Paul says ἀκούω σχίσματα ἐν ὑμῖν ὑπάρχειν (I hear that there are divisions among you). Paul had heard about the divisions perhaps from those in Chloe's household (1:11), but the memory of that communication remains vividly on his mind. In Matthew 6:2 Jesus says that they have received (ἀπέχουσιν) their reward. Sometimes the present of existing results is called the perfective present.

Performative Present

A performative is a verb that accomplishes something by merely uttering it, such as "I hereby pronounce you man and wife." The action is perceived almost instantaneously as the notion of progress is reduced to the circumstances of the utterance. This function is normally called the aoristic present, but this terminology implies that the present depicts an action in its entirety without reference to its progress. The aoristic present would then deviate from the sense of the imperfective aspect (action viewed as a progress) and overlap with the perfective aspect (action viewed as a whole). There is no need for an aoristic present, for if one wanted to express simple action (action viewed as a whole) in the present time, one could use the aorist (as suggested by the epistolary and dramatic aorists; cf. Turner 1963:60).

In this category are such examples as Luke 17:4 Μετανοῶ (I repent); John 11:41 εὐχαριστῶ (I give thanks); Acts 19:13 ὁρκίζω (I adjure you); 25:11 ἐπικαλοῦμαι (I appeal); 26:1 Ἐπιτρέπεται (I permit); 26:17 ἀποστέλλω (I send); and Romans 16:1 Συνίστημι (I commend). Verbs of speaking used to introduce direct or indirect speech can also be included in this category (e.g., Matt. 3:9 λέγω; Acts 16:18 παραγγέλλω). See Fanning (1990:202–5) for discussion.

In Mark 2:5 Jesus says Τέκνον, ἀφίενταί σου αἱ ἁμαρτίαι (Child, your sins are forgiven). Divine forgiveness of sins is not something that we think of as progressive (Your sins are in the process of being forgiven). There is no problem understanding this as a performative, "I hereby pronounce that your sins are forgiven."

There could be a problem, however, in applying this idea to Acts 9:34 (another passage often cited as aoristic present), where Peter says Αἰνέα, ἰᾶταί σε Ἰησοῦς Χριστός (Aeneas, Jesus Christ heals you). This assumes ἰᾶται (present) to be correct over ἴαται (perfect). A present continuous translation would be misleading (Jesus Christ is healing you). Aeneas would probably respond, "Well, how long will it take?" Peter gave forth a simple pronouncement, and the healing was instantaneous and complete. This appears to be aoristic. If we interpret the verb as performative, the translation would be, "I hereby pronounce that you are healed through the power of Jesus Christ." However this could give the impression that the spoken word by humans has efficacious power in itself or at least that humans can manipulate divine power at will. It could instead be interpreted as a present of existing state (Jesus Christ has healed you). The focus would then be on the continued outcome. Peter simply declares what Christ had already done.

The Imperfect Form

The imperfect is, along with the present, part of the imperfective aspect. It grammaticalizes the speaker's perception of the progressive nature of an action. The imperfect is commonly found in historical narrative, most frequently in Mark and least frequently in Matthew (perhaps due to the stylistic temperament of each writer). It is only because imperfects are found most often in historical narrative that they appear to express continuous action in the past.

Descriptive Imperfect

A writer or speaker will employ the descriptive imperfect to paint a picture of the unfolding, progressive nature of a past event. Again the time frame comes from the context. Robertson (1934:883) states, "The aorist tells the simple story. The imperfect draws the picture. It helps you to see the course of the act. It passes before the eye the flowing stream of history." One example is Luke 17:27 ἤσθιον, ἔπινον, ἐγάμουν, ἐγαμίζοντο ἄχρι ἧς ἡμέρας εἰσῆλθεν Νῶε εἰς τὴν κιβωτόν (They were eating, drinking, marrying, giving in marriage until the day Noah entered the ark). This gives a vivid picture of continual sin before the flood. Other examples include Mark 12:41, where the rich were casting in (ἔβαλλον) much; and Luke 15:16, where the prodigal son was desiring (ἐπεθύμει) to eat carob pods.

Iterative Imperfect

As in the present, the iterative expresses an action that occurs at repeated intervals. This would include customs and habits. The context and the verb stem contribute the information that the time frame is past and that the action is iterative. The tense morphology contributes only the idea of a perceived continuing process. The iterative imperfect may be rendered in English with such phrases as "kept on," "repeatedly," "used to," and "were accustomed to."

In the feeding of the five thousand (Mark 6:41) Jesus broke the bread and kept on giving (ἐδίδου) it to His disciples. As the disciples kept coming back for more to distribute among the people, Jesus kept on giving them more. A miracle indeed. In Mark 15:6 the imperfect refers to a custom: Κατὰ ἑορτὴν ἀπέλυεν αὐτοῖς ἕνα δέσμιον (It was Pilate's practice to release a prisoner to the Jews at each Passover). Other examples include Luke 2:41 where Jesus' parents were in the habit of going (ἐπορεύοντο) to Jerusalem every year for the feast and Acts 3:2 where a lame man was carried (ἐβαστάζετο) and put (ἐτίθουν) every day at the temple gate. It is obvious from these examples that the iterative idea comes from the context.

Tendential Imperfect

The tendential imperfect is similar to the tendential present. In both, the context points to an action that was begun, attempted, or proposed, but not carried out. Sometimes this is called the conative imperfect. It may be brought out in English by supplying such words as "trying" or "attempting." In Matthew 3:14 John was trying to prevent Jesus from being baptized: ὁ Ἰωάννης διεκώλυεν αὐτόν. The translation "John was preventing him" would be misleading. John was not preventing Jesus from being baptized, only trying to prevent him, for John finally acquiesced and performed the baptism. In Mark 15:23 the soldiers tried to give (ἐδίδουν) Jesus wine mixed with myrrh, in Luke 1:59 the relatives and neighbors were going to name (ἐκάλουν) Elizabeth's baby Zechariah, in Acts 18:4 Paul was trying to persuade (ἔπειθεν) Jews and Gentiles, and in Galatians 1:23 Paul was trying to destroy (ἐπόρθει) the church.

Inceptive Imperfect

The inceptive imperfect focuses on the beginning of an action. The temporal and inceptive information comes from the context and verbal idea. The inceptive idea can be expressed in English with such words as "began," "was beginning," or "started." The inceptive imperfect is sometimes called the inchoative or ingressive imperfect. One example is Mark 1:21 καὶ εὐθὺς τοῖς σάββασιν εἰσελθὼν εἰς τὴν συναγωγὴν ἐδίδασκεν (and immediately on the Sabbath he entered into the synagogue and began teaching). The progressive idea is conveyed by "began teaching" rather than "began to teach." See also Matthew 4:11 διηκόνουν (began ministering), Mark 14:72 ἔκλαιεν (started weeping), and Luke 19:7 διεγόγγυζον (started grumbling).

Durative Imperfect

The durative imperfect refers to an action that began in the past, continued for some time, and may or may not be separated by an interval from the time frame of the speaker. Some grammarians call it the progressive imperfect or the imperfect of prolonged action. The temporal and durative ideas are derived from the context. There are two types:

Without interval—When the context indicates a past durative action that continues up to the time frame of the speaker, it is best rendered into English with a perfect. Examples include Luke 2:49 Τί ὅτι ἐζητεῖτέ με (Why have you been seeking me?) and 1 John 2:7 ἦν εἴχετε ἀπ᾽ ἀρχῆς (which you have had from the beginning).

Interval—When the context indicates a past durative action that preceded another event mentioned in the context, it is best rendered into English with a past perfect. For example, the imperfect ἔκειτο (was lying) in John 20:12 cannot mean that Jesus was lying there when Mary saw the angels, for He had already risen: θεωρεῖ δύο ἀγγέλους . . . ἕνα πρὸς τῇ κεφαλῇ καὶ ἕνα πρὸς τοῖς ποσίν, ὅπου ἔκειτο τὸ σῶμα τοῦ Ἰησοῦ (She saw [historical present] two angels . . . one at the head and one at the feet, where the body of Jesus had been lying). Another example is Matthew 14:4, where John had been saying (ἔλεγεν) to Herod that he should not have his brother's wife.

Voluntative Imperfect

The imperfect may be used to express a continuing desire that is not being realized. Thus the desire has a present reference. Some grammarians classify this use under the tendential category. It has several different nuances. First, it can be used to express the speaker's non-fulfillment of a desire or activity in a polite way. In Galatians 4:20 Paul uses the voluntative imperfect to express something which could not be realized at that time because of the circumstances. He tells the Galatians that he would like (ἤθελον) to be with them. To say that he was wishing to be with them misses the point.

Second, it can be used to camouflage the speaker's desire, that is, to state the desire in an unoffensive way to avoid undue implications of a more direct statement. In Acts 25:22 Agrippa would like to hear what Paul had to say, but he was more concerned with protecting his reputation and social status. An exuberant and direct "Yes, I want to hear what Paul has to say" would have blown his stately facade. Instead, he says Ἐβουλόμην καὶ αὐτὸς τοῦ ἀνθρώπου ἀκοῦσαι (I would sort of like to hear the fellow myself). The imperfect enables Agrippa to express himself, but without appearing overly eager about it.

Third, the voluntative imperfect may be used for a desire which is impossible to fulfill. In Romans 9:3 Paul says ηὐχόμην γὰρ ἀνάθεμα εἶναι αὐτὸς ἐγὼ ἀπὸ τοῦ Χριστοῦ ὑπὲρ τῶν ἀδελφῶν μου (I could wish that I be accursed from Christ for the sake of my brothers). Paul recognizes that it would be impossible for him to be consigned to damnation in place of his fellow Jews because God would never condemn a believer and because only Christ could die in place of another. The voluntative imperfect enables Paul to express his deep and continuing concern for his fellow Jews (cf. Cranfield 1979:454–57 for various views).

The Future Form

Some regard the future as an absolute tense that serves to express future events. However, not all future tenses describe events that will take place in the future (e.g., the imperatival and gnomic future). Others interpret the future form as expressing a non-indicative mood (akin to subjunctive). Still others interpret it as having both modal and temporal functions. Whether the future grammaticalizes aspect is also debated. Some argue that it has no aspect while others contend that it expresses simple action. If time is a function of context and the aspect of the future is vague, then it might be best to view it as grammaticalizing the speaker's expectation of a possible event (cf. Porter 1989:403).

Predictive Future

Often the future is used to predict a future event, as when Agabus in Acts 21:11 predicted that if Paul went to Jerusalem, the Jews would bind (δήσουσιν) and deliver (παραδώσουσιν) him over to the Gentiles. The form grammaticalizes the expectation, and the context suggests a certainty on the part of Agabus. When an expectation gains certainty for an individual and then is dogmatically expressed, it becomes a prediction. The objective certainty of the prediction depends on whether the speaker is deity or a person giving a divine pronouncement. In Mark 1:8 John the Baptist predicts that Jesus will baptize (βαπτίσει) people with the Holy Spirit. See also John 14:26 (διδάξει).

Progressive Future

Sometimes the verbal idea and/or context suggests that the expected event is progressive. The normal way to express a continuous future action, however, is with the future periphrastic participle. In Philippians 1:18 Paul says ἀλλὰ καὶ χαρήσομαι (and indeed, I will continue to rejoice). The ἀλλά is interpreted as an intensive particle. Other examples include Philippians 1:6 ἐπιτελέσει (will carry it on to completion) and 2 Thessalonians 3:4 ποιήσετε (you will continue to do).

Imperatival Future

The future is often used to express commands. The same idiom occurs in English. When parents tell their teenager, "You will be home by eleven," they are not predicting, they are commanding. It is a categorical command that can be rendered in English with the emphatic "you will be . . ." or "you must." It is almost always found in the second person.

In Matthew 1:21 καλέσεις τὸ ὄνομα αὐτοῦ Ἰησοῦν (You shall name him Jesus) the angel was not predicting that Joseph and Mary would name their son Jesus, he is commanding that this was to be his name (You must name him Jesus). The imperatival future in Matthew 5:48 Ἔσεσθε οὖν ὑμεῖς τέλειοι (Be perfect) sometimes causes trouble. There is no need to interpret it as pertaining to the future kingdom, as some do. It is a loving command accompanied with divine grace to enable believers to progress toward the goal of being like the Father. Other examples include commands, such as Galatians 5:14 Ἀγαπήσεις τὸν πλησίον σου ὡς σεαυτόν (Love your neighbor as [you love] yourself), and prohibitions, such as in Romans 7:7 Οὐκ ἐπιθυμήσεις (You must not lust). Prohibitions (negative commands) using οὐ or οὐ μή with the future tense form reflect LXX usage (cf. 1 Tim 5:18; Deut. 25:4). It is especially observed in the Decalogue (cf. Matt. 19:18; Exod. 20:13–16).

Deliberative Future

The future is often used in questions where there is some uncertainty as to one's direction. The questions usually employ the first person. They may either be (a) real questions that ask for the advice or judgment of another, as in Luke 22:49 where the disciples asked Jesus whether they should strike (πατάξομεν) with the sword; (b) rhetorical questions in which the speaker is debating with him or herself what to do, as in Romans 9:14 where Paul asks, "What then shall we say (ἐροῦμεν)"; or (c) rhetorical questions that challenge the readers or listeners to ponder the implications of the question and to respond appropriately, as in Hebrews 2:3 "How shall we escape (ἐκφευξόμεθα), if we neglect so great salvation?" The rhetorical question actually expresses an implicit statement, "We will surely not escape." The third person is used in Romans 3:6 where Paul asks, "How shall God judge (κρινεῖ) the world?" See also John 6:68 and 1 Corinthians 15:29.

Gnomic Future

The future may also be used to express timeless truths or omnitemporal actions. The gnomic idea is more often expressed by the present or aorist. One clear example is Romans 5:7 μόλις γὰρ ὑπὲρ δικαίου τις ἀποθανεῖται (Rarely would one ever die for a righteous person). Paul is not predicting an unusual event, he is stating what is always the case. Thus the word "ever" is added to the translation. Other examples include Matthew 4:4, where Jesus says that people do not live (ζήσεται) by bread alone, and Galatians 6:5, where Paul says that everyone is to carry (βαστάσει) his own burden.

Exercises

In the following examples, parse the form and then evaluate the significance of the aspect, the nature of the verb, and the context. Then determine the best semantic function. Translate the passage in such a way as to convey the use(s) you have chosen.

1. Matt. 23:13   κλείετε, εἰσερχομένους
2. Matt. 26:24   ὑπάγει, ἦν
3. Matt. 26:63   ἐσιώπα, Ἐξορκίζω
4. Matt. 27:48   ἐπότιζεν
5. Matt. 28:20   εἰμι
6. Mark 3:2   παρετήρουν, θεραπεύσει
7. Mark 5:42   περιεπάτει
8. Mark 6:1   ἔρχεται, ἀκολουθοῦσιν
9. Mark 8:2   Σπλαγχνίζομαι, προσμένουσιν
10. Mark 14:35   προσηύχετο
11. Luke 13:7   ἔρχομαι, εὑρίσκω
12. John 14:18   ἀφήσω, ἔρχομαι
13. Rom. 6:2   ζήσομεν
14. Gal. 1:13   ἐδίωκον, ἐπόρθουν
15. Heb. 3:4   κατασκευάζεται
16. 1 Pet. 1:16   ἔσεσθε

8

Aorist, Perfect, and Pluperfect

As mentioned in chapter 7, the verb system is divided into three aspects: (1) perfective (aorist), (2) imperfective (present/imperfect), and (3) stative (perfect/pluperfect). In this chapter we will continue the discussion of aspect by taking up the perfective and stative, represented by the aorist, perfect, and pluperfect.

The Aorist Form

The aorist has been interpreted in various ways: as conveying (a) an objectively instantaneous (point) action, (b) an objectively completed action (i.e., past time), (c) a subjectively indefinite action (i.e., not defined in any way), or (d) a subjectively whole action (cf. Fanning 1990:86–97). By "subjectively" we mean how the writer perceives the action rather than how it "objectively" exists. Sometimes the terms are confused. The aorist is commonly said to convey punctiliar or point action, when what is meant is that the action is viewed as a whole. The "punctiliar" or "point" terminology should be avoided, since it can lead to the erroneous idea that the aorist refers to an action that occurred at one particular moment of time.

Examples of resulting misinterpretations abound in the literature, especially in holiness circles to support a "crisis" nature of sanctification. For example, in Matthew 16:24 Jesus teaches His disciples to deny themselves once for all, take up their cross once for all, and to follow Him forevermore. In Acts 2:38 Peter exhorts his audience to make a decisive once-for-all time repentance. In Romans 5:12 all have sinned once for all in Adam. In Romans 12:1 we are to make a decisive, once-for-all presentation of our lives to God, something that never needs to be done again (Morris 1988:433). Lenski often interprets the aorist as a point action, as in Romans 6:2, where the believer's death to sin was one punctiliar act; and Romans 7:3, where the death of the husband was a "single brief act" (Lenski 1936:389, 446). Such information cannot be extracted from the aorist form.

Ward (1969:13–28) devotes an entire chapter to "Pinpoints," in which he presents some interesting, but dubious, translations of the aorist. For example, the disciples "were gripped by great fear" (Mark 4:41); the prophets wanted to "catch a glimpse" of coming things (Luke 10:24); the "pain of compassion pierced" the father of the prodigal son (Luke 15:20); a ruler "fired a question" at Jesus, asking what "one noble deed" can merit salvation (Luke 18:18); and believers do not have "a High-Priest incapable of a stab of sympathy" (Heb. 4:15). For discussion of the abuse of the aorist, see Stagg (1972:222–31).

It would be better to view the aorist as grammaticalizing the speaker's perception of an event in its entirety or as a single whole. As mentioned in chapter 7, the difference between the perfective aspect (aorist) and the imperfective aspect (present and imperfect) is the difference between viewing an entire parade from a helicopter (perfective) and viewing one float at a time pass by from the curb or grandstand (imperfective). The event does not have to be objectively completed in order to be perceived as a whole (e.g., futuristic aorists). The idea that the aorist indicative refers only to the past is misleading, for it can refer to something past, present, future, or even to something that is beyond time. Also the aorist may contextually refer to something that happens in a moment or to something that continues over a span of time. The time frame, duration, and other nuances, such as with the constative and ingressive aorists, are derived from the interaction between form and context (both literary and situational contexts). This interaction between form and context is the normal way any language conveys information.

In narrative material the aorist is used to develop the nucleus or backbone of the story. As such, it is the normal tense form in narrative. In contrast, the present and imperfect are used to introduce significant participants and background information and to highlight certain features of the story.

Constative Aorist

The constative aorist reflects the root idea of the perfective aspect. It expresses the action as a complete whole without regard to the length of time it took to accomplish it. This use is sometimes called the *historical aorist*, since the time reference is past. The action may have objectively taken place (1) in a moment of time, as in Mark 1:41 ἐκτείνας τὴν χεῖρα αὐτοῦ ἥψατο (having stretched out his hand, he touched him); (2) during a succession of events, as in Romans 1:13 πολλάκις προεθέμην ἐλθεῖν πρὸς ὑμᾶς (oftentimes I determined to come to you); or (3) over an extended period of time, as in John 2:20 Τεσσεράκοντα καὶ ἒξ ἔτεσιν οἰκοδομήθη ὁ ναὸς οὗτος (This temple was built in forty-six years). The actual length of time the action took is determined by the verbal idea and contextual pointers. For example, in Acts 11:26 Paul and Barnabas gathered (συναχθῆναι) with the church for a whole year and taught (διδάξαι) the people. In Acts 18:11 Paul continued (Ἐκάθισεν) in Corinth a year and a half.

Ingressive Aorist

The contextual focus of the ingressive aorist is on the beginning of an action or entrance into a state. Whether it refers to an action or state depends on the verbal idea. It is sometimes called the inceptive aorist. The ingressive idea can be expressed in English by using "began" or "became."

The classic example is 2 Corinthians 8:9 δι' ὑμᾶς ἐπτώχευσεν πλούσιος ὤν (although he was rich, for you he became poor). The aorist ἐπτώχευσεν in this context cannot mean "he was poor." Christ was exceedingly rich, but for us He became poor, that is, He left one state and entered into another (cf. Phil. 2:7–8). This was done so that we might become rich (another ingressive aorist). The context in John 11:35 ἐδάκρυσεν ὁ Ἰησοῦς (Jesus wept) suggests the aorist should be taken as ingressive. When Jesus saw where Lazarus was buried, He began to weep. The ingressive idea could be captured in various ways, such as "Jesus burst into tears." In John 4:52 the official asked what hour his son began to improve (κομψότερον ἔσχεν).

Culminative Aorist

The contextual focus of the culminative aorist is on the completion of an action which then often issues into another action or state. It is normally rendered into English with a perfect tense. The culminative aorist usually occurs with verbs that imply an effort or a process. This usage is quite common. In Philippians 4:11 Paul says ἐγὼ γὰρ ἔμαθον ἐν οἷς εἰμι αὐτάρκης εἶναι (for I have learned to be content in whatever the circumstance). To say that Paul "learned" to be content implies that Paul learned to be content through some particular event, a misleading idea. Learning to be content was a process throughout his Christian life. The aorist conceives it as a whole, and the context highlights the application of that past learning to his present situation. Other examples include Matthew 2:2 "We have come (ἤλθομεν) to worship him" and 1 John 2:11 "The darkness has blinded (ἐτύφλωσεν) his eyes."

Gnomic Aorist

The gnomic idea can be either omnitemporal (happens or exists all the time) or timeless (lies beyond time). The gnomic idea is normally rendered into English by a present tense. Some grammarians question the validity of the gnomic aorist, arguing that the examples normally cited could be explained in other ways, usually constative or culminative aorists. However the contextual pointers regarding time are different in the gnomic aorist. They point to something that happens all the time rather than to something that did happen. The gnomic aorist (in contrast with the gnomic present) grammaticalizes the speaker's perception of the actions or truths in their entirety.

An example of an omnitemporal aorist is 1 Peter 1:24–25 ἐξηράνθη ὁ χόρτος καὶ τὸ ἄνθος ἐξέπεσεν· τὸ δὲ ῥῆμα κυρίου μένει εἰς τὸν αἰῶνα (grass always dries up, and flowers always drop off, but the Word of the Lord continues forever). It is commonly recognized that things of this realm are subject to decay and death. The Word of the Lord, however, does not fit into this category; it remains forever. Other examples of omnitemporal aorists include Ephesians 5:29 and James 1:11.

An example of a timeless aorist is Luke 7:35 ἐδικαιώθη ἡ σοφία ἀπὸ πάντων τῶν τέκνων αὐτῆς (wisdom is proved right by all her children, i.e., by all those who practice it). Other examples of timeless aorists include Matthew 7:24–27 and Mark 1:11.

Epistolary Aorist

The epistolary aorist, as normally interpreted, refers to a writer placing himself or herself in the time frame of future readers. Thus something that is a present or future reality to the author may be expressed as a past fact for the sake of the readers' viewpoint. By the time the readers received the epistle, the event the author had mentioned would have already taken place. Yet this presupposes that the aorist indicative had a past reference. Otherwise, the explanation does not work. Porter (1989:228) suggests that the author composes the letter within his or her own time frame (using contextual pointers) and the readers interpret it accordingly. The aorist merely focuses on the act as a whole. The epistolary aorist occurs most often in the Epistles and is normally rendered into English with the present or future tense.

In Philemon 12 Paul writes ὅν ἀνέπεμψά σοι, which would be translated "whom I sent back to you" if the aorist indicative were always past referring. There are, however, several temporal pointers in the context that will not allow this rendering. Paul had not yet sent Onesimus back to Philemon, for Onesimus was the carrier of the epistle, and the epistle was not quite finished. The context makes it clear that the reference is yet future to Paul; thus "whom I am going to send to you." By the use of such pointers, Paul conveyed a future reference which the readers would have properly deciphered, especially now that Onesimus was there standing in front of them. In Galatians 6:11 Paul writes Ἴδετε πηλίκοις ὑμῖν γράμμασιν ἔγραψα τῇ ἐμῇ χειρί. The context is ambiguous regarding the time frame. If it is present, then the aorist ἔγραψα refers to the large letters of the ending (See what large letters I use when I write to you with my own hand). It would be similar to a sprawling signature. If the time frame were past, then the large letters would refer to the entire epistle (See what large letters I have written to you). Most take it as present reference.

Futuristic Aorist

The aorist is sometimes used in reference to a future event: Jude 14 Ἰδοὺ ἦλθεν κύριος ἐν ἁγίαις μυριάσιν αὐτοῦ (the Lord is coming with myriads of his saints) and John 17:18 καθὼς ἐμὲ ἀπέστειλας εἰς τὸν κόσμον, κἀγὼ ἀπέστειλα αὐτοὺς εἰς τὸν κόσμον (Just as you sent me into the world, I will send them into the world). The futuristic (or prophetic) aorist often occurs in the apodosis ("then" clause) of a future conditional with ἐάν in the protasis ("if" clause); compare with Matthew 18:15 (then you will have won back your brother).

What is sometimes called proleptic aorists could also fit into this category. Prolepsis refers to the speaker's treatment of a future event as if it had already happened. The time frames are entirely contextual: John 13:31 Νῦν ἐδοξάσθη ὁ υἱὸς τοῦ ἀνθρώπου (Now is the Son of Man glorified).

Dramatic Aorist

The aorist is sometimes used in reference to actions that just happened. English translations use a perfect tense with the word "just." For example, Mark 5:35 Ἡ θυγάτηρ σου ἀπέθανεν (Your daughter has just died). Sometimes the verbal notion and context indicate that the action is still being experienced. In Luke 16:4 ἔγνων τί ποιήσω (I know what I shall do) the solution to the dilemma had just dawned on the steward. Here the time frame is not limited to the past, since the action of knowing continues. In idiomatic English we would say, "I got it!" A past translation, "I knew what I shall do," would be out of place, as would the translation, "I have just known what I would do." The context indicates that the action was sudden and that it lingers into the present.

The Perfect Form

The perfect is normally interpreted temporally as expressing a completed act with continuing results. There are problems with this definition if time is not a function of form, for completed acts are always past. Contextually the perfect may refer to something past (Matt. 19:8), present (Matt. 27:43), possibly future (Matt. 20:23; John 5:24; Jas. 5:2–3), omnitemporal (Rom. 7:2), or timeless (John 3:18). It seems better to view the perfect and pluperfect as members of the stative aspect in which the speaker conceives the verbal idea as a condition or state of affairs. Continuing the parade analogy, it would be when the parade manager considers all the arrangements, conditions, and accompanying events in existence at the parade, rather than viewing the parade itself as a whole or one float at a time. The following functions are derived in conjunction with the context, not from the form alone. The first four have a contextually derived past time reference.

Consummative Perfect

A perfect is called *consummative* when the verbal idea and context suggest that the state of affairs had continued for awhile but has now come to an end. Paul says in 2 Timothy 4:7 τὸν καλὸν ἀγῶνα ἠγώνισμαι, τὸν δρόμον τετέλεκα, τὴν πίστιν τετήρηκα (I have fought a good fight, I have finished the course, I have kept the faith). Paul remained faithful to his calling throughout a difficult ministry. That particular state of affairs is about over, and Paul is now anticipating the rewards that await him. Another example is John 2:10, where the headwaiter said, "You have kept (τετήρηκας) the good wine until now." See also Galatians 1:9.

Iterative Perfect

A perfect is called *iterative* when the context suggests that the state of affairs took place at intervals. For example, 1 John 1:1 Ὃ ἦν ἀπ᾿ ἀρχῆς, ὃ ἀκηκόαμεν, ὃ ἑωράκαμεν τοῖς ὀφθαλμοῖς (that which was from the beginning, that which we have heard, that which we have seen with our eyes). The state of affairs in which the disciples were in the very presence of the Lord occurred at repeated intervals for a period of three and a half years. In John 5:37 Jesus says that the Father had repeatedly testified (μεμαρτύρηκεν) of Him.

Intensive Perfect

A perfect is called *intensive* when the context depicts a prior act which issued in a new state of affairs. How long the new state continues is contingent on contextual pointers. In 1 Corinthians 15:3–4 Paul summarizes the gospel: ὅτι Χριστὸς ἀπέθανεν . . . καὶ ὅτι ἐτάφη καὶ ὅτι ἐγήγερται τῇ ἡμέρᾳ τῇ τρίτῃ (that Christ died and that he was buried and that he was raised on the third day). Christ not only entered into a new state on the third day, but the extended context suggests that the risen state continues; otherwise, our faith is in vain. Other examples include Mark 5:33, where the woman realized what had happened (γέγονεν) to her; John 16:28, where Jesus said, "I have come (ἐλήλυθα) into the world"; and Romans 5:2, where Paul says that we have gained access (ἐσχήκαμεν) into the experience of God's grace.

The perfect τετέλεσται in John 19:30 has been interpreted either as consummative or intensive: ὅτε οὖν ἔλαβεν τὸ ὄξος ὁ Ἰησοῦς εἶπεν, Τετέλεσται (Then when Jesus took the sour wine, he said, "It is finished"). Some say it is consummative, meaning that Jesus was looking backward to the state of affairs that had just been drawn to a close: the Old Testament sacrifices, rituals, typology, as well as His own life and sufferings. All this has finally been brought to completion. Others interpret it as intensive, meaning that Jesus was looking ahead to the benefits of His death. They say it refers to the continuing state of a debt that has forever been paid and which is available to all. The verbal idea in τετέλεσται argues heavily in favor of a consummative perfect.

Dramatic Perfect

The perfect is sometimes used to vividly describe a past state of affairs. Translation into English will normally be with a simple past. John 1:15 Ἰωάννης μαρτυρεῖ περὶ αὐτοῦ καὶ κέκραγεν (John testified concerning him and cried out). The historical present μαρτυρεῖ introduces a new paragraph, and the dramatic perfect κέκραγεν highlights the state of affairs involving John's forceful proclamations. Other examples include Matthew 13:46 πέπρακεν πάντα (he sold everything) and Revelation 5:7 ἦλθεν καὶ εἴληφεν (he came and took the scroll).

Perfect of Present State

Often the context, verbal idea, and perfect form will convey a present state of affairs with no antecedent action. This is common with οἶδα (e.g., Matt. 21:27, John 16:30). It also employs other verbs, as in Matthew 24:25 ἰδοὺ προείρηκα ὑμῖν (I am telling you beforehand); John 8:52 Νῦν ἐγνώκαμεν ὅτι δαιμόνιον ἔχεις (now we know that you have a demon); and John 20:29 Ὅτι ἑώρακάς με πεπίστευκας (Do you believe because you see me?).

Gnomic Perfect

Again we are defining *gnomic* as either an omnitemporal action or a timeless truth. A common formula for introducing Scripture is γέγραπται (it has been written; cf. Matt. 4:4, 7, 10). This could be understood as a timeless perfect. The state of affairs involving the validity of recorded Scripture stands beyond time; that is, God's Word is valid regardless of the time or even if time ceased to be. An omnitemporal perfect is illustrated by 2 Peter

2:19 ᾧ γάρ τις ἥττηται, τούτῳ δεδούλωται (for by what a person is overcome, by this he is enslaved). This happens all the time as people become addicted to alcohol or drugs.

The Pluperfect Form

The pluperfect is normally described like the perfect, but is placed antecedent to the temporal framework of the passage. This temporal notion often does not conform to the way it is used. For instance, in Acts 1:10 one cannot interpret the pluperfect παρειστήκεισαν in such a way as to suggest that the angelic personages "had stood" there. Rather they "were standing" there as the disciples looked into heaven. This past continuous force is commonly acknowledged for the pluperfect of οἶδα. As with the perfect, the pluperfect grammaticalizes a state of affairs. In addition, Porter (1989:289) suggests that it grammaticalizes remoteness. The time reference (antecedent, past, present, or timeless) is irrespective of whether it has an augment (often there is no augment).

Consummative Pluperfect

A pluperfect is called *consummative* when the context indicates that a state of affairs is finished and that some event separates it from the main event line or from the time of the speaker. Since the time frame is antecedent to the context, a past perfect translation is used. For example, the disciples had gone (ἀπεληλύθεισαν) into town when Jesus asked the woman for a cup of water (John 4:8). In reference to Jesus' statement that Lazarus sleeps, John interjects that Jesus had spoken (εἰρήκει) concerning Lazarus' death (John 11:13).

Intensive Pluperfect

The intensive pluperfect focuses on a state that is concurrent with the time frame of the context. A simple past translation is used in historical narrative: John 18:16 ὁ Πέτρος εἰστήκει πρὸς τῇ θύρᾳ ἔξω (Peter stood outside near the door). In John 19:25 several women stood near (εἰστήκεισαν) the cross, not "had stood near." This could be rendered "were standing near," but it is not necessary because the verb suggests a continued state of affairs.

Pluperfect of Past State

Most pluperfects convey (along with verbal idea and context) a past state with no antecedent action. Although the majority of pluperfects fall into this category, there are only five different verbs involved: thirty-two times with οἶδα (I know), fourteen times with ἵστημι (I stand), two times with εἴωθα (I am accustomed), and one time each with πείθω (I persuade) and παρίστημι (I am present). For example, John 1:31 κἀγὼ οὐκ ᾔδειν αὐτόν (and I did not know him). In Mark 1:34 Jesus did not permit the demons to speak, because they knew Him (ᾔδεισαν αὐτόν), not because they had known Him. In Mark 10:1 Jesus was teaching the people as was His custom (ὡς εἰώθει), not as had been His custom.

Iterative Pluperfect

On rare occasions the context suggests an iterative force, as in Luke 8:29 πολλοῖς γὰρ χρόνοις συνηρπάκει (for the evil spirit seized him many times).

Exercises

In the following examples, parse the form (one is imperfect) and then evaluate the significance of the aspect and the influence of the verbal idea and context. Then determine the best semantic function and translate the passage in such a way as to convey the use(s) you have chosen.

1. Matt. 2:3   ἐταράχθη
2. Matt. 12:46   εἰστήκεισαν
3. Matt. 19:6   συνέζευξεν
4. Matt. 19:20   ἐφύλαξα
5. Mark 14:44   δεδώκει
6. Luke 1:30   εὗρες
7. Luke 19:41   ἔκλαυσεν
8. John 1:14   ἐγένετο, ἐσκήνωσεν, ἐθεασάμεθα
9. John 15:6, 8   ἐβλήθη, ἐδοξάσθη
10. Acts 4:10   παρέστηκεν
11. Acts 28:30   Ἐνέμεινεν, ἀπεδέχετο
12. 1 Cor. 7:39   δέδεται
13. Eph. 6:22   ἔπεμψα
14. 1 John 4:1   ἐξεληλύθασιν
15. 1 John 4:12   τεθέαται
16. Rev. 20:4   πεπελεκισμένων, ἐβασίλευσαν

9 Voice and Mood

Voice

Voice is a morphological feature that conveys the relation of the subject to the action of the verb. In general, the active voice means that the subject *performs* the action (John cuts the bread), the middle voice means that the subject *participates* in the results of the action (John cuts the bread for himself), and the passive means that the subject *receives* the action (The bread is cut by John). The selection of voice is often a subjective decision on the part of the writer or speaker. Matthew, for example, has actives in three passages where Mark has middles (Matt. 19:20 and Mark 10:20; Matt. 26:23 and Mark 14:20; Matt. 26:51 and Mark 14:47).

If we define voice as the relation of the subject to the action of the verb, then stative verbs, such as εἰμί, have no voice, for there is no action. Stative verbs accordingly are excluded from this analysis of voice functions.

Active Voice

Simple active—The most common use of the active voice is to indicate that the subject directly performs the action of the verb: Romans 5:8 Χριστὸς ὑπὲρ ἡμῶν ἀπέθανεν (Christ died for us).

Causative active—Sometimes an active voice is used when the subject indirectly causes the action to take place. Examples include Matthew 5:45, where God causes His sun to shine on the good and bad (ἀνατέλλει); John 19:1, where Pilate had Jesus taken and whipped (ἔλαβεν, ἐμαστίγωσεν); and 1 Corinthians 3:6, where Paul planted, Apollos watered, but God caused it to grow (ηὔξανεν). Absurdities could result if the causative idea were not observed: "God shines His sun," "Pilate took and whipped Jesus," and "Paul planted, Apollos watered, but God was growing." Sometimes the verb itself is causative; other times causation is determined by context.

Reflexive active—The reflexive active occurs when the active voice is used with a reflexive pronoun. The subject then acts upon itself, much like the direct middle (below): Matthew 23:12 ὅστις ταπεινώσει ἑαυτὸν ὑψωθήσεται (whoever humbles himself shall be exalted).

Middle Voice

The middle voice is difficult to express in English, since English does not have a corresponding idiom. The student should avoid the idea that it is always reflexive (I loose myself). The basic notion is that the subject intimately participates in the results of the action. It is the voice of personal involvement. Even though deponent verbs are translated with an active sense, they often convey the idea of interest or involvement.

Direct middle—This is sometimes called the reflexive middle. The subject directly performs the action on itself. The classic example is in Matthew 27:5, where Judas went out and hanged himself (ἀπελθὼν ἀπήγξατο) (cf. Luke 12:15). The direct middle is relatively rare. The reflexive idea is normally expressed with the active voice and a reflexive pronoun.

Indirect middle—The indirect middle can express a variety of nuances that convey the subject's special interest in the action. For example, the subject may do something (1) in reference to itself, as in Acts 25:11, where Paul appealed to Caesar on his own behalf (ἐπικαλοῦμαι); (2) by itself, as in 1 Corinthians 13:8, where tongues will cease by themselves (παύσονται); or (3) in reference to others with whom it happens to be intimately and personally involved, as in 1 Thessalonians 1:2, where Paul says he mentions (μνείαν ποιούμενοι) the Thessalonians in his prayers. It also occurs in Acts 18:26 when Priscilla and Aquila took Apollos aside (προσελάβοντο) to instruct him more fully. Interaction between the context, the verbal idea, and the middle voice will help determine these and other nuances of the indirect middle.

The switching between middle and active voice in James 4:2–3 is somewhat problematic: "You do not have because you do not ask (αἰτεῖσθαι); you ask (αἰτεῖτε) and you do not receive, because you ask (αἰτεῖσθε) amiss." Some say the switching is arbitrary (BDF 1961:166). Others suggest that it is merely stylistic variation. Mayor (1897:133) suggests that the active represents mere vocalizing of words, while the middle represents prayer of the heart.

Permissive middle—The subject may either seek to have an action done in regards to itself or permit it to take place. Joseph, in Luke 2:4–5, went to Bethlehem to have himself registered (ἀπογράψασθαι). Paul argues in Galatians 5:2 that if a man allows himself to become circumcised (περιτέμνησθε), Christ will be of no value to him. In Acts 22:16 Ananias told Paul to permit himself to be baptized (βάπτισαι) and to allow God to wash away his sins (ἀπόλουσαι).

Reciprocal middle—Sometimes the plural subject of a middle voice verb interacts with other members of the subject. John 9:22 ἤδη γὰρ συνετέθειντο οἱ Ἰουδαῖοι (for the Jews had already decided among themselves).

Deponent middle—Most middle voice verbs in the New Testament are deponent verbs. A deponent verb is one that has a middle voice form but active voice meaning. Mark 1:40 ἔρχεται πρὸς αὐτὸν λεπρός (a leper came to him).

Passive Voice

Thematizing the subject—The most common function of the passive voice is to keep the topic of the passage or the previous subject as the subject of the sentence. The passive in Romans 1:17 ἀποκαλύπτεται (is revealed) keeps Paul's theme of "the righteousness of God" in the forefront.

Omitting the agent—The agent in an active sentence (John ate the sandwich) can be omitted in a passive sentence (The sandwich was eaten). The agent is omitted for several reasons. The theological passive circumvents using the word *God,* perhaps due to Jewish tradition. The Jews avoided unnecessary use of the divine name to protect them from frivolously uttering the sacred name and thus violating the Third Commandment (Ex. 20:7). This circumlocution occurs most often in the Gospels. The passives in the Beatitudes (Matt. 5:4–9), for example, are theological passives: παρακληθήσονται (they shall be comforted = God will comfort them), χορτασθήσονται (they shall be satisfied = God will satisfy them), ἐλεηθήσονται (they will be shown mercy = God will be merciful to them), and κληθήσονται (they will be called = God will call them) (cf. Zerwick

1963:76). Other reasons for using the passive to omit the agent are when the agent is irrelevant or obvious from the context (cf. J. Callow 1986:32–33).

Emphasizing the agent—When the agent is named in a passive construction, it is part of a prepositional phrase with ἀπό, διά, ἐκ, παρά, or ὑπό. This tends to highlight the agent, as in Matthew 1:22: "All this took place in order that what was spoken *by the Lord* might be fulfilled" (cf. NIV and TEV for active rendering).

Passive with middle sense—Sometimes a passive verb will have a middle meaning: 1 Peter 5:6 Ταπεινώθητε οὖν ὑπὸ τὴν κραταιὰν χεῖρα τοῦ θεοῦ (Humble yourselves under the mighty hand of God).

Deponent passive—Some verbs with passive forms have active meanings, such as ἐγενήθην, ἐπορεύθην, and ἐφοβήθην. It is very common with the passive of ἀποκρίνομαι (I answer), as in Matthew 27:14 οὐκ ἀπεκρίθη αὐτῷ (he did not answer him). The passive of ἐγείρω often has an active sense, as in Luke 7:14 ἐγέρθητι (Arise!). Thus the passive of ἐγείρω does not necessarily imply a direct action of God (i.e., a theological passive).

Mood

Mood is a morphological feature that indicates how the speaker regards what he or she is saying with respect to its factuality. There are four moods. In general, the *indicative* represents something as factual (John ate dinner), the *subjunctive* represents something as possible (John might eat dinner), the *optative* represents something as a wish (I wish John were eating dinner), and the *imperative* represents something as a command (Eat dinner). The four moods are divided into two groups: factual *(indicative)* and non-factual or potential (subjunctive, optative, imperative). It should be noted that moods only express the speaker's perception of the action or state in relation to reality, not the objective nature of that relationship.

Indicative

The indicative mood is used to express an action or state as if it were a reality. The sentence "John is at the circus" may or may not be objectively true. Nevertheless, the sentence is framed in the indicative mood that expresses a proposition as if it were a matter of fact. The first two functions discussed below represent the basic notion of the indicative, whereas the last four show overlap with the potential moods and could be combined as the potential indicative.

Declarative indicative—A declarative indicative makes a statement or an assertion. In Matthew 16:16 Peter affirmed Σὺ ͺεῖ ὁ Χριστὸς ὁ υἱὸς τοῦ θεοῦ τοῦ ζῶντος (You are the Christ, the Son of the living God).

Interrogative indicative—An interrogative indicative is used in questions. It is basically a statement that has undergone a transformation. Thus the question "Is John here?" has at the deep structure level the statement "John is here." In John 1:19 the priests and Levites asked John the Baptist Σὺ τίς εἶ (Who are you?).

Indicative of Command—The future indicative can be used as a command: Matthew 1:21 καλέσεις τὸ ὄνομα αὐτοῦ Ἰησοῦν (You must name him Jesus) and James 2:8 Ἀγαπήσεις τὸν πλησίον σου ὡς σεαυτόν (Love your neighbor as yourself). This is sometimes called the cohortative indicative.

Indicative of obligation—The indicative is used to express an obligation using the verbs δεῖ (it is necessary) or ὀφείλω (I ought): 1 John 4:11 ὀφείλομεν ἀλλήλους ἀγαπᾶν (we ought to love one another).

Indicative of wish—The indicative is used to express a wish with such verbs as θέλω (I wish), βούλομαι (I wish), and ὄφελον (I would that): 1 Corinthians 7:32 θέλω ὑμᾶς ἀμερίμνους εἶναι (I wish you to be free from worry).

Indicative of condition—Indicative verbs are found in first and second class conditions. First Corinthians 7:15 is a first class condition: εἰ δὲ ὁ ἄπιστος χωρίζεται, χωριζέσθω (But if the unbelieving husband departs, let him depart). The verb χωρίζω is often used in the papyri as a technical term for divorce in marriage contracts and divorce documents. Thus if an unbelieving partner initiates the divorce, the believer is to permit it.

Subjunctive

The subjunctive conveys the idea that the speaker regards what is expressed by the verb as a possibility, supposition, or desire rather than as a fact. It appears to express more of a visualization of the action becoming factual than the optative. The potential moods do not grammaticalize an objective future reference, only a subjective projection beyond the present. Moreover, students should be aware that the translation using "may" or "might" (as commonly taught in Elementary Greek) cannot be universally applied to the subjunctive.

Subjunctive in dependent clauses—The most common use of the subjunctive is in dependent clauses, of which there is a great variety. Some of the more common clauses are the following:

(1) Purpose clauses can be formed with ἵνα + subjunctive, as in Matthew 1:22 Τοῦτο ὅλον γέγονεν ἵνα πληρωθῇ (This all came to pass that it might be fulfilled). Purpose clauses can also be formed with ὅπως + subjunctive, as in Hebrew 2:9.

(2) Result clauses can be formed with ἵνα + subjunctive, as in Romans 11:11 μὴ ἔπταισαν ἵνα πέσωσιν (Did they stumble so as to fall beyond recovery? NIV). See also John 9:2. The second subjunctive in 1 John 1:9 does not convey doubt that God will forgive our sins: ἐὰν ὁμολογῶμεν τὰς ἁμαρτίας ἡμῶν, πιστός ἐστιν καὶ δίκαιος, ἵνα ἀφῇ ἡμῖν τὰς ἁμαρτίας. It is part of a ἵνα clause that could be interpreted as result (If we confess our sins, he is faithful and just so as to forgive our sins) or as a noun clause of apposition (If we confess our sins, he will remain faithful and just, that is, he will forgive our sins).

(3) Third class conditional clauses are formed with ἐάν + subjunctive, as in John 6:51 ἐάν τις φάγῃ ἐκ τούτου τοῦ ἄρτου ζήσει εἰς τὸν αἰῶνα (If anyone eats this bread, he will live forever).

(4) Indefinite local clauses can be formed with ὅπου and either ἄν or ἐάν + subjunctive, as in Matthew 26:13 ὅπου ἐὰν κηρυχθῇ τὸ εὐαγγέλιον (wherever the gospel is preached).

(5) Temporal clauses can be formed with ὅταν or with various words meaning "until" + subjunctive, as in Mark 13:30 οὐ μὴ παρέλθῃ ἡ γενεὰ αὕτη μέχρις οὗ ταῦτα πάντα γένηται (This generation will not pass away until all these things come to pass).

(6) Noun clauses are often formed with ἵνα + subjunctive, as in Mark 6:12 ἐκήρυξαν ἵνα μετανοῶσιν (They preached that the people should repent). The ἵνα clause is the object of the verb ἐκήρυξαν and thus functions as a noun clause of indirect discourse (cf. Matt. 4:3). In John 15:12 a noun clause of apposition is also formed by ἵνα + subjunctive: αὕτη ἐστὶν ἡ ἐντολὴ ἡ ἐμή, ἵνα ἀγαπᾶτε ἀλλήλους (this is my commandment, that you love one another). See Matthew 10:25 for an example of subject ἵνα clause with subjunctive.

(7) Relative clauses can be formed with the relative and ἄν or ἐάν + subjunctive, as in 1 John 2:5 ὃς δ' ἂν τηρῇ αὐτοῦ τὸν λόγον (whoever keeps his word).

Deliberative subjunctive — Subjunctives are used in questions where there is some uncertainty as to one's direction. The speaker is either (a) asking others for guidance regarding the proper course of action or (b) debating with him or herself about what to do. The first represents a real question where an answer is expected, as in Mark 6:37 ἀγοράσωμεν δηναρίων διακοσίων ἄρτους (Do you want us to buy two hundred denarii of bread?). The second represents a rhetorical question where no answer is expected, as in 1 Corinthians 11:22 τί εἴπω ὑμῖν (What should I say to you?). As with the deliberative future, the deliberative subjunctive can also be used in rhetorical questions that challenge the audience to ponder the implications of the question, as in Romans 10:14.

Subjunctive of emphatic negation — The aorist subjunctive with οὐ μή is used to emphatically deny that something will happen. This idiom can be translated with an emphatic negative future tense using "never." For example, John 10:28 οὐ μὴ ἀπόλωνται εἰς τὸν αἰῶνα (they will never perish) and Hebrew 13:5 Οὐ μή σε ἀνῶ οὐδ' οὐ μή σε ἐγκαταλίπω (I will never leave you, and I will never, for any reason, forsake you). The future indicative can also be used, but it is not nearly as frequent as the aorist subjunctive. Both are found in John 6:35 ὁ ἐρχόμενος πρὸς ἐμὲ οὐ μὴ πεινάσῃ, καὶ ὁ πιστεύων εἰς ἐμὲ οὐ μὴ διψήσει πώποτε (The one who comes to me will never hunger, and the one who believes on me will never thirst). Moulton (1978:192) reasons that since ninety percent of the New Testament occurrences of οὐ μή occur in Old Testament quotations and in the sayings of Christ, the cause is "a feeling that inspired language was fitly rendered by words of a peculiarly decisive tone."

Subjunctive of Prohibition — A prohibition is a negative command (Don't do it). Prohibitions are formed in one of four ways: (1) with μή and the present imperative; (2) with μή and the aorist subjunctive; (3) with οὐ and the future indicative (Matt. 5:21); and (4) sometimes with μή and the aorist imperative (Mark 13:15). Examples of the aorist subjunctive of prohibition with a second person verb include Matthew 5:17 Μὴ νομίσητε ὅτι ἦλθον καταλῦσαι τὸν νόμον (Do not think that I have come to destroy the law) and Matthew 1:20 μὴ φοβηθῇς παραλαβεῖν Μαρίαν τὴν γυναῖκά σου (You must not be afraid to take Mary as your wife). In the latter example the aorist is used to prohibit an action already in progress (cf. John 3:7). Occasionally the verb will be third person, as in 1 Corinthians 16:11 μή τις οὖν αὐτὸν ἐξουθενήσῃ. This could be rendered "Let no one despise him" or "No one is to despise him."

The difference between prohibitions using aorist subjunctives and those using present imperatives lies in the difference in aspect. With the aorist the speaker prohibits an activity in its totality (Don't do it) (cf. McKay 1985:216). It is possible, depending on the context and verbal idea, that the aorist used in prohibitions can assume other nuances of the aorist, such as the ingressive idea (Don't begin to do it). With the present the speaker views the prohibition as a process or something that pertains to habitual activities (Don't be in the habit of doing it).

Hortatory subjunctive—First person plural subjunctives may function as hortatory subjunctives. The speaker uses it to exhort others to join him or her in a certain activity. The expression "let us" is normally used in English translation: 1 John 4:7 Ἀγαπητοί, ἀγαπῶμεν ἀλλήλους (Brothers, let us love one another). Not all first person plural subjunctives are hortatory (cf. 1 John 3:11, 5:2).

The hortatory subjunctive may be either present or aorist. The present conveys the progressive idea, as in Galatians 6:10 ἐργαζώμεθα τὸ ἀγαθὸν πρὸς πάντας (Let us do good to all persons). Whenever people cross our path, we should treat them kindly. The aorist conveys the exhortation as a whole, as when Peter remarked in Mark 9:5 ποιήσωμεν τρεῖς σκηνάς (Let us build three shelters). Peter does not conceive of the action in segments, to be done one at a time, but as a whole.

Optative

The optative is not common in the New Testament, occurring only sixty-eight times (forty-five aorists and twenty-three presents). It conveys the idea that the speaker regards what is expressed by the verb as a wish or as an uncertainty rather than as a fact. It appears to express more hesitation than the subjunctive.

Optative of wish or prayer—Optatives occur most often in liturgical and devotional contexts, such as in prayers, blessings, benedictions, imprecations, and pious rejections. For example, liturgical optatives are found in formal benedictions, where a spiritual leader uses a set formula to invoke divine blessing. This is common in the opening and closing of epistles: 1 Peter 1:2 χάρις ὑμῖν καὶ εἰρήνη πληθυνθείη (May grace and peace be multiplied to you). An informal blessing is found in 2 Timothy 1:16 δῴη ἔλεος ὁ κύριος τῷ Ὀνησιφόρου (May the Lord grant mercy to the household of Onesiphorus). An imprecatory prayer is found in Acts 8:20 Τὸ ἀργύριόν σου σὺν σοὶ εἴη εἰς ἀπώλειαν (May your money perish with you). The stereotyped expression μὴ γένοιτο (may it never be) occurs fifteen times (fourteen in the Pauline Epistles and once in Luke 20:16). It expresses a strong rejection based on devotion to the truth. The AV paraphrases the expression "God forbid," a rendering unsurpassed by any modern version. In Luke 1:38 (May it be to me as you have said) Mary uses the optative to express devotional submission to God's will.

Optative of deliberation—The second most common use of optatives is in questions (usually indirect) when the speaker is pondering such things as the meaning of something, the identity of someone, the truth of something, what should be done, whether something is able to be done, or what happened. Examples include Luke 1:29 διελογίζετο ποταπὸς εἴη ὁ ἀσπασμὸς οὗτος (she was pondering what kind of salutation this might be) and Acts 8:31 Πῶς γὰρ ἂν δυναίμην ἐὰν μή τις ὁδηγήσει με (How can I unless someone guide me?). See also Luke 3:15, 6:11, 22:23, Acts 5:24, and 17:11.

Optative of possibility—A few optatives occur in the protasis ("if" clause) of conditional sentences. In 1 Peter 3:17 Peter says that it would be better to suffer for doing good, if this should be God's will (εἰ θέλοι τὸ θέλημα τοῦ θεοῦ) than for doing wrong (cf. Acts 24:19; 1 Pet. 3:14). See Boyer (1988:129–40) for further discussion of optatives.

Imperative

The imperative expresses an attempt to bring about a desired action through the agency of another, that is, to impose one's will on another or to give another direction. It grammaticalizes the speaker's perception of an action or state which could become factual provided the directions were acted upon.

Imperative of command—The most common use of the imperative is in commands. The distinction between present and aorist commands is the same for prohibitions. Following the parade analogy, the present imperative commands that we sit at the curb and focus our attention on one float at a time. We only see a progression; we do not know how long the parade will last or if it will continue indefinitely. The speaker envisions the command being acted upon in stages, whenever the situation arises, or the like. Thus the present imperative calls attention to the details or individual segments of the activity. The aorist imperative focuses our attention on the activity as a whole. It appears to be the speaker's subjective choice to grammaticalize the command, prohibition, or request as a whole or as a process. The same request, for example, "Give us our daily bread" is framed with an aorist imperative in Matthew 6:11 and with a present imperative in Luke 11:3.

A popular view of the role of aspect in commands and prohibitions is that the aorist refers to specific situations (Do [or don't do] this particular thing at this particular time) and the present refers to general precepts (Always [or don't ever] be doing it). This view finds support in the distribution of aorist and present imperatives in the New Testament. As expected, one finds more specific commands in narrative material and more general principles in didactic material. Commands in the Gospels commonly use the aorist, whereas commands in the Epistles commonly use the present (cf. Fanning 1990:327–32).

There are, however, several difficulties with this idea. One is that it tends to interpret the aorist as objectively taking place at a point of time. Another is that both the present and aorist imperatives can convey general principles and specific commands. Which one a command pertains to is actually determined by temporal pointers in the context, not by the form of the imperative. For example, both an aorist imperative (μείνατε) and a present imperative (γρηγορεῖτε) are found in Mark 14:34 μείνατε ὧδε καὶ γρηγορεῖτε (remain here and watch). The context suggests a specific command for both. Before Jesus raised the young girl from the dead (Matt. 9:24), He told the mourners to depart (Ἀναχωρεῖτε). The present imperative could hardly be a general principle. The same is true for the series of present imperatives in Jesus' instruction to the twelve (Matt. 10:8): i.e., heal the sick, raise the dead, cleanse the lepers, and cast out demons. Present imperatives that pertain to specific situations abound in the Gospels (cf. Matt. 2:20; 8:32; 9:2, 9; 14:18; 16:23; 17:17; 21:2; 27:65).

Conversely, Paul regularly uses aorist imperatives for general precepts. Examples include Romans 6:13 παραστήσατε ἑαυτοὺς τῷ θεῷ (present yourselves to God) and Colossians 3:8 ἀπόθεσθε καὶ ὑμεῖς τὰ πάντα (get rid of all these things). These passages pertain to the Christian life for which one might expect present imperatives to be used rather than aorists. Some suggest that the aorist calls for a once-for-all act, but the transformation of life is hardly ever achieved in a single act, as Paul himself realized (cf. Phil. 3:12–15). Some say that the aorist may be used in place of a present because it implies more urgency. Urgency, however, is derived from the situation and the authority of the speaker, as Boyer (1987:45–46) suggests, not from the tense form. Others suggest that Paul employs the aorist with an ingressive idea to focus on the need for all Christians to break from the past life and to begin living the new life. While this is plausible, it seems best to view Paul's use of aorist imperatives as focusing on the whole act, and to let the context determine other nuances.

The imperative of command can be in the third person, as in James 1:5–6 αἰτείτω παρὰ τοῦ διδόντος θεοῦ (he should ask from God, the one who gives) . . . αἰτείτω δὲ ἐν πίστει (but he must ask in faith; cf. NIV, TEV). The idea of permission misses the point in the second phrase, "he is permitted to ask in faith," and is questionable in the first phrase, "If anyone lacks wisdom, he is permitted to ask God." See also James 1:19. The third person imperative βαπτισθήτω in Acts 2:38 is normally taken as a command in parallel with the preceding second person imperative (Repent and be baptized). However, could the change in person have any significance on the soteriological necessity of the two actions?

Passive imperatives are somewhat problematic in that they command the recipient of the action rather than the doer of the action. For example, how is one to comply with the commands "Be saved" and "Be baptized"? Boyer (1987:49) divides passive imperatives into two categories: (1) those in which the recipient allows the action to take place, as in Mark 1:41 (Be cleansed), and (2) those in which the recipient has a responsibility to see that the action gets done, as in Romans 12:2 (Be transformed).

Imperative of prohibition — Present imperatives preceded by μή are used in prohibitions (negative commands) that convey a process. Thus "Don't get into the habit of doing it" or "Don't make it part of your life-style." It is often found in the Epistles where Paul calls for a new life in Christ: Romans 12:2 μὴ συσχηματίζεσθε τῷ αἰῶνι τούτῳ, ἀλλὰ μεταμορφοῦσθε τῇ ἀνακαινώσει τοῦ νοός (Do not be conformed to this world, but be transformed by the renewing of the mind). The first imperative συσχηματίζεσθε is a prohibition, and the second μεταμορφοῦσθε is a positive command. Both are present imperatives that focus on the details one encounters as the injunctions are undertaken. Another example is 1 John 4:1 Ἀγαπητοί, μὴ παντὶ πνεύματι πιστεύετε (Beloved ones, do not believe every spirit).

Traditionally, μή with the present imperative has been interpreted as "Stop what you are doing" (DM 1955:301; BW 1979:127). Although this meaning does highlight the progressive nature of the present, the vast majority of cases would result in forced exegesis, as Boyer (1987:42–45) has shown, such as trying to prove that the Ephesians were drunkards (Eph. 5:18). It should only be applied where the context suggests that the undesired action was in progress. There are no contextual clues that those Jesus was addressing in Matthew 6:19 had been laying up treasures on earth, as the Williams translation implies, "Stop storing up your riches on earth." There might be come credence for this idea in certain contexts. For example, the disciples were terrified when they saw a figure walking toward them on the water (Matt. 14:26). In the following verse Jesus says μὴ φοβεῖσθε (stop being afraid) (cf. Matt. 19:14; Mark 16:6; Luke 1:13; 2:10; 8:49, 52; 11:7; John 2:16; Rev. 1:17; 5:5).

Imperative of entreaty—When the strength of a command would be improper because of the social positions of the parties involved, the imperative is reduced to the force of a request. That is, subordinates do not normally command their superiors to do something, they politely request it. However, there is not an exact correlation between social position and imperatival force. Sometimes commands can be given by inferiors to superiors and requests from superiors to those of lesser rank.

Imperatives of entreaty are often found in prayers. In the Lord's Prayer (Matt. 6:9–13) both second and third person imperatives are used: ἐλθέτω ἡ βασιλεία σου (Please send your kingdom), ἄφες ἡμῖν τὰ ὀφειλήματα ἡμῶν (Please forgive us of our wrongdoings), and ῥῦσαι ἡμᾶς ἀπὸ τοῦ πονηροῦ (Please keep us safe from the evil one). These certainly cannot be commands, nor can the third person forms be permission, as if we were permitting God to act. Aorist imperatives are usually found in prayers to God (New Testament exceptions are Luke 11:3 [δίδου] and 22:42 [γινέσθω], where present imperatives are used). Some think that the aorist in prayers is milder and more reverent, whereas the present is more harsh. Turner (1963:75) says that the aorist is used for specific prayers and the present for general prayers. Specific prayers would naturally have more of a sense of urgency; but it is best to regard the aorist as grammaticalizing the entirety of the request; that is, when we pray, we normally commit the whole matter to God.

Imperatives that express invitations can also be regarded as imperatives of entreaty: John 1:46 Ἔρχου καὶ ἴδε (Come and see) (cf. John 11:34, Rev. 22:17).

Imperative of permission—The imperative can be used to grant permission. The social positions of the parties involved are usually reversed from the imperative of entreaty. The person who grants permission is usually superior, whereas the person who asks a request is usually subordinate. The translation could employ "let" (Let John do it) or "may" (John may do it). It normally occurs with the third person imperative, as in 1 Corinthians 7:36 ὃ θέλει ποιείτω (let him do what he wishes), but may also be found with second person imperatives, as in Jesus' response to the demons' request to enter the swine (Matt. 8:32) εἶπεν αὐτοῖς, Ὑπάγετε (he said to them, you may go).

Third person imperatives do not all convey permissions, as suggested by the stereotyped translation in some elementary grammars (let him loose). They can be used in commands, prohibitions, entreaties, suggestions, or permissions. See Boyer (1987:47–48) for discussion of third person imperatives.

Imperative of condition—The imperative can function as a conditional. In John 2:19, for example, the imperative cannot be taken as a command, request, or permission: Λύσατε τὸν ναὸν τοῦτον καὶ ἐν τρισὶν ἡμέραις ἐγερῶ αὐτόν (If you destroy this temple, I will raise it up in three days). See also Luke 6:37–38 and James 4:7–8.

Imperative of greeting—Greetings are often expressed with an imperative: Matthew 26:49 προσελθὼν τῷ Ἰησοῦ εἶπεν, Χαῖρε ῥαββί (He came to Jesus and said, "Greetings, Rabbi") (cf. Acts 15:29).

Imperative of warning—Imperatives of warning are translated with such expressions as "look out," "beware," or "take care," depending on the verb involved: Acts 13:40 Βλέπετε οὖν μὴ ἐπέλθῃ τὸ εἰρημένον ἐν τοῖς προφήταις (Take care that what was spoken by the prophets does not happen to you). See also Mark 8:15, 12:38, Phil. 3:2, and Col. 2:8.

Exercises

In the following examples, parse the form and then interpret the voice or
mood in light of the aspect, verbal idea, and context. Translate the passage
in such a way as to convey the function(s) you have chosen.

1. Matt. 5:18   παρέλθῃ (mood), both occurrences
2. Matt. 5:37   ἔστω (mood)
3. Matt. 7:2   κριθήσεσθε (voice)
4. Matt. 7:6   δῶτε (mood)
5. Matt. 14:10   ἀπεκεφάλισεν (voice)
6. Matt. 26:4   συνεβουλεύσαντο (voice)
7. Matt. 28:9   Χαίρετε (mood)
8. Mark 6:24   αἰτήσωμαι (mood)
9. Mark 7:4   βαπτίσωνται (voice)
10. Mark 9:22   ἀπολέσῃ (mood), βοήθησον (mood)
11. John 11:7   Ἄγωμεν (mood)
12. John 20:17   ἅπτου (mood)
13. Eph. 4:26   ὀργίζεσθε (mood)
14. 1 Thess. 5:23 ἁγιάσαι (mood)
15. 1 John 2:28   φανερωθῇ (mood)
16. 1 John 5:16   ἴδῃ, ἐρωτήσῃ (mood)

10 Participles

Grammarians classify participles as verbal adjectives because they have both verb and adjective characteristics. Like a verb, they have aspect and voice and may take an object. Like an adjective, they have gender, number, and case and will agree with a noun or pronoun in the sentence. Both the verb and adjective characteristics are important for the interpretation of the participle regardless of its function. Participles usually function semantically as the verb of deep structure clauses, which, when transformed into English, become adverbial or adjectival clauses. Thus the modifying force of the participle is central to most of its functions.

It is often said that the time of the participle is relative to the time of the main verb; a present participle expresses action taking place at the same time as the main verb, and an aorist participle expresses action taking place before the main verb. While this happens to be the case much of the time, it is probably not the morphology that is doing it. The time relation between the participle and main verb is conveyed by the sense of the context, not by the tense form of the participle (Porter 1989:378; cf. BDF 1961:174–75). The participle itself is timeless (Robertson 1934:1111). The so-called tense indicators merely indicate aspect. The present indicates that the speaker perceives an action in progress, and the aorist indicates that the speaker perceives it as a whole. There is evidence that the time relation between the participle and main verb is signaled by their relative positions: a participle before the verb indicating antecedent time and a participle after the verb indicating subsequent time (Porter 1989:381).

Participles Functioning in Noun Phrases

A noun phrase can be defined as a group of words that function as a noun. This may include a verb or participle. For example, the sentence "The man who came to our house is good" contains a subject noun phrase — "The man who came to our house" — that has a relative clause with a verb. The sentence represents two kernel clauses at the deep structure level: (1) "The man is good" and (2) "The man came to our house." In English if we wanted to fuse the second kernel into the first to make one sentence, we could transform it into a relative clause. We could also make relative clauses in Greek, but Greek has other ways to fuse the two kernels together. We could, for example, transform the verb in the second kernel clause into a participle: ὁ ἐλθὼν πρὸς τὸν οἶκον ἡμῶν ἐστιν ἀγαθός. The noun phrase that functions as the subject of ἐστίν is ὁ ἐλθὼν πρὸς τὸν οἶκον ἡμῶν. The English surface structure with a relative clause is semantically equivalent to the Greek surface structure with a participle. Both were generated from the same two kernel clauses. The same analysis could be applied to complement clauses.

Participles that function in noun phrases are usually preceded by an article. This function is commonly called a substantival participle. A substantive is a word or group of words that can be used as a noun. As we have noted, however, the participle actually represents a deep structure verb, not a noun. Noun phrases containing participles function as subject, direct object, indirect object, object of preposition, apposition, or predicate nominative.

Subject

Mark 4:3 ἐξῆλθεν ὁ σπείρων σπεῖραι (The one who is sowing [i.e., the sower] went out to sow). Often an article and participle can be transformed into a noun rather than into a relative clause: ὁ κλέπτων (the thief), ὁ κρίνων (the judge).

The time frame of the participle is determined by contextual pointers: Galatians 1:23 Ὁ διώκων ἡμᾶς ποτε νῦν εὐαγγελίζεται τὴν πίστιν (The one who formerly persecuted us is now proclaiming the faith). The entire noun phrase "The one who formerly persecuted us" functions as the subject of the sentence. The action of the participle takes place before the main verb, even though a present tense form is used.

Direct Object

Regular direct object—Mark 1:32 ἔφερον πρὸς αὐτὸν . . . τοὺς δαιμονι-
ζομένους (They were bringing to him the ones possessed with demons).

Indirect discourse—The noun phrase direct object that follows a verb of
speaking is called indirect discourse. Indirect discourse is the report of what
someone said; for example, "John said that he would be in class." It is distinguished from direct discourse in which the actual words are quoted; for
example, "John said, 'I will be in class tomorrow.'" Indirect discourse is usually formed with ὅτι but can also be formed with an infinitive or participle.

When a participle is used, both the participle and its subject will be in
the accusative case, since the noun phrase of which they are a part is actually
the object of a verb of speaking: for example, 1 John 4:2 πᾶν πνεῦμα ὃ
ὁμολογεῖ Ἰησοῦν Χριστὸν ἐν σαρκὶ ἐληλυθότα ἐκ τοῦ θεοῦ ἐστιν (Every
spirit which confesses that Jesus has come in the flesh is from God). The
subject of the complement clause is the accusative "Jesus Christ," and the
verb is the accusative participle "has come." The entire construction "that
Jesus has come in the flesh" is the noun phrase direct object of the verb
"confesses." Sometimes the complementizer "that" is not needed in the
translation.

Direct object after verbs of perception and cognition—Participles following
verbs of perception and cognition, such as ἀκούω, βλέπω, γινώσκω, εἶδον,
εὑρίσκω, θεωρέω, οἶδα, or ὁράω, function in the same way as participles
following verbs of speaking. They can also form noun phrase direct objects
with an oblique case participle: Mark 1:10 εἶδεν σχιζομένους τοὺς
οὐρανούς (he saw that the heavens were being divided). As with indirect
discourse, the complementizer (that) need not be present (he saw the heavens being divided). Other examples include John 1:37 ἤκουσαν . . . αὐτοῦ
λαλοῦντος (they heard him speaking) and 3 John 4 ἀκούω τὰ ἐμὰ τέκνα
ἐν τῇ ἀληθείᾳ περιπατοῦντα (I hear that my children are walking in the
truth). In each of the examples there is a noun or pronoun in the same case
as the participle that functions as the subject of the clause. Participle objects
after verbs of perception are more common than after verbs of speaking.

Complement after other verbs—A complement is a word or group of words
that completes the meaning and syntactical structure of the predicate. Some
verbs, especially those of ceasing and completing, such as τελέω (I finish) or
παύομαι (I cease), require a participle or infinitive to complete the verbal

idea. The verbal sense is incomplete without the entire verb chain: Ephesians 1:16 οὐ παύομαι εὐχαριστῶν ὑπὲρ ὑμῶν (I do not cease giving thanks for you) and Luke 5:4 ἐπαύσατο λαλῶν (he ceased speaking).

Indirect Object

John 1:22 ἵνα ἀπόκρισιν δῶμεν τοῖς πέμψασιν ἡμᾶς (That we might give an answer to the ones who sent us). The dative participle τοῖς πέμψασιν is the indirect object of the verb δῶμεν.

Object of Preposition

Substantival participles functioning as objects of prepositions are more common than normally recognized in grammars: Matthew 5:44 προσεύχεσθε ὑπὲρ τῶν διωκόντων ὑμᾶς (Pray for the ones persecuting you).

Apposition

Some examples of participles functioning in appositional noun phrases include Matthew 1:16 Ἰησοῦς ὁ λεγόμενος Χριστός (Jesus, the one called Christ); Mark 6:14 Ἰωάννης ὁ βαπτίζων (John the Baptist); and 1 Thessalonians 1:10 Ἰησοῦν τὸν ῥυόμενον ἡμᾶς ἐκ τῆς ὀργῆς τῆς ἐρχομένης (Jesus, the one who delivers us from the coming wrath) (cf. Phil. 4:7).

Predicate Nominative

1 John 5:6 Οὗτός ἐστιν ὁ ἐλθὼν δι' ὕδατος καὶ αἵματος (This is the one coming through water and blood).

Participles Functioning in Adjectival Phrases

Participles often function in adjectival phrases, modifying a noun or pronoun. The participle will agree in gender, number, and case with the word it modifies and will function as restrictive adjective phrases, as descriptive adjective phrases, and as predicate adjectives.

Restrictive Adjective Phrases

A restrictive adjective phrase is one that is essential for the proper identification of the head noun. It will limit the noun to a particular individual, thing, or group in order for the readers to identify it. Without the modifier, they would not know for sure which of the many possible referents of the noun is being discussed. Such modifiers are therefore essential to the meaning of the sentence. The restrictive use is by far the most common type of adjectival participle. When it is transformed into a restrictive relative clause in English, it is not to be set off by commas. The restrictive adjectival participle occurs in three basic forms.

Article-participle-noun—Examples include Romans 3:25 (τῶν προγεγονότων) ἁμαρτημάτων (the sins which happened before) and Luke 15:12 τὸ ἐπιβάλλον μέρος (the part which belongs to me).

Article-noun-article-participle—This is the most common position for adjectival participles: John 6:50 ὁ ἄρτος (ὁ ἐκ τοῦ οὐρανοῦ καταβαίνων) (the bread which comes down from heaven). Whether to insert a present or past verb in the relative clause is determined by context, not by the tense form of the participle.

Noun-participle—Galatians 5:3 παντὶ ἀνθρώπῳ περιτεμνομένῳ (to every man who allows himself to be circumcised).

Descriptive Adjective Phrases

When the readers already know what is being discussed, a modifier is not necessary to identify the head term for them. When a modifier does occur, it simply gives additional description. This is called a *descriptive* or *non-restrictive adjective phrase*. A non-restrictive adjective is not essential to the meaning of the sentence: Matthew 16:16 τοῦ θεοῦ (τοῦ ζῶντος) (the living God). Phrases with words meaning "surpassing" are descriptive: "the surpassing grace of God" (2 Cor. 9:14), "the surpassing greatness" (Eph. 1:19), and "the surpassing riches" (Eph. 2:7).

Predicate Adjective

A predicate adjective makes a descriptive affirmation about the subject; for example, "The ball is red." When an adjectival participle is used in the predicate along with a linking verb, such as εἰμί, it is called a predicate adjective participle. One example is Revelation 1:18 καὶ ἰδοὺ ζῶν εἰμι (and behold I am the living one).

The construction in Galatians 1:22 ἤμην ἀγνοούμενος τῷ προσώπῳ ταῖς ἐκκλησίαις (I was unknown in person to the churches) is often cited as a predicate adjective (e.g., BW 1979:145). However, does the participle function as an adjective, attributing a quality to Paul (e.g., Paul was short, nearsighted, unknown), or does it function as part of a verb chain, expressing a progressive notion? The first represents a predicate adjective, and the second an imperfect periphrastic construction (discussed later in the chapter). In predicate adjectives the verbal sense resides more in the copulative verb, whereas in periphrastic participles the verbal sense resides more in the participle. Burton (1980:62–63), Bruce (1982:103), and Longenecker (1990:41) are undoubtedly correct when they call it a periphrastic construction emphasizing the continuity of his being unknown.

Participles Functioning in Adverbial Phrases

Adverbial participles modify the verb of a main clause or another subordinate clause. As with regular adverbs, they answer such questions as When? How? By what means? Why? and Under what circumstances? The particular way they modify the verb is not grammaticalized in Greek; that is, the adverbial force is not indicated by the grammar. The adverbial force can usually be determined by analyzing the relation between the participle and verb in light of the context. This use of the participle is sometimes called circumstantial because it describes the circumstances of the verbal action or state. Adverbial participles are never preceded by an article.

Adverbial participles are best translated into English with an adverbial clause. Grammatically, however, they are merely individual words or phrases in the Greek surface structure, not clauses; but the Greek surface structure represents a deep structure kernel clause with a subject and verb. As we transform the kernel clause into the English surface structure, the clause construction is often retained along with an adverbial conjunction to denote the particular way it relates to the main verb. For example, the participle in Mark 12:14 ἐλθόντες λέγουσιν αὐτῷ (having come they said to him) has for its kernel clause "they came." We now have two deep structure kernel clauses, "they came" and "they said." The first clause modifies the second by denoting time. Thus when transformed into English, a temporal adverbial conjunction is inserted at the beginning of the initial clause, "When they came, they said." If the participle is in the nominative case, then its subject will be the same as the subject of the sentence. If the participle is in an oblique case, then its subject will be another noun in the sentence with which it will agree. It is up to the expertise of the exegete to determine the proper adverbial force.

Time

If the participle is interpreted as conveying a temporal relation to the leading verb, insert "when," "while," or "after" in the translation at the beginning of the adverb clause. The particular adverbial conjunction to use is determined by context, not by morphology. The aspect, however, does seem to influence the choice of terms to a certain degree. "While" (during which time) is more congenial with a present participle because the speaker perceives the event in progress. "When" (at which time) is more suitable with the aorist participle because the speaker perceives the action as a whole.

Acts 19:2 Εἰ πνεῦμα ἅγιον ἐλάβετε πιστεύσαντες (Did you receive the Holy Spirit when you believed?). Some interpret the aorist participle as antecedent time, contending that a person receives the Holy Spirit after conversion. Whether or not this is true cannot be determined from the tense form of the participle.

Hebrews 9:12 εἰσῆλθεν ἐφάπαξ εἰς τὰ ἅγια αἰωνίαν λύτρωσιν εὑράμενος (He entered once into the holy place, after he had obtained eternal redemption). The NRSV (following Dods 1974:333 and Burton 1898:66) suggests that the time of the participle should be subsequent to the main verb: "he entered . . . , thus obtaining eternal redemption." Hughes (1977:328, 337), however, argues that the time of the aorist participle is antecedent, that Christ had already obtained redemption before entering the holy place. The question is whether redemption is contingent on entering the heavenly sanctuary, the entire priestly act, or only on the sacrifice. Again the answer must be found in the context, not in the form of the participle.

Manner

The participle of manner modifies the main verb by telling how something is done. Some grammarians call this the *modal* function. In Luke 19:5

σπεύσας κατάβηθι (come down quickly) the participle is translated with a simple adverb of manner.

Sometimes ὡς is used with the participle: Mark 1:22 ἦν γὰρ διδάσκων αὐτοὺς ὡς ἐξουσίαν ἔχων (for he was teaching them as having authority; or in an authoritative manner, with authority, or authoritatively). Christ's teachings were not based on what previous rabbis had said, as in traditional rabbinical teaching. He spoke with divine authority.

One may rightly question some examples of manner participles cited in grammars; for example, Matthew 3:1 παραγίνεται Ἰωάννης ὁ βαπτιστὴς κηρύσσων ἐν τῇ ἐρήμῳ (John the Baptist came preaching in the desert). The participle does not really tell *how* John appeared, only what he was do-ing when he did appear. It might be better to classify this example as atten-dant circumstance.

Means

Participles can be used to convey the means by which a person accomplishes something. This is sometimes called the *instrumental* use of the participle. The key to distinguish means from manner is to see whether the phrase "by means of" can be inserted in the translation. In the sentence, "John vigor-ously hit the ball with a bat," the adverb "vigorously" indicates how John hit the ball (manner), and the phrase "with a bat" indicates the instrument he used (means).

Matthew 6:27 τίς ἐξ ὑμῶν μεριμνῶν δύναται προσθεῖναι ἐπὶ τὴν ἡλικίαν αὐτοῦ πῆχυν ἕνα (Which one of you by means of worrying is able to add one cubit to his stature). An aorist participle perceives the action as a whole: Acts 22:16 ἀπόλουσαι τὰς ἁμαρτίας σου ἐπικαλεσάμενος τὸ ὄνομα αὐτοῦ (wash away your sins by calling on his name).

Reason

The reason participle expresses the unintentional cause that brought about some circumstance. This is commonly called the *causal participle*. It is best translated using "because" or "for," as in Matthew 22:29 Πλανᾶσθε μὴ εἰδότες τὰς γραφάς (You are deceived because you do not know the Scriptures) and John 20:20 ἐχάρησαν οὖν οἱ μαθηταὶ ἰδόντες τὸν κύριον (the disciples rejoiced because they saw the Lord). Neither the ignorance of the Scriptures nor the seeing of the Lord was intended to produce the result which happened. See also Matthew 1:19 and John 2:23.

Grounds

Participles often give the grounds for a conclusion or exhortation. *Grounds* refers to the evidence or facts upon which a conclusion or exhortation is based. To test for a grounds-conclusion relation, try inserting "therefore in conclusion" before the main clause. In translation, however, the word "since" before the participial clause is sufficient, for example, Romans 5:1 Δικαιωθέντες ἐκ πίστεως εἰρήνην ἔχομεν πρὸς τὸν θεόν (Since we have been justified by faith, we have peace with God). In Matthew 27:4 Ἥμαρτον παραδοὺς αἷμα ἀθῷον (I have sinned since I have betrayed innocent blood) the betrayal was the evidence that led Judas to the conclusion that he sinned. It was not the cause of the sin. See also Galatians 4:9.

A debated passage is Philemon 9 διὰ τὴν ἀγάπην μᾶλλον παρακαλῶ, τοιοῦτος ὢν ὡς Παῦλος πρεσβύτης (I appeal rather on the basis of love, since I am such a person as Paul, an old man). The problem is whether the participle ὢν lays down the basis for the appeal (grounds) or the right to command which Paul is laying aside (concession). Those who interpret πρεσβύτης as "old man" prefer grounds. The following phrase "and now also a prisoner for Christ Jesus" seems to evoke empathy and love from Philemon, thus supporting the grounds use of the participle. Those who interpret πρεσβύτης as "ambassador" prefer the concessive use: "I appeal rather on the basis of love, although I am such a person as Paul, an ambassador" (O'Brien 1982:289–90; Moule 1957:144; cf. Lightfoot [1879] 1959:337–38). The thought would be that, although Paul could have used his authority as ambassador to command Philemon to accept Onesimus, he based his appeal instead on love.

Condition

The conditional participle states a condition that, when fulfilled, issues into a certain consequence indicated by the main clause. Thus the participle functions as the verb in the protasis ("if" clause) of a conditional sentence: Matthew 21:22 καὶ πάντα ὅσα ἄν αἰτήσητε ἐν τῇ προσευχῇ πιστεύοντες λήμψεσθε (and whatever you ask in prayer, if you believe, you will receive).

In Hebrews 6:6 the AV, RSV, and NIV render the participle παρα-
πεσόντας as conditional, "if they fall away." This suggests (although does
not require) that the author may be using a hypothetical case that could
never happen to true believers. It seems better to view the participle as the
last in a series of five substantival participles that identify the apostates, all
governed by the article in verse 4: "For it is impossible to renew to repentance those who have been once enlightened, who have tasted the heavenly
gift, . . . and who have fallen away." The REB, NJB, NRSV, and TEV interpret the participle as substantival.

Concession

The concessive participle states a circumstance in spite of which the action
or state of the main verb is realized. The main clause therefore is contrary to
what one would expect. The words "though" or "although" are inserted at
the beginning of the adverbial clause to bring out the idea of concession.
John 9:25 τυφλὸς ὢν ἄρτι βλέπω (although I was blind, now I see). The
particles καίπερ, καὶ γε, or καίτοι are occasionally used to clarify the concessive force of the participle.

Translators sometimes transform the subordinate concessive clause into
an independent clause and insert a "but" or "yet" in the translation:
Philippians 2:6 ἐν μορφῇ θεοῦ ὑπάρχων οὐχ ἁρπαγμὸν ἡγήσατο τὸ
εἶναι ἴσα θεῷ (Although he existed in the very nature of God, he did not
consider equality with God something to cling on to). This could also be
rendered, "He has always had the very nature of God, yet he did not consider equality with God something to cling on to" (cf. TEB, NEB, JB). This
does not change the focus, since clauses introduced with adversative conjunctions (but, yet) tend to be semantically prominent.

Purpose

The purpose participle reveals the intent behind the action of the leading
verb. Some grammarians call this the *telic* or *final* participle. The participle
may be translated using "to," "in order to," "for the purpose of," or "so that"
(with a modal auxiliary, such as "may" or "might"). It is equivalent to infinitives and ἵνα clauses that express purpose: Romans 15:25 πορεύομαι εἰς
Ἰερουσαλὴμ διακονῶν τοῖς ἁγίοις (I am going to Jerusalem to minister to

the saints) and John 6:6 τοῦτο δὲ ἔλεγεν πειράζων αὐτόν (But he was saying this to test him).

Some suggest that purpose participles are usually future tense (Moule 1968:140). However, many are present (cf. the above examples and Matt. 22:35; 27:55; Mark 10:2; Luke 2:45; 7:3; 10:25; 13:6–7; John 6:24; 12:33). Acts 25:13 is a clear case of an aorist participle expressing purpose: κατήντησαν εἰς Καισάρειαν ἀσπασάμενοι τὸν Φῆστον (they arrived at Caesarea to pay their respects to Festus; cf. AV, NIV, TEV, NRSV). Knowling (1974:496) says that if we adopt the aorist reading rather than the future, then it would refer to antecedent action (i.e., After Agrippa and Bernice had greeted Festus they went to Caesarea). Festus, however, ruled from Caesarea (cf. Metzger 1975:492). Burton remarks, "The assumption that the Aorist Participle properly denotes past time, from the point of view either of the speaker or of the principle verb, leads to constant misinterpretation of the form" (1898:59).

Result

The result participle is a debated category; several grammars do not even list it. Result refers to the consequence of an action and is to be translated using "so that" or "with the result that." If this is a legitimate function, it is rather rare. One possibility is Mark 7:12–13 οὐκέτι ἀφίετε αὐτὸν οὐδὲν ποιῆσαι τῷ πατρὶ ἢ τῇ μητρί, ἀκυροῦντες τὸν λόγον τοῦ θεοῦ (You no longer permit him to do anything for his father or mother, with the result that you are making void the word of God; cf. NIV, NRSV). Another possibility is John 5:18 πατέρα ἴδιον ἔλεγεν τὸν θεὸν ἴσον ἑαυτὸν ποιῶν τῷ θεῷ (He is calling God his own father, so that he is making himself equal with God; cf. Phillips).

The participles in Ephesians 5:19–20 (λαλοῦντες, ᾄδοντες, ψάλλοντες, εὐχαριστοῦντες) are often interpreted as the result of being filled with the Spirit. Although some contend that the speaking, singing, praising, and thanking are the means of being filled, it is best to view them as the consequences of a Spirit-filled person (cf. Lincoln 1990:345). Other possible result participles include Ephesians 2:15 (ποιῶν), Hebrews 12:3 (ἐκλυόμενοι), 2 Peter 2:1 (ἐπάγοντες), and 2:6 (τεθεικώς).

Attendant Circumstance

The participle of attendant circumstance expresses an action or circumstance that accompanies the action of the leading verb. This function is sometimes called *circumstantial.* The best translation in English is to transform the participle into a finite verb of the same mood as the leading verb and insert "and" between the two verbal expressions. This, however, leads one to suspect a coordinate relation between the two verbs. The participle is still grammatically subordinate to the leading verb, even though it does not fall into one of the adverbial categories cited above: Mark 1:18 ἀφέντες τὰ δίκτυα ἠκολούθησαν αὐτῷ (They left their nets and followed him). Besides being grammatically subordinate, the participial phrase represents a deep structure proposition that is semantically less prominent than that represented by the main clause (a step-GOAL relation; cf. chapter 17).

Sometimes the attendant circumstance participle is used along with an infinitive. In such cases, the participle is to be translated as a second infinitive, connected to the regular infinitive by the word "and": Mark 1:7 οὐκ εἰμὶ ἱκανὸς κύψας λῦσαι (I am not worthy to bend down and loose).

The participle πορευθέντες in Matthew 28:19 has long prompted discussion. The AV translates it as an attendant circumstance and therefore with the same mood (imperative) as the leading verb: πορευθέντες οὖν μαθητεύσατε πάντα τὰ ἔθνη (Go ye therefore, and teach all nations). Some interpret the participle as temporal, "Having gone, make disciples of all nations" (cf. Lenski 1943:1172). The exegete must ask whether the Lord assumed that the disciples were ready to depart or whether the disciples needed the added command. Most versions follow the AV and interpret it as attendant circumstance.

One participle that especially challenges the exegete is ἐνεργουμένη in James 5:16 πολὺ ἰσχύει δέησις δικαίου ἐνεργουμένη. (1) The participle could function as an adjective modifying the subject δέησις (prayer): "The *energetic* prayer of a righteous man avails much" (Laws [1980] 1987:234, AV, NJB, Phillips). (2) The participle could denote time: "The prayer of a righteous man avails much, *when it is at work*" (Ropes 1978:309, Williams). (3) The participle could express attendant circumstance: "The prayer of a righteous man is powerful *and effective*" (NIV, REB). (4) The participle could be understood in the passive voice with a temporal force: "The prayer of a righteous man avails much, *when it is put into effect* [by God]" (Mayor

1897:171–73; Davids 1982:196–97). The question is whether effective prayer is contingent on (1) a certain kind of prayer, (2) the perseverance in prayer, (3) the character of the person praying, or (4) God. The reader is invited to consult the commentaries for the arguments.

Genitive Absolute

The genitive absolute construction consists of a participle and a noun, both in the genitive case. Occasionally the noun is absent (Matt. 17:14, 26; Luke 12:36; Acts 21:31; Rom. 9:11). The genitive absolute functions as a subordinate adverbial clause, modifying the leading verb with one of the above adverbial uses, the most common being time and reason. The genitive noun is the subject, and the genitive participle is the verb of the clause. Not all genitive participles, however, are genitive absolutes.

It is called "absolute" because supposedly the subject of the adverbial clause is not mentioned elsewhere in the sentence; for example, "When *John* came home from the war, the family rejoiced." However, the term is somewhat of a misnomer, since forty-two percent of the 313 genitive absolutes in the New Testament are coreferential with another element in the UBS sentence and twenty-nine percent are coreferential with another element in the main clause (Healey and Healey 1990:186–87). It is coreferential with the main subject in Matthew 1:18, with a genitive in Matthew 12:46, with a dative in Matthew 1:20, and with an accusative in Matthew 22:41. The purpose of the construction then is not to construct a clause with a subject that is not mentioned elsewhere in the same sentence. Rather it seems to serve within the sentence as a switch-reference device to show that the subject of the main clause is different from its own subject (Healey and Healey 1990:188). There are only four exceptions to this observation. It also seems to have a discourse function at the beginning of paragraphs (or subparagraphs) to indicate a change in setting. This is especially true in narrative.

An example of a genitive absolute of time which marks a new paragraph is Matthew 2:13 Ἀναχωρησάντων δὲ αὐτῶν ἰδοὺ ἄγγελος κυρίου φαίνεται (and when they departed an angel of the Lord appeared). Genitive absolutes may also express grounds (1 Pet. 4:1), reason (Acts 27:7), condition (Heb. 10:26), concession (John 20:26), and attendant circumstance (Eph. 2:20).

Pleonastic Participles

There are two types of pleonastic (redundant) expressions that involve participles and verbs of speaking: (1) participle-verb, such as ἀποκριθεὶς εἶπεν (having answered he said); and (2) verb-participle, such as ἐλάλησεν λέγων (he spoke saying). Zerwick (1963:127) calls the first an *empty formula*. It is often translated with a single word, such as "replied" or "said," depending on the context. John, however, prefers two finite verbs separated by καὶ: ἀπεκρίθη καὶ εἶπεν. This could also be reduced to simply "he answered."

Participles Functioning as Verbs

Imperatival Participles

The use of the participle as an imperative is sometimes debated, since it is not found in classical Greek. Some regard it as a Hebraism conveying a rule for daily living and thus not a true imperative (Daube [1947] 1981:467–88). Others contend that it is found in the papyri and is therefore a peculiarity of koine Greek (Moulton 1978:180–83). Some regard it as an anacoluthon (Boyer 1984:173; cf. Robertson 1934:1133) in which the imperative ἔστε is omitted (an imperative form that does not occur in the New Testament). The imperatival participle occurs most frequently in Romans 12 and 1 Peter. For example, 1 Peter 3:1 γυναῖκες ὑποτασσόμεναι τοῖς ἰδίοις ἀνδράσιν (Wives, be in subjection to your husbands); compare with Mark 5:23 (ἐλθών) and perhaps Hebrews 13:5 (ἀρκούμενοι). The imperatival participle should not be confused with the attendant circumstance participle with an imperative main verb.

Indicative Participles

In addition to functioning as imperatives, the participle can function as indicative verbs, a use Moulton says is fairly well established in the papyri (Moulton 1978:222–25; Moule 1968:179): Romans 5:11 ἀλλὰ καὶ καυχώμενοι ἐν τῷ θεῷ (But we also rejoice in God) (cf. 2 Cor. 4:8–10; 5:6, 12; 7:5; 8:4; 9:11, 13).

Periphrastic Participles

The word *periphrastic* refers to the use of several words where one would do. It is a roundabout way of speaking or writing, being derived from περί (around) and φράζω (I explain). For example, εἰμὶ ποιῶν says the same thing as ποιῶ. The participle ποιῶν functions as the major component in a two-part main verb chain. The periphrasis is usually constructed with some form of εἰμί (sometimes γίνομαι, ὑπάρχω, ἔχω) and then a participle. Only on a rare occasion does the participle precede the auxiliary verb. The interpretations of the various periphrastic constructions should be in accordance with the aspect of the participle. Also the frequency of this construction in the New Testament (especially Luke, Mark, and John) raises the question whether it gives added emphasis in every case.

Present periphrastic—The present periphrastic participle is constructed with a present form of εἰμί and a present participle: Matthew 27:33 ὅ ἐστιν Κρανίου Τόπος λεγόμενος (which is called "The Place of a Skull"; cf. Mark 5:41; Col. 1:6).

Imperfect periphrastic—The imperfect periphrastic is constructed with an imperfect form of εἰμί and a present participle. It is very common in the New Testament: Mark 1:22 ἦν γὰρ διδάσκων αὐτούς (for he was teaching them; cf. Luke 2:51). The participle ἐρχόμενον in John 1:9 ῏Ην τὸ φῶς τὸ ἀληθινόν, ὃ φωτίζει πάντα ἄνθρωπον, ἐρχόμενον εἰς τὸν κόσμον has been variously interpreted. The options are (1) periphrastic, "The true light which illuminates every man was coming into the world" (cf. NIV, NRSV, REB); (2) adjectival modifying φῶς, "This was the real light—the light that comes into the world and shines on all mankind" (TEV); or (3) adjectival modifying ἄνθρωπον, "That was the true Light, which lighteth every man that cometh into the world" (AV). Barrett (1978:160–61) and Brown (1966:9) argue for the periphrastic construction in that it highlights the incarnation.

In some cases the εἰμί and participle retain their independent force (Zerwick 1963:126): Acts 19:14 ἦσαν τινος Σκευᾶ Ἰουδαίου ἀρχιερέως ἑπτὰ υἱοὶ τοῦτο ποιοῦντες (There were seven sons of Sceva, a Jewish high priest, who were doing this; cf. AV, REB). The NIV and NRSV interpret the participle as periphrastic rather than adjectival.

Future periphrastic—The future periphrastic is constructed with a future form of εἰμί and a present participle. It is translated as a progressive future:

Luke 5:10 ἀπὸ τοῦ νῦν ἀνθρώπους ἔσῃ ζωγρῶν (from now on you will be catching men; cf. Matt. 24:9, Luke 22:69).

Perfect periphrastic—The perfect periphrastic is constructed with a present form of εἰμί and a perfect participle. It enhances the force of the perfect: Ephesians 2:8 τῇ γὰρ χάριτί ἐστε σεσῳσμένοι (for by grace you are saved). The present tense translation focuses on the stative idea of the perfect. See also Matthew 10:26 and 18:20.

Pluperfect periphrastic—The pluperfect periphrastic is constructed with an imperfect form of εἰμί and a perfect participle: John 3:24 οὔπω γὰρ ἦν βεβλημένος εἰς τὴν φυλακὴν ὁ Ἰωάννης (For John had not yet been cast into prison; cf. Luke 8:2, John 1:24). This construction is fairly common.

Future perfect periphrastic—The future perfect periphrastic is constructed with a future form of εἰμί and a perfect participle. The translation (following English grammar) is said to be "shall have been." It is rather rare in the New Testament. One example that provokes debate is Matthew 16:19 ὃ ἐὰν δήσῃς ἐπὶ τῆς γῆς ἔσται δεδεμένον ἐν τοῖς οὐρανοῖς (whatever you bind upon earth shall have already been bound in heaven; cf. Williams). If the notion of an English future perfect is pressed, then Peter is to proclaim only what has previously been decreed in heaven. His actions then do not dictate heavenly ordinances (cf. JB). This, however, assumes that the perfect is temporally based. Hence the binding and loosing had already been decreed before the time of speaking. Porter (1989:471–74) argues that the perfect conveys only the state without reference to its inception or permanence. If these temporal ideas could be derived from the context, then the interpretation implied by an English future perfect could still be maintained. Other examples include Matthew 18:18 and Hebrews 2:13.

Exercises

Cite the best participial use for the following examples and, if appropriate, give alternate possibilities. Translate the participial construction in such a way as to bring out the force of the use(s) you have chosen.

1. Matt. 9:6   Ἐγερθείς
2. Matt. 11:1   διατάσσων
3. Matt. 11:18   ἐσθίων, πίνων
4. Matt. 14:5   θέλων
5. Matt. 19:22   ἀκούσας, λυπούμενος, ἔχων
6. Matt. 21:23   ἐλθόντος, διδάσκοντι, λέγοντες
7. Matt. 25:25   φοβηθείς, ἀπελθών
8. Matt. 26:60   προσελθόντων
9. Matt. 27:49   σώσων
10. Matt. 28:19–20   βαπτίζοντες, διδάσκοντες
11. Mark 11:9–10   Εὐλογημένος, ἐρχόμενος, Εὐλογημένη, ἐρχομένη
12. Mark 11:11   περιβλεψάμενος, οὔσης
13. Mark 12:28   προσελθών, ἀκούσας, συζητούντων, ἰδών
14. Mark 14:22   ἐσθιόντων, λαβών, εὐλογήσας
15. Mark 16:5   εἰσελθοῦσαι, καθήμενον, περιβεβλημένον
16. Luke 6:30   αἰτοῦντι, αἴροντος
17. Luke 9:25   κερδήσας, ἀπολέσας, ζημιωθείς
18. John 20:30–31   γεγραμμένα, πιστεύοντες
19. Acts 3:26   ἀναστήσας, εὐλογοῦντα
20. Acts 7:12   ἀκούσας, ὄντα

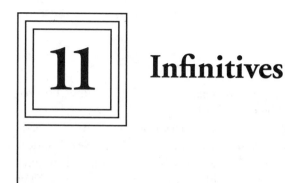

Infinitives

Grammarians classify infinitives as verbal nouns. Like a verb the infinitive will have aspect and voice. The relative temporal relation to the rest of the sentence, like the participle, must be established by context, not by the form of the infinitive. Temporal contextual pointers include the prepositions often used in infinitive constructions, such as ἐν, πρό, πρίν, and μετά. Its noun characteristics are not grammaticalized on the infinitive form, but they are sometimes found on accompanying articles. The categories *verbal adjective* and *verbal noun* for the participle and infinitive are based on historical linguistics and are somewhat misleading, for their functions in koine Greek far transcend these limiting labels.

Infinitives Functioning in Adverbial Phrases

Infinitives often function adverbially, either alone, preceded by a genitive article, or as the object of a preposition in a prepositional phrase functioning adverbially. The adverbial infinitive modifies a verb in various ways: time, reason, purpose, result, means, or manner. In a prepositional phrase the infinitive will be preceded by a preposition and usually a neuter article and usually followed by an accusative noun or pronoun. Such constructions cannot be translated literally into English. The phrase must be transformed into an English adverbial clause with the accusative noun or pronoun becoming the subject, the infinitive becoming the verb, and with the appropriate adverbial conjunction (e.g., before, after, while, because) at the beginning of the clause.

Time

An infinitive can be used to express the relative time of the main verb in relation to the action expressed by the infinitive.

Antecedent time—Antecedent time means that the action of the main verb takes place before the action expressed by the infinitive. To convey this idea, "before" is used at the beginning of the adverbial clause. Antecedent time may be expressed with πρὸ τοῦ + infinitive (nine times in the New Testament), πρίν + infinitive (eight times), or πρὶν ἤ + infinitive (three times). Aorist infinitives are used despite the fact that the action of the infinitive follows that of the verb. The only exception is the present infinitive in John 17:5. In Luke 22:15 Jesus told His disciples that He desired to eat the Passover with them πρὸ τοῦ με παθεῖν (before I suffer). The accusative με is transformed into the subject of the clause, and the infinitive παθεῖν becomes the verb of the clause. In John 8:58 πρὶν Ἀβραὰμ γενέσθαι ἐγὼ εἰμί (before Abraham came into existence, I am) the indeclinable Ἀβραάμ functions as the accusative subject. With the divine ἐγὼ εἰμί the idea is more than Christ's existing before Abraham; it means that He eternally exists (Barrett 1978:352).

Contemporaneous time—Contemporaneous time means that the action of the main verb takes place at the same time as that of the infinitive. This notion is commonly expressed by ἐν τῷ + infinitive with the infinitive being either present (usually) or aorist. The tense form of the infinitive indicates aspect rather than time: the speaker views the action as in progress with the present and as a whole with the aorist. The construction can be translated using "when," "while," "as," or "just as." One example is Matthew 13:4 ἐν τῷ σπείρειν αὐτόν (while he was sowing). The construction occurs more often in Luke's writings than anywhere else (forty-one of the fifty-four New Testament occurrences). There is a possibility that on occasion ἐν τῷ + infinitive could convey subsequent time and be translated "after" (cf. TEV on Luke 3:21; Turner 1963:145).

The exegete should be aware that the phrase ἐν τῷ + infinitive does not always express time. It can express other adverbial notions, such as reason (Luke 1:21, because he delayed in the temple), means (Acts 3:26, by turning; cf. Burton 1898:162), or epexegetical (Luke 12:15). See the discussions of reason and means below.

Subsequent time—Subsequent time means that the action of the main verb takes place after that of the infinitive. To convey this idea, "after" is used at the beginning of the adverbial clause. Subsequent time is expressed by μετὰ τὸ + infinitive. The infinitive is aorist except for one instance of a perfect. Luke's writings account for eight of the fifteen occurrences. Mark 14:28 μετὰ τὸ ἐγερθῆναί με (after I am raised). This construction, unlike ἐν τῷ + infinitive, always conveys time.

Reason

An infinitive may be used to express the unintentional cause for what took place. The most common way to express reason using an infinitive is in the form διὰ τό + infinitive. The tense form is usually present. The construction is to be translated into English using "because." For example, in Mark 4:6 the plants dried up because they had not been able to develop their roots (διὰ τὸ μὴ ἔχειν ῥίζαν). In John 2:24 Jesus did not trust Himself to the people because He knew all persons (διὰ τὸ αὐτὸν γινώσκειν πάντας). He innately knew that their belief was superficial and that they considered Him to be merely another wonder worker. Luke's writings account for eighteen of the thirty-two occurrences of this construction.

There are other ways to express reason using the infinitive, such as with ἐν τῷ + infinitive. Turner (1963:145) suggests that ἐν τῷ + infinitive is causal in Acts 2:1 (because the day of Pentecost had arrived) and Romans 15:13 (because you believe) (cf. BDF 1961:208). The occurrence in Romans 15:13 is debatable. Is Paul praying for God to fill the Roman Christians with joy and peace by means of their faith in Him (TEV, NEB), when they believe in Him (NIV, REB), or because they believe in Him? The latter seems most probable. The construction with a causal sense is also found in Hebrews 2:8 (because he subjected all things to him, nothing was left outside of his control) and Hebrews 8:13 (Because he speaks of a new covenant, he makes the first old) (cf. Turner 1963:146).

Reason is once expressed with τῷ + infinitive (2 Cor. 2:13, because I did not find Titus) and once with ἕνεκεν τοῦ + infinitive (2 Cor. 7:12, because your zeal for us is manifest before God). Burton (1898:161) is most likely correct in saying the infinitives in Mark 5:4 are not strictly causal, but express evidence of the demoniac's strength.

Purpose

Purpose infinitives express the intent or goal for which something is done (e.g., Mary went to the store to buy food). Translation into English may take various forms, such as "in order to," "in order that," "to," "that," "so that," or "for the purpose of." English phrases containing "that" must also be followed by a modal auxiliary, such as "may" or "might," to convey purpose; otherwise, they would convey result. Purpose infinitives are equivalent to ἵνα + subjunctive, which also can express purpose. Purpose clauses often occur after verbs of motion (such as ἔρχομαι, -βαίνω, and πορεύομαι), sending (such as ἀποστέλλω), giving (such as δίδωμι), and choosing (such as ἐκλέγομαι). There are various infinitive constructions that can express purpose:

Simple Infinitive — The simple infinitive is a very common way to express purpose: Mark 10:45 ὁ υἱὸς τοῦ ἀνθρώπου οὐκ ἦλθεν διακονηθῆναι ἀλλὰ διακονῆσαι καὶ δοῦναι τὴν ψυχὴν αὐτοῦ λύτρον ἀντὶ πολλῶν (the Son of Man did not come to be served, but to serve and to give his life a ransom for many) and Matthew 5:17 Μὴ νομίσητε ὅτι ἦλθον καταλῦσαι τὸν νόμον (Do not think that I have come to destroy the law). For other examples, see Matthew 2:2; Mark 1:24; Luke 2:22; 15:15; 18:10; Acts 10:33; and 1 Corinthians 1:17.

Infinitive with εἰς τό — Acts 3:19 μετανοήσατε οὖν καὶ ἐπιστρέψατε εἰς τὸ ἐξαλειφθῆναι ὑμῶν τὰς ἁμαρτίας (Repent therefore and turn to God, so that your sins might be wiped out). Paul favors this construction (forty-eight of seventy-one occurrences) but often uses it in senses other than purpose; other New Testament writers use it more consistently as purpose. For examples of purpose in Romans, see 1:11, 3:26, 4:16, 7:4, 8:29, 15:8, 13, 16. Westcott (1974:118) suggests that ἵνα + subjunctive indicates direct and immediate purpose, whereas εἰς τό + infinitive indicates "more remote result aimed at or reached" (cf. Rom. 1:20).

The construction εἰς τό + infinitive can express result (Rom. 4:18), less frequently indirect discourse (1 Thess. 2:12), once manner (Rom. 12:3), and once as a complement (Phil. 1:23). It is sometimes used epexegetically to explain an adjective (1 Thess. 4:9, Jas. 1:19).

Infinitive with τοῦ — Matthew 13:3 ἐξῆλθεν ὁ σπείρων τοῦ σπείρειν (The sower went out to sow). Luke uses τοῦ with the infinitive more than any other New Testament writer (approximately forty times) with about half expressing purpose. Paul uses it about thirteen times, but only two clearly express purpose (cf. Rom. 6:6; Phil. 3:10). The infinitive with τοῦ may express functions other than purpose, such as result, subject, direct object, and epexegetical.

Infinitive with πρὸς τό—Ephesians 6:11 ἐνδύσασθε τὴν πανοπλίαν τοῦ θεοῦ πρὸς τὸ δύνασθαι ὑμᾶς στῆναι (Put on the whole armor of God, so that you might be able to stand). This construction occurs eleven times in the New Testament.

The construction πρὸς τό + infinitive almost always expresses purpose. Twice it is weakened to reference or manner, as in Matthew 5:28 ὁ βλέπων γυναῖκα πρὸς τὸ ἐπιθυμῆσαι (everyone who looks on a woman lustfully [or in such a way as to arouse his desires]; cf. NIV, RSV, NJB, REB, Turner 1963:144; BDF 1961:207). The difficult construction πρὸς τὸ δεῖν in Luke 18:1 probably expresses reference (Marshall 1978b:671). Jesus spoke a parable in reference to (or about) the need to pray at all times and not faint. Rarely is the significance of the parable given prior to the parable, as it is here.

Infinitive with ὥστε—Matthew 27:1 συμβούλιον ἔλαβον πάντες οἱ ἀρχιερεῖς . . . ὥστε θανατῶσαι αὐτόν (All the chief priests took counsel . . . for the purpose of putting him to death). This is an uncommon usage; compare with Matthew 10:1 (twice), 15:33, 24:24, Luke 4:29, and 20:20, but see Boyer (1985:11). Normally ὥστε with an infinitive expresses result.

Infinitive with ὡς—This only occurs twice denoting purpose. There is no case of its denoting result in the New Testament: Luke 9:52 εἰσῆλθον εἰς κώμην Σαμαριτῶν ὡς ἑτοιμάσαι αὐτῷ (They went into a Samaritan village in order to prepare for him; cf. Acts 20:24). There are textual variants on both verses with ὥστε listed as an alternate reading.

Result

Result refers to the consequence of an action. The result can be either intentional (John fixed the car, so that it now runs smoothly) or unintentional (The wind blew so hard that it knocked over the tomato cage). It is often difficult to distinguish between purpose and intended result, because when a purpose is fulfilled, it may be regarded an intended result. The difficulty is to determine the vantage point of the speaker or writer with respect to the fulfilled intent, whether before (purpose) or after (result). The form may help some, but most of the infinitive constructions used for purpose can also be used for result. The problem is compounded when it involves divine action, for with the omnipotent and omniscient God who dwells beyond time, His purposes are always realized, and everything realized is either planned or permitted for some reason. Moulton (1978:219) says that in passages dealing with divine action "contemplated and actual results, final and consecutive clauses, necessarily lose their differentia."

Result is expressed in English with such expressions as "that," "so that," "so as to," and "as a result." Some grammarians use "final" for purpose clauses and "consecutive" for result clauses.

Infinitive with ὥστε — This is the most common way to express result using an infinitive: Mark 1:27 ἐθαμβήθησαν ἅπαντες ὥστε συζητεῖν πρὸς ἑαυτούς (They were all amazed, so that they were questioning one another). The subject of the infinitive (they) must be supplied. See also Luke 12:1, Acts 16:26, 1 Corinthians 13:2, and Hebrews 13:6. The construction ὥστε + infinitive occurs forty-five times as clearly result, seven times as possibly purpose (see above under purpose), and once as apposition (1 Cor. 5:1).

Simple infinitive — Hebrews 11:8 Πίστει καλούμενος Ἀβραὰμ ὑπήκουσεν ἐξελθεῖν (When Abraham was called, he obeyed, and as a result he stepped out by faith). For other possible examples, see Luke 10:40, Acts 5:3, Romans 1:10, Ephesians 3:17, Colossians 4:6, Revelation 2:20 (twice), and 5:5. Romans 1:28 could be purpose, intentional result, or unintentional result: παρέδωκεν αὐτοὺς ὁ θεὸς εἰς ἀδόκιμον νοῦν, ποιεῖν τὰ μὴ καθήκοντα (God gave them over to corrupted minds, so that they do things that are not proper). One could argue that if this were God's intent, it would implicate Him as the author of evil. However in the sovereign mind of God, this may have been allowed to happen to show them the futility of their going their own way.

Infinitive with εἰς τό — Romans 1:20 εἰς τὸ εἶναι αὐτοὺς ἀναπολογήτους (so that they are without excuse). God's intent in revealing Himself through nature was not to render people without excuse when they sinned; it was to display His glory. The consequence of this display of glory is that when humans do forsake God, they have no excuse. Both Käsemann (1980:42) and Cranfield (1975:116) follow this reasoning to argue for result. However, in the omniscient mind of God, could not the rendering of humans without excuse be a secondary purpose for His revealing Himself? Sanday and Headlam (1902:44) argue that the infinitive does not denote "primary purpose, but indirect, secondary or conditional purpose. God did not design that man should sin; but He did design that if they sinned they should be without excuse." Turner (1963:143) says, "as the passage deals with divine action, however, it is better to retain the usual near-final meaning of εἰς τό, whatever theologians may say." Other possible examples of εἰς τό + infinitive denoting result include Romans 4:11, 18, 6:12, 7:5, 12:2, 1 Corinthians 8:10, 2 Corinthians 7:3, 8:6, Galatians 3:17, 1 Thessalonians 2:16, and Hebrews 11:3.

Infinitive with τοῦ—Matthew 21:32 οὐδὲ μετεμελήθητε ὕστερον τοῦ πιστεῦσαι αὐτῷ (You did not even repent so as to believe on him) (cf. Acts 18:10, Romans 7:3). Romans 1:24 could be either purpose or result: Διὸ παρέδωκεν αὐτοὺς ὁ θεὸς ἐν ταῖς ἐπιθυμίαις τῶν καρδιῶν αὐτῶν . . . τοῦ ἀτιμάζεσθαι τὰ σώματα αὐτῶν (wherefore God gave them over to the desires of their heart, so that they dishonored their bodies). This is parallel with the simple infinitive ποιεῖν in Romans 1:28, and both should be taken the same way. Käsemann (1980:48) argues that both infinitives denote result, but adds that the infinitive in Romans 1:24 should be taken as passive (cf. Cranfield 1975:122). Barrett ([1957] 1987:38,40), however, argues that the infinitives are epexegetical, explaining what is meant by having a corrupt mind and a lustful heart. Some argue for purpose (Denney 1974:593). It is probably best to view it as result.

Means

The infinitive can on occasion express means. This is sometimes called the *instrumental infinitive*.

Simple infinitive—In Revelation 2:14 Balaam taught Balak to induce the Israelites to sin by eating (φαγεῖν) food sacrificed to idols and by committing sexual immorality (πορνεῦσαι). Boyer (1985:18), however, interprets these infinitives as appositives to σκάνδαλον. Other possible examples include Acts 15:10 and Hebrews 5:5.

Infinitive with ἐν τῷ—The prepositional phrase ἐν τῷ + infinitive can also expresses means, as in Acts 3:26 (God sent him to bless you by turning you). The expression ἐν τῷ τὴν χεῖρά σου ἐκτείνειν in Acts 4:30 (by stretching forth your hand) probably expresses means (AV, NJB), although it is sometimes translated as an imperative (NIV, TEV, REB). The example often cited in Hebrews 3:12 (by departing from the living God) is probably epexegetical rather than means (cf. Turner 1963:146, TEV, NIV).

Infinitive with ἐκ τοῦ—Second Corinthians 8:11 ἐκ τοῦ ἔχειν (by means of what you have; cf. NASB, TEV).

Manner

Infinitive with εἰς τό—In Romans 12:3 the infinitive is used as an object of a preposition in a phrase that functions as an adverb of manner εἰς τὸ σωφρονεῖν (soberly, reasonably). One is not to think more highly of oneself than he or she ought, but to think soberly or with sober judgment.

Infinitive with πρὸς τό—Matthew 5:28 πρὸς τὸ ἐπιθυμῆσαι (lustfully or with a lustful eye). Manner infinitives are rather rare.

Explaining an Adjective

Infinitives also function adverbially when they explain or modify adjectives. This function is sometimes called *epexegetical.* The more common adjectives that are modified by infinitives are ἄξιος, δυνατός, ἕτοιμος, and ἱκανός: Luke 15:19 οὐκέτι εἰμὶ ἄξιος κληθῆναι υἱός σου (I am no longer worthy to be called your son). The infinitive κληθῆναι modifies the adjective ἄξιος by answering the question "Worthy in what way?" For other examples, see Mark 1:7, Romans 4:21, Hebrews 5:11, James 1:19.

Infinitives Functioning as Nouns

Subject

When acting as a subject, the infinitive will always be an impersonal subject. This also occurs in English. In the sentence "To read is enjoyable", the infinitive "to read" is the subject. It is smoother English, however, to insert the dummy pronoun "it" at the beginning of the sentence to signal that the subject follows the verb: "It is enjoyable to read." The use of the infinitive subject parallels ἵνα + subjunctive, which also may be used as a subject (1 Cor. 4:2).

Subject of impersonal verbs—The verbs δεῖ and ἔξεστιν are classified as impersonal verbs. They commonly occur in the third person singular indicative and take impersonal subjects. Noun phrases that act as the subject of δεῖ and ἔξεστιν are almost always formed with an infinitive: Luke 4:43

εὐαγγελίσασθαί με δεῖ τὴν βασιλείαν τοῦ θεοῦ. This can be translated various ways: "To preach the kingdom of God is necessary for me," "It is necessary that I preach the kingdom of God," or "I must preach the kingdom of God." The first translation, although somewhat awkward in English, shows that the infinitive functions as the subject of the verb.

Verbs classified as impersonal, such as δεῖ and ἔξεστιν, may be something other than a third person singular indicative and still take an infinitive subject (Matt. 12:4; Luke 18:1; Acts 2:29; 19:36; 25:24; 26:9; 2 Cor. 12:4). The verb μέλει is an impersonal verb occurring only in the third person singular, but uses other noun phrases as subjects, not infinitives.

Subject of εἰμί — Often the third person singular of εἰμί is used as an impersonal verb with an infinitive for its subject: Mark 7:27 οὐ γάρ ἐστιν καλὸν λαβεῖν τὸν ἄρτον τῶν τέκνων καὶ τοῖς κυναρίοις βαλεῖν (For it is not good to take the bread from the children and throw it to the dogs). The infinitives "to take" and "to throw" are subjects of the predication "is not good." Infinitives in such constructions are usually anarthrous. Sometimes the verb must be supplied: Philippians 1:21 ἐμοὶ γὰρ τὸ ζῆν Χριστὸς καὶ τὸ ἀποθανεῖν κέρδος (For to me to live *is* Christ and to die *is* gain).

Subject of passive verbs — Matthew 13:11 ὑμῖν δέδοται γνῶναι τὰ μυστήρια τῆς βασιλείας τῶν οὐρανῶν (To you it has been given to know the mysteries of the kingdom of heaven). The infinitive "to know" is the subject of the passive verb "has been given" (to know has been given).

Subject of other verbs — Certain other verbs may also function as impersonal and take infinitive subjects. These include δοκέω, συμφέρει, and γίνομαι (when it means "it came to pass that"). There are two infinitive subjects in Romans 7:18 τὸ γὰρ θέλειν παράκειταί μοι, τὸ δὲ κατεργάζεσθαι τὸ καλὸν οὔ (For to will is present with me, but to accomplish the good is not). For other examples, see Matthew 15:20 and 2 Corinthians 7:11.

Direct Object

Infinitives may also function as direct objects, either alone or as part of a larger noun phrase. As with participles, complements of non-linking verbs are considered noun phrase direct objects.

Natural complement — Some verbs require an additional thought to complete the verbal sense: Matthew 6:24 Οὐδεὶς δύναται δυσὶ κυρίοις δουλεύειν (No one is able to serve two masters). The fragment "no one is able" leaves the reader with the question "Able to do what?" Thus a comple-ment "to serve" is necessary to complete the idea.

Verbs that require complements fall into several categories: (a) verbs ex-pressing will or desire, such as βούλομαι and θέλω; (b) verbs expressing in-tention, such as ἄρχομαι, ζητέω, μέλλω, ὀκνέω, ποιέω, τολμάω; (c) verbs expressing permission, such as ἀφίημι, ἐπιτρέπω, κωλύω; (d) verbs express-ing ability, such as δύναμαι and ἰσχύω; (e) verbs expressing worthiness, such as ἀξιόω; and (f) verbs expressing obligation, such as ὀφείλω (Boyer 1985:6–7). Complementary infinitives rarely have an article.

Direct object of verbs denoting mental activity—Verbs denoting mental ac-tivity often take an infinitive as a complement: Luke 2:44 νομίσαντες αὐτὸν εἶναι ἐν τῇ συνοδίᾳ (supposing that he was in the caravan). The verb of thinking νομίσαντες is followed by the infinitive εἶναι which rep-resents a deep structure verb. When transformed into English, it becomes the verb of a complement clause. The subject of the clause is the accusative pronoun αὐτόν (thus "he was"). The complementizer "that" is sometimes inserted in the translation to indicate a complement clause. The more com-mon verbs of mental activity that take infinitive complements are δοκέω, ἐλπίζω, κρίνω, λογίζομαι, and νομίζω.

Indirect discourse—Verbs of speaking often take an infinitive complement clause as their direct object. Mark 12:18 οἵτινες λέγουσιν ἀνάστασιν μὴ εἶναι (who say that there is no resurrection). The more common verbs of speaking that take infinite complements are αἰτέω, διατάσσω, εἶπον, ἐρωτάω, εὔχομαι, κελεύω, λέγω, παραγγέλλω, and παρακαλέω.

Regular direct object—An infinitive may function as the regular direct ob-ject. Examples include 2 Corinthians 8:11 τὸ ποιῆσαι ἐπιτελέσατε (finish the work) and Philippians 2:13 θεὸς γάρ ἐστιν ὁ ἐνεργῶν ἐν ὑμῖν καὶ τὸ θέλειν καὶ τὸ ἐνεργεῖν (for God is the one who is working in you the de-sire and the ability) (cf. NJB, REB). Other possible examples include Luke 1:9, John 5:26, and Philippians 4:10.

Apposition

Infinitives may function as a noun in apposition to a preceding noun or pronoun. Apposition is the explaining of a preceding nominal by giving more specific information. Although not usually needed, words such as "namely" or "that is" may be supplied in the translation: James 1:27 θρησκεία καθαρὰ . . . αὕτη ἐστίν, ἐπισκέπτεσθαι . . . τηρεῖν (Pure religion . . . is this, namely, to visit . . . and to keep; cf. Acts 15:29; 24:15, Rom. 4:13; 1 Cor. 7:37; 2 Cor. 2:1; 1 Thess. 4:3, 4, 6 (twice); Heb. 9:8; 1 Pet. 2:15; Rev. 12:7).

Infinitives Functioning as Adjectives

The use of the infinitive as a modifier is sometimes called *epexegetical*. The infinitive will define, limit, or explain a noun or adjective. Its use to explain an adjective is treated under adverbial functions. Epexegetical infinitives are usually anarthrous, but sometimes they are preceded with a genitive article and rarely by an accusative article.

The more common nouns that are modified by infinitives are ἀνάγκη, ἐξουσία, καιρός, and χρεία: Matthew 3:14 Ἐγὼ χρείαν ἔχω ὑπὸ σοῦ βαπτισθῆναι (I am having need to be baptized by you). The infinitive βαπτισθῆναι explains what is meant by the noun χρείαν. Mark 2:10 ἐξουσίαν ἔχει ὁ υἱὸς τοῦ ἀνθρώπου ἀφιέναι ἁμαρτίας (The Son of Man has authority to forgive sins). The infinitive ἀφιέναι qualifies the kind of authority being discussed. See also John 1:12, 19:10, and Hebrews 3:12.

Infinitives Functioning as Main Verbs

Imperatives

On occasion an infinitive may function as an imperative main verb in an independent clause. Some (e.g., Boyer 1985:15) question this category, arguing that the infinitives could be explained as complementary or indirect discourse by supplying a verb (cf. BDF 1961:196–97). Moulton (1978:179) notes that the imperatival infinitive "was familiar Greek, especially in laws and in maxims," and is surprised at its infrequency in the New Testament. One example is Romans 12:15 χαίρειν μετὰ χαιρόντων, κλαίειν μετὰ κλαιόντων (Rejoice with the ones rejoicing, weep with the ones weeping; cf. Phil. 3:16; 2 Thess. 3:14).

Many clauses that appear as imperatival could be explained other ways, as Boyer suggests: the εἶναι in Titus 2:2 could be apposition rather than imperative, and the ἀποθέσθαι, ἀνανεοῦσθαι, and ἐνδύσασθαι in Ephesians 4:22–24 could be considered indirect discourse after the ἐδιδάχθητε in

Ephesians 4:21 (You have been taught that you are to put off the old self . . .). The imperative verb παρακάλει is to be supplied in Titus 2:9 (cf. 2:6), making ὑποτάσσεσθαι indirect discourse rather than imperatival. Plummer (1922:240) suggests that ἔχειν in Luke 9:3 is best explained as an anacoluthon (cf. Moulton 1978:179). The ὀμόσαι in Matthew 5:34 could also be indirect discourse rather than imperative (But I am saying to you that you should not swear at all), but the imperatival force seems more in keeping with Jesus' authoritative manner of teaching (But I tell you, "Do not swear at all").

Periphrasis for Future Verb

The construction μέλλω with the infinitive is often translated as a simple future (e.g., Matt. 2:13; 17:12). The event, however, is conceived to be imminent or to take place very soon. In Revelation 3:10 John writes, "I will keep you from the time of trouble which is about to come on the entire inhabited world." The imminency conveyed by the construction harmonizes with an important motif in Revelation and should not be ignored.

Infinitives Functioning as Interjections

Three times in the New Testament the infinitive is used as an interjection of greeting, equivalent to our "Hi!" or "Hello!" As with all interjections, it is grammatically independent from the rest of the sentence. Thus it is commonly called an *infinitive absolute*. The infinitive of χαίρω (I rejoice) is a standard element in the opening salutation of letters of the day and simply means "greetings": Ἀπολλώνιος Ζήνωνι χαίρειν (P. Cairo Zen. 59154; Apollonius to Zenon, greetings). All three New Testament occurrences are in the salutation of letters. James is the only New Testament Epistle that opens with the secular formula: Ἰάκωβος . . . ταῖς δώδεκα φυλαῖς . . . χαίρειν (James . . . to the twelve tribes . . . , greetings; cf. Acts 15:23; 23:26). Burton (1898:154) regards these examples as objects of an unexpressed verb of bidding rather than an independent interjection.

Exercises

Cite the best infinitive use for the following examples and, if appropriate, give alternate possibilities. Translate the passage in such a way as to bring out the force of the use(s) you have chosen.

1.	Matt. 6:1	ποιεῖν, θεαθῆναι
2.	Matt. 20:19	ἐμπαῖξαι, μαστιγῶσαι, σταυρῶσαι
3.	Matt. 24:24	πλανῆσαι
4.	Mark 1:45	κηρύσσειν, διαφημίζειν, δύνασθαι, εἰσελθεῖν
5.	Mark 3:14–15	κηρύσσειν, ἔχειν, ἐκβάλλειν
6.	Mark 8:31	διδάσκειν, παθεῖν, ἀποδοκιμασθῆναι, ἀποκτανθῆναι, ἀναστῆναι
7.	Luke 11:18	ἐκβάλλειν
8.	Luke 19:11	εἶναι, δοκεῖν, ἀναφαίνεσθαι
9.	Luke 22:40	εἰσελθεῖν
10.	Luke 22:61	φωνῆσαι
11.	John 13:19	γενέσθαι
12.	Acts 1:3	παθεῖν
13.	Acts 7:42	λατρεύειν
14.	Acts 11:15	ἄρξασθαι, λαλεῖν
15.	Acts 16:30	ποιεῖν
16.	Acts 19:21	πορεύεσθαι, γενέσθαι, ἰδεῖν
17.	Rom. 12:3	ὑπερφρονεῖν, φρονεῖν, φρονεῖν, σωφρονεῖν (more challenging)
18.	Rom. 14:13	τιθέναι
19.	1 Thess. 1:8	ἔχειν, λαλεῖν
20.	Rev. 5:2	ἀνοῖξαι, λῦσαι

12 Conjunctions

A conjunction is a word used to link words, phrases, clauses, sentences, and even paragraphs. Coordinating conjunctions (e.g., and, but, or) can connect any size unit (from words to paragraphs) of equal structural rank. This is called a paratactic relation. Subordinating conjunctions (e.g., when, because, if) are used to connect dependent clauses to independent (main) clauses. This is called a hypotactic relation. A clause is a group of related words that has both a subject and predicate. An independent clause can stand alone as a complete sentence, whereas a subordinate clause cannot. For example, "Mary went to the store because they needed food." The first clause "Mary went to the store" can stand alone, but the second clause "because they needed food" cannot. It is a subordinate clause and is introduced by a subordinate conjunction (because).

Conjunctions and Relationships

Most of sentences in the Greek New Testament begin with a conjunction. The New Testament writers follow the classical practice of using conjunctions to indicate semantic relations between sentences and paragraphs. Robertson (1934:443) remarks that "this was not merely an artistic device, but a logical expression of coherence of thought." Among the more common conjunctions used to link independent units are καί, δέ, ἀλλά, γάρ, and οὖν. Of particular interest is γάρ, which can be used to show that one sentence or paragraph gives the reason, grounds, or explanation for another sentence or paragraph (cf. Robertson 1934:962). It is still called a coordinating conjunction in such cases, since grammatically it links units of equal structural rank. Semantically, however, reason, grounds, and explanation give support to another unit that is more prominent. In addition, οὖν is often used to show that one grammatically independent unit is the conclusion of another. Semantically, the conclusion is more prominent than the grounds or evidence upon which it is based. These observations lead us to the idea that there is not an exact correspondence between surface structure taxis (coordination and subordination) and deep structure prominence (cf. chapter 17).

Although most sentences begin with a conjunction, some do not. The absence of a conjunction at the beginning of a sentence is called *asyndeton*. At times asyndeton is deliberate to gain a desired rhetorical effect (Luke 17:27; 1 Cor. 13:4–7; Phil. 3:2). Sometimes it simply reflects the author's rapidity of thought, excitement, urgency, or the like (1 Cor. 15:43–44a; Gal. 5:4, 7–10). Asyndeton may also be used to introduce major sections (Rom. 9:1; 10:1; 13:1). A semantic relationship still exists between sentences and paragraphs, even though a conjunction may be absent.

The Major Conjunctions

The following list surveys the semantic nuances of the major conjunctions. There are at least twenty-four Greek conjunctions and many more when compound forms are considered. Some of the more common ones not covered in the following discussions are the temporal conjunctions ὅτε and ὅταν (when, whenever), the local conjunction ὅπου (where), and the disjunctive conjunction ἤ (or). There are also other meanings than those listed, especially when the conjunction is used in combination with other conjunctions, particles, and adverbs. Other conjunctions and meanings can be found in standard lexicons.

ἀλλά

Contrast—Ἀλλά usually functions as a coordinating, adversative conjunction. An adversative conjunction marks a contrast between the two joined elements and is translated "but" or "however": Matthew 5:17 (I did not come to destroy the law but [ἀλλά] to fulfill it). Ἀλλά is normally regarded as a stronger adversative than δέ. Semantically, propositions introduced with adversative conjunctions (e.g., "I came to fulfill the law") are more prominent than the propositions with which they are contrasted (e.g., "I did not come to destroy the law").

Emphasis—Sometimes ἀλλά is used as an emphatic particle rather than as a conjunction. Examples include Acts 19:2 (We indeed [ἀλλά] have not even heard that there is a Holy Spirit) and 1 Corinthians 3:2 (Indeed [ἀλλά], you are not even ready now) (cf. 2 Cor. 7:11). The emphatic use of ἀλλά is common when used with καί, γέ, ἤ, or οὐδέ (cf. 1 Cor. 9:2). When used with an imperative, it strengthens the command and could be translated "now" or "then."

Exclusion—Sometimes ἀλλά is the equivalent of ἐὰν μή and can be translated "except," as in Mark 4:22.

Transition—Ἀλλά is also used to mark a transition to a new topic or thought rather than to convey a sharp contrast with the preceding: Mark 16:6–7 (See the place where they laid him. Now [ἀλλά] go and tell his disciples) (cf. Rom. 8:37; Gal. 2:3).

ἄρα

Conclusion—Ἄρα is most commonly used as an inferential conjunction. An inferential conjunction draws a conclusion from a previous statement and can be translated "so," "then," "therefore," or "consequently": Romans 7:21 (Therefore [ἄρα] I find a principle in me). Paul is fond of the phrase ἄρα οὖν (so then), which could be considered as "an emphatically inferential connective" (Thrall 1962:10; cf. Rom. 5:18; 7:3, 25; 8:12; 9:16).

Emphasis—Ἄρα can also function as an emphatic particle. In Acts 12:18 the soldiers wondered what had indeed (ἄρα) happened to Peter (cf. Matt. 18:1; Luke 12:42). The lexicons distinguish between ἄρα and the interrogative particle ἆρα (Luke 18:8). They say that ἆρα expects a negative response or indicates anxiety or impatience. Dana and Mantey (1955:241) argue that this distinction is unnecessary. They contend that in questions it serves as an emphatic particle, not an interrogative particle. Thus in Acts 8:30 they read ἄρα instead of ἆρα (as in UBS³) and translate, "Do you really (ἄρα) know what you are reading?" Some of the examples given for the emphatic ἄρα could be treated as modal particles of possibility or uncertainty rather than emphasis. For example, Acts 12:18 could be rendered "what perchance had happened to Peter" (cf. Matt. 24:45; Mark 4:41). Some suggest that ἄρα expresses interest or surprise (cf. Thrall 1962:10)

γάρ

Syntactically γάρ can function either as a coordinate conjunction to link independent units or as a subordinate conjunction to introduce dependent clauses. As mentioned in the opening remarks of this chapter, γάρ is often used to show that one independent unit semantically supports another. For example, γάρ may give the reason, grounds, or clarification for an adjoining sentence (cf. Col. 2:5; 3:3, 25) or paragraph (cf. Rom. 8:18; 2 Tim. 4:6).

This poses a problem in a meaning-based translation, because English does not allow a subordinate conjunction to link independent sentences and paragraphs. When γάρ introduces an independently standing unit that gives the reason for another semantic unit, it must be translated with the ambiguous "for," left untranslated, or perhaps with a phrase such as "the reason for this is that. . . ." Simple sentences cannot start with "because" for it would produce a sentence fragment in English.

Reason—A common use of γάρ is to express the unintentional cause that brought about a certain result. In Matthew 19:22 the young man went away sad because (γάρ) he had many possessions. In Mark 16:8 the women fled from the tomb because (γάρ) they were afraid.

Grounds—The causal use of γάρ represents two distinct semantic functions: reason (discussed above) and grounds. Grounds is the basis or supporting evidence for a conclusion, question, or exhortation. Reason is part of a direct cause/effect relationship; grounds is not. For example, in Colossians 3:20 Paul exhorts the children to obey their parents since (γάρ) this will please God. In Matthew 22:28 the Sadducees asked Jesus, "In the resurrection whose wife will she be, since (γάρ) all seven had been married to her?" (cf. Matt. 1:21).

Explanation—Γάρ is often used to introduce an explanatory statement. Semantically, an explanation is less prominent than what is being clarified, even when the explanation that γάρ introduces happens to be a grammatically independent unit, such as a sentence or paragraph. Γάρ may be translated "for," "for example," "for instance," "that is," or the like. In Matthew 12:39 Jesus mentions "the sign of Jonah." Jesus' application of the Jonah story would be a rather obscure sign for His audience. He therefore explains what He meant in the next verse: "for [γάρ] just as Jonah was three days and nights in the belly of a huge fish, so will the Son of Man be three days and nights in the heart of the earth" (cf. Matt. 12:50). Mark uses γάρ in 5:42

as a parenthetical explanation to his readers that Jairus' daughter was old enough to walk.

Emphasis—As an emphatic particle, γάρ can be translated "indeed," "certainly," "surely," "actually," or the like. For example, John 9:30 (This is surely marvelous!), Acts 8:31 (How indeed can I unless someone guide me?), Acts 16:37 (No indeed!), 1 Thessalonians 2:20 (Indeed, you are our pride and joy!), and 1 Pet. 4:15 (If any of you suffer, it certainly should not be as a murderer or thief).

Transition—Γάρ can indicate the transition of a discourse into a new discussion, as in 1 Corinthians 10:1 (moreover; cf. Gal. 1:11). As a transitional device, γάρ is often translated "now," "and," or left untranslated. The TR reads δέ rather than γάρ in both 1 Corinthians 10:1 and Galatians 1:11.

δέ

Contrast—Δέ often marks a contrast between two elements and is translated "but," "however," or "yet." It is said that δέ is a weaker adversative than ἀλλά, yet the contrast can still be rather pronounced, as in Matthew 6:19–20 (Do not lay up treasures on earth . . . , but lay up treasures in heaven). The contrast between elements is more pronounced when μέν introduces the first element and δέ introduces the second (on the one hand . . . on the other hand). This rendering is not often used in translations because of its awkwardness (Matt. 3:11).

Addition—As a copulative conjunction, δέ joins members in an additive relation and is translated "and." In James 1:13 we read that God cannot be tempted with evil and (δέ) cannot tempt anyone. Sometimes it is used in a sequential sense, as in Matthew's genealogy (Matt. 1:2–16).

Transition—In narrative discourse δέ often introduces a shift or change in thought: either a new development, the introduction of a new character, a change in temporal setting, the introduction of parenthetical material, or the resumption of the main event line. For example, in Mark 1:30 δέ introduces a new participant (Peter's mother-in-law) and in Mark 1:32 a new development (the bringing of all the sick people) (cf. Levinsohn 1981a-b, Buth 1981). An important function of δέ is to shift the reader off the main event line (for background information or parenthetical material) and then back to it. In addition, it can indicate a movement from one episode to another in historical narrative (Matt. 2:19, 3:1). As such, it can be rendered "now," "then," or left untranslated. As mentioned in chapter 4, when used with a nominative case article (without a noun), it functions as a switch-reference device, showing a shift in subject from the previous sentence (e.g., οἱ δέ in John 2:9).

Explanation—The explanatory δέ is rare: John 6:6 (Now he said this to test Philip), and 1 Corinthians 1:12 λέγω δὲ τοῦτο (Now what I mean is this). This use could be considered as transition to indicate a shift to parenthetical material.

Emphasis—Acts 3:24 (Indeed, all the prophets), 2 Corinthians 10:2 (I indeed beg you), and Galatians 4:20 (I would certainly [δέ] like to be present with you).

διό

The primary function of διό is to introduce a conclusion. It is a strong inferential conjunction, meaning "therefore" or "wherefore": Matthew 27:8 (Therefore that field was called the Field of Blood).

ἐάν

Condition—Ἐάν is normally used with the subjunctive (but sometimes with the indicative) in third class conditional sentences (cf. Luke 19:40).

Time—Ἐάν can be used as a temporal conjunction to convey a future event that is contemporaneous with another future event. 1 John 3:2 (We know that when [ἐάν] he appears, we shall be like him; cf. John 12:32; Heb. 3:7; 1 John 2:28).

Indefiniteness—Ἐάν is often used as a modal particle after relatives to make them indefinite, with the meaning "whoever," "wherever," or "whatever": Mark 13:11 (But say whatever [ὃ ἐάν] is given you at that time; cf. 1 Cor. 16:6). This use is equivalent to ἄν after relatives (cf. Matt. 23:16).

Exclusion—The construction ἐὰν μή serves as a negative condition (Matt. 10:13) or exception clause (Luke 13:3), meaning "unless," "if not," or "except."

εἰ

Condition—*Εἰ* regularly introduces the premise (protasis) of a conditional sentence. It is found in first, second, and fourth class conditions: Galatians 3:29 (If [εἰ] you belong to Christ, then you are Abraham's seed). See chapter 15 for a fuller treatment of conditionals.

Grounds—*Εἰ* often introduces the grounds for a conclusion or exhortation, with the meaning of "since." About one third of the sentences with the form of a first class condition semantically convey a grounds-conclusion relation between the propositions rather than a condition-consequence relation; i.e., "Since John is absent, he will miss the lecture." These should not be classified as conditional sentences. The first proposition establishes the grounds for the second proposition, the conclusion. The conclusion is the main clause and may have the form of a statement, exhortation, or rhetorical question (e.g., Gal. 2:14). Examples include Colossians 3:1 (Since [εἰ] you are risen with Christ, seek the things above) and 1 John 4:11 (Since [εἰ] God so loved us, we should also love one another; cf. Matt. 7:11; John 7:23; 10:35; Acts 4:9; 11:17; Rom. 6:8; 15:27; Col. 2:20; Heb. 7:15).

Concession—The construction εἰ καί introduces a concession clause, meaning "although": Luke 18:4–5 (Although [εἰ καί] I do not fear God or care about people, I will see that this widow is treated right because she is troubling me so). Sometimes εἰ alone can introduce a concession clause (1 Cor. 9:2). Sentences that semantically convey a concession-contraexpectation relation between the propositions should not be classified as conditional, even though they have the form of a first class condition and employ εἰ or εἰ καί (the reverse καὶ εἰ is probably conditional rather than concessional). The first proposition expresses a situation which one expects to turn out a certain way, and the second states the unexpected result. In English we would say, "Although John came, he did not hear the lecture." Examples include Mark 14:29, Luke 11:8, 1 Corinthians 8:5–6, 2 Corinthians 7:8, 11:6, and Colossians 2:5.

Noun Clauses—*Εἰ* functions as a complementizer to transform an embedded sentence into a complement noun clause. This function is common after verbs of emotion or wonder, but occurs with other verbs as well: 1 John 3:13 (Do not marvel that [εἰ] the world hates you). Perhaps the εἰ in Luke 12:49 should also be interpreted as a complementizer (How I wish that [εἰ] it were already kindled!). Other examples include Mark 15:44a, Acts

26:22–23, Romans 1:10, and 2 Corinthians 11:15. The usual complementizers in Greek are ὅτι and ἵνα.

Questions — As an interrogative particle εἰ introduces either direct or indirect questions. Questions involving εἰ will be yes/no questions, not content questions. (1) When εἰ introduces a direct question, it will not be translated: Matthew 12:10 ἐπηρώτησαν αὐτὸν λέγοντες, Εἰ ἔξεστιν τοῖς σάββασιν θεραπεῦσαι (They asked him saying, "Is it lawful to heal on the Sabbath?"; cf. Acts 7:1; 19:2; 21:37; 22:25). This is similar to the dropping of ὅτι when it introduces direct quotations. The εἰ does not need to be capitalized, as in Luke 13:23, 22:49, and Acts 1:6. (2) When εἰ introduces an indirect question, it might be preferable to translate it as "whether" rather than "if," although both are acceptable in English. "Whether" is less ambiguous. Examples include Matthew 26:63 ἡμῖν εἴπῃς εἰ σὺ εἶ ὁ Χριστός (Tell us whether you are the Christ) and Mark 15:44b ἐπηρώτησεν αὐτὸν εἰ πάλαι ἀπέθανεν (Pilate asked him whether Jesus had already died). The direct forms would be yes/no questions, "Are you the Christ?" and "Has Jesus already died?" Indirect questions will not have question marks. See also Matthew 27:49 and Acts 17:11.

Direct and indirect questions are similar to direct and indirect quotations. The indirect forms are reports of what was asked or said. What was actually uttered would be the direct form. Indirect speech may not have the same words, but they will have the same meaning.

Emphasis — Sometimes εἰ will function as an emphatic particle, meaning "indeed," "surely," or the like: Ephesians 3:2 NIV (Surely [εἰ] you have heard . . .).

ἵνα

Purpose — Ἵνα with the subjunctive or future indicative often forms a purpose clause and is translated "in order that," "that," or "so that": John 3:14–15 (It is necessary for the Son of Man to be lifted up, so that [ἵνα] those who believe might have eternal life). The ἵνα in Mark 4:12 poses special problems (But to those outside I speak in parables, so that [ἵνα] they might be looking and never perceiving . . .). It seems as if Jesus is purposefully denying the kingdom to certain people. Cranfield (1959:156) argues that the final (purpose) clause should not be weakened into a causal or relative clause, contending that it is within the purpose of God to withhold the secrets of the kingdom of God from those not ready to hear. The problem is compounded in that Matthew used ὅτι instead of ἵνα (Matt. 13:13). This leads Zerwick (1963:140–41) to suggest the possibility that ἵνα in Mark 4:12 could be causal, giving the reason for speaking in parables. He notes, however, that the causal ἵνα is commonly rejected for the New Testament (cf. John 8:56 for a possible causal ἵνα).

Noun Clauses—There are four types of noun clauses. (1) *Complement clause:* Ἵνα with the subjunctive may serve as a complement noun clause following verbs of speaking (Matt. 4:3; Mark 6:12), wishing (Matt. 7:12), asking or praying (Eph. 1:16–17), exhorting (1 Cor. 1:10). (2) *Subject clause:* Ἵνα with the subjunctive may serve as a subject noun clause, as in Matthew 10:25 (It is sufficient for the disciple that [ἵνα] he become as his teacher; cf. John 16:7). (3) *Appositional clause:* Ἵνα with the subjunctive may also serve as a noun clause in apposition to another noun: John 6:29 (This is the work of God, that [ἵνα] you believe; cf. 1 John 3:11). (4) For other types of noun clauses introduced by ἵνα, see John 2:25 (epexegetical) and 4:34 (predicate nominative).

Result—Although not very common, ἵνα with the subjunctive can also express result: John 9:2 (Rabbi, who sinned, this man or his parents, so that [ἵνα] he was born blind? cf. Rom. 11:11).

Imperative—The imperatival use of ἵνα is debatable. For example, Mark 5:23 ἵνα ἐλθὼν ἐπιθῇς τὰς χεῖρας αὐτῇ could be interpreted "Please come and lay your hands on her" (cf. Eph. 5:33). See Zerwick (1963:141–42) and Turner (1965:145–48) for discussions. Turner suggests that the problematic ἵνα in John 9:3 should be imperatival: "But let the works of God be manifest" rather than "This happened so that the works of God might be manifest." Most of the examples commonly set forth could be explained as having an elliptical verb with ἵνα forming a purpose, result, or noun clause.

Time—Sometimes the formula ἔρχεται ὥρα ἵνα stands for ἔρχεται ὥρα ὅτε (the time is coming when) (cf. John 12:23; 13:1; 16:32). For the parallel ἔρχεται ὥρα ὅτε, see John 4:21, 23.

καί

The basic syntactic function of καί is simply to join two coordinate elements together. Semantically, however, καί displays a wide variety of meanings. Some have felt that this is due to the influence of the Hebrew *waw* consecutive. In Hebrew the *waw* consecutive was used to express many co-ordinating and subordinating relations. In literal translations (e.g., NASB) it is usually translated as "and," but in idiomatic translations (e.g., NIV) the semantic force is made explicit, with the *waw* consecutive being translated with such words as "but," "yet," "when," or "because." Although the Greeks preferred to make the subordination explicit, the New Testament writers often echoed the use of the *waw* consecutive. Some have called this the Semitic καί, but others question this label, because a wide variety of meanings has also been found in the papyri.

Addition—There are four subtypes of addition. (1) *Simple additive.* The most common use of καί is to join two coordinate elements without specifying any particular relationship or focus (Rev. 7:12). The translation will simply be "and." (2) *Combining additive.* The correlative expression καί . . . καί (both . . . and) combines two elements into a single unit. (3) *Discourse additive. Καί* usually functions within a narrative episode to join elements that continue the main line of the plot. Elements in plot development that represent a shift in thought (e.g., new participants, change in background, or change in focus) are usually signaled by δέ, not by καί. (4) *Focusing additive.* Quite often καί is used to add something to the discussion and, at the same time, to highlight it. That is, the utterance is especially true with respect to the focused element that was added. *Καί* functions to raise the addition to semantic prominence, even though it might be syntactically coordinate or subordinate. There are two types: ascensive and adjunctive.

(i) *Ascensive* ("even"). The ascensive idea is a focusing addition that further develops the previous thought: 1 Corinthians 2:10 (NIV) (The Spirit searches all things, even [καί] the deep things of God). The ascensive use of καί could explain John 3:5 (Unless a person is born of water, even [καί] of the Spirit, he cannot enter the kingdom of God). The ascensive idea elaborates on the same thought, bringing it to a climax. Both the water and the Spirit pertain to inward cleansing: water is the symbol, and the Spirit is the effective agent. Other examples include Matthew 8:33 (They told everything, including [καί] all that had happened to the demoniacs) and 1 Corinthians 2:2 (Jesus Christ, and especially [καί] his death on the cross).

(ii) *Adjunctive* ("also"). The adjunctive idea is a focusing additive that introduces another thought into the discussion. Examples include Matthew 12:45 (So shall it also [καί] be with this wicked generation) and John 7:3 (Go into Judea, so that your disciples may also [καί] see the works you do) (cf. Matt. 5:39–40; 19:28; 20:4; Mark 1:38).

Emphasis—Sometimes καί has an emphatic force and could be rendered "indeed," "certainly," or the like: 1 Corinthians 14:19 (But in church worship, I would rather speak five words with understanding, in order that I might indeed [καί] instruct others).

Reason—Mark 8:3 (NIV) (They will collapse on the way, because [καί] some of them have come a long distance). Another example is Revelation 12:11c (cf. JB, NRSV, NEB).

Contrast—Καί sometimes functions as an adversative conjunction and can be translated "but," "however," "and yet," or "nevertheless": James 4:2 (NIV) (You want something but [καί] don't get it). See also Matthew 6:26, 13:17, Mark 4:16–17, 7:24c, 12:12, Luke 10:24, John 1:10c, 3:19, and 1 Corinthians 16:12.

Purpose—Matthew 5:15 (They put it on a stand in order that [καί] it might give light to everyone in the house; cf. Rev. 14:15).

Condition—Matthew 26:15 (NIV) (What are you willing to give me if [κἀγώ] I hand him over to you?). Κἀγώ is a crasis (joining) of καί and ἐγώ.

Consequence—Καί can also function to introduce the apodosis of a conditional sentence: Revelation 14:9–10 (If anyone worships the beast and his image, . . . then [καί] he will drink the wine of God's wrath).

Concession—Luke 18:7 (AV) (And shall not God avenge his own elect, which cry day and night unto him, though [καί] he bear long with them?).

Time—Mark 15:25 (NIV) (It was the third hour when [καί] they crucified him; cf. Luke 19:43; Acts 5:7; Heb. 8:8). Sometimes it has a sequential notion of time: John 4:35 (There are four months, and then [καί] comes the harvest; cf. John 7:33).

Relative—Luke 6:6 (There was a man who [καί] had a withered hand).

Conclusion—Καί can also introduce the conclusion to some facts or evidence: Matthew 3:14 (Since I have need to be baptized by you, then [καί] why do you come to me?) and Mark 10:26 (who then [καί] can be saved?).

Comparison—Zerwick (1963:152) suggests that the καί in 1 Corinthians 12:3 should be understood as expressing a comparison: "Just as no one led by the Spirit of God can say 'Jesus be cursed,' so [καί] no one can say 'Jesus is Lord' unless he is led by the Holy Spirit."

ὅπως

Purpose—Ὅπως is used with the subjunctive to denote purpose: Matthew 5:16 (In order that [ὅπως] they might see your good works).

Noun Clauses—Ὅπως with the subjunctive may be used after verbs of asking, exhorting, and praying to form a complement noun clause: Matthew 8:34 (They asked that [ὅπως] he depart from their region).

ὅτι

Reason—As mentioned with γάρ, what is commonly called cause covers two semantic relations: reason (i.e., unintentional cause) and grounds (i.e., basis or evidence). Reason is illustrated by John 3:23 (John was baptizing in Aenon, because [ὅτι] there was plenty of water; cf. Mark 6:34; John 6:2; 10:4).

Grounds—In Luke 13:2 (Do you think these Galileans were worse sinners than all the others, since [ὅτι] they suffered these things?) the ὅτι clause gives the grounds or basis for supposing the first clause to be true (it did not cause it; cf. TEV, Moule 1968:147).

Noun Clauses—There are three types of clauses. (1) *Complement clause.* Ὅτι functions as a complementizer after verbs of speaking (e.g., λέγω), perception (e.g., ἀκούω), thinking (e.g., νομίζω), and emotion (e.g., χαίρω) to form complement noun clauses: Matthew 5:21 (You have heard that [ὅτι] it was said by the ancients). This is commonly called indirect discourse. Ὅτι also introduces direct discourse, in which case it is not to be translated. Grammarians call this ὅτι *recitativum*. In some edited Greek testaments the beginning of a direct quotation is indicated with a capital letter. In English the entire quotation is set off by quotation marks: Matthew 7:23 ὁμολογήσω αὐτοῖς ὅτι Οὐδέποτε ἔγνων ὑμᾶς (I will confess to them, "I never knew you"; cf. Matt. 2:23). (2) *Subject clause.* John 8:17 (That [ὅτι] the witness of two men is true has been written in your law). (3) *Appositional clause.* Ὅτι often introduces an appositional clause after a cataphoric demonstrative pronoun: 1 John 1:5 (This is the message we heard from his Son, that [ὅτι] God is light and that there is no darkness in him at all). Sometimes what appears as apposition is the result of raising the subject of the complement clause into the matrix (main) clause: Acts 9:20 (He preached Jesus, that [ὅτι] he is the Son of God). Ὅτι in such cases introduces a complement clause and would be translated, "He preached that Jesus is the Son of God."

Result—On rare occasions ὅτι can express result (John 7:35).

οὖν

Conclusion—The primary use of οὖν is as an inferential conjunction. An inferential conjunction signals that what follows is the conclusion or inference from what precedes. The translations may be "therefore," "wherefore," "then," "consequently," or "accordingly." The οὖν in Romans 12:1 draws the conclusion from the previous eleven chapters of Romans. Semantically, the conclusion is more prominent than its grounds or evidence, even though both units are grammatically independent and therefore syntactically coordinate.

Transition—In historical narrative οὖν is often used to resume the main event line after an interruption, such as a parenthesis, quotation, or introduction of background material (Luke 3:7; 7:31 [also inferential]; John 4:28; 7:45). The resumptive οὖν could be translated "now" or "then."

Response—Οὖν can also function as a narrative link that introduces an action in response to a previous action or utterance: John 1:39 (Jesus said to them, "Come and see." So [οὖν] they went and saw where he was staying) (cf. John 5:18; 11:47). As such it continues the development of the plot line instead of shifting away from it or back to it. Although the word "therefore" may be used, οὖν does not denote a logical inference. Οὖν can also signal a reply in a dialogue. The translation "in reply" is sufficient in such cases (John 4:52b).

Emphasis—Οὖν also serves as an emphatic particle, being translated "certainly," "indeed," "really," or the like (John 20:30, REB).

Contrast—Sometimes οὖν is used as an adversative conjunction, meaning "but" or "however" (John 9:18; Rom. 10:14; cf. TEV).

ὡς

Comparison—Ὡς can introduce a comparison between words, phrases, or clauses. The comparison often conveys how something is done and could be classed adverbially as manner, as in Ephesians 5:33 (Let each one love his wife as [ὡς] he loves himself). The comparative ὡς can also function as a preposition, as in Matthew 18:3 (If you do not become as little children).

Time — "When," "while" (Luke 1:23).

Purpose — "In order that" (Acts 20:24).

Reason — Ὡς sometimes gives the reason for an action (Acts 28:19).

Noun Clauses — Ὡς is used after verbs of knowing, speaking, or hearing to introduce a complement noun clause. It would be equivalent in such cases to ὅτι (Rom. 1:9; 1 Thess. 2:11a).

With numbers — Ὡς is used adverbially meaning "about" (Mark 5:13).

ὥστε

Conclusion — When ὥστε is followed by the indicative, it usually introduces a conclusion or inference from the preceding thought, as in Matthew 19:6 (Therefore [ὥστε] they are no longer two but one flesh).

Result — When ὥστε is followed by an infinitive, it usually introduces a result. The result is most often unintentional (part of a reason-result relation), as in Mark 15:5 (Jesus did not answer anything, so that Pilate marveled). This could be restated as "Because Jesus did not answer, Pilate marveled." Sometimes ὥστε conveys intentional result (part of a means-result relation), as in Matthew 12:22 (He healed him, so that the man could talk and see). Syntactically, a result clause is subordinate, but semantically a result proposition could be the more prominent element (e.g., Mark 2:2; Acts 16:26). This happens when the ensuing context develops the thought in the result proposition rather than the thought in the adjoining proposition (cf. chapter 17). Twice in the New Testament ὥστε with the indicative expresses result (John 3:16; Gal. 2:13).

Purpose — On a few occasions ὥστε with an infinitive can express purpose (Matt. 24:24; cf. chapter 11).

Exercises

Interpret the following conjunctions and then translate the phrase or passage. Many are dependent on a reading of the wider context.

1. Matt. 6:30   εἰ
2. Matt. 15:27   δέ, καί, γάρ (somewhat challenging)
3. Matt. 19:3   Εἰ
4. Matt. 27:43   εἰ, γάρ, ὅτι
5. Mark 5:11   δέ
6. Luke 4:1   δέ
7. Luke 7:47   ὅτι (See Zerwick 1963:144–45, Moule 1968:147)
8. John 3:19   δέ, ὅτι, γάρ
9. John 4:1–2   οὖν, ὅτι, ὅτι, καί, ἀλλά
10. John 4:8   γάρ, ἵνα
11. John 9:22   ὅτι, γάρ, ἵνα, ἐάν
12. John 16:1–2   ἵνα, ἀλλά, ἵνα
13. John 17:3   δέ, ἵνα, καί
14. Gal. 6:16   καί (third occurrence; check commentaries)
15. Eph. 4:1   οὖν
16. 1 John 5:15   ἐάν, ἐάν

13 Adverbs and Particles

Adverbs and particles are not inflected forms, that is, they do not have prefixes or suffixes. The spelling remains the same, except for an occasional removable sigma on some adverbs. For example, οὕτως sometimes occurs as οὕτω (thus).

Adverbs

Adverbs modify verbs, adjectives, or adverbs. An adverbial idea can be conveyed in various ways. Adverbial conjunctions introduce adverbial clauses: John 2:22 "When (ὅτε) he was risen from the dead." Prepositions usually introduce adverbial phrases: Revelation 4:6 "around (κύκλῳ) the throne." Other words that can function adverbially include nouns, participles, and infinitives. The present discussion focuses on words that are used primarily as independent adverbial modifiers. There are four basic categories of independent adverbs: time, place, manner, and degree.

Adverbs of Time

Adverbs of time answer the question "When?" and generally precede the word modified. Some examples are ἅπαξ (once), εὐθύς (immediately), νῦν (now), πάλιν (again), ποτέ (formerly), πρωΐ (early), and τότε (then). The interrogative adverb of time is πότε (when?). In Mark 16:2 the women came to the tomb very (λίαν) early (πρωΐ) in the morning. The adverb λίαν modifies the adverb πρωΐ by expressing degree. Πρωΐ is an adverb of time and modifies the following verb ἔρχονται. The πάντοτε (always) in Colossians

1:3, however, probably modifies the preceding verb (we give thanks) rather than the following participle (praying).

Words normally classified as adverbs may at times function as other parts of speech. In Romans 3:26 νῦν functions as an adjective, ἐν τῷ νῦν καιρῷ (in the present time), and in Luke 1:48 it functions as a noun, ἀπὸ τοῦ νῦν (from the present). Sometimes πάλιν is used as a discourse marker to introduce another quotation in a chain of quotes (John 12:39).

The temporal adverb ταχύ occurs six times in Revelation, five times in the expression ἔρχομαι ταχύ (I am coming soon; cf. Rev. 2:16, 3:11, 22:7, 12, 20). One question is whether it always refers to the second advent of Christ at the end of the age. Ladd (1972:49) argues that in Revelation 2:16 it refers to a historical visitation of Christ, whereas elsewhere in Revelation it refers to the second advent. Caird ([1966] 1987:41, 54, 283) consistently interprets it as Christ's coming to help us in times of need. A second question, which is partially contingent on the first, is the meaning of the expression. If the reference is to historical visitations, then there is no problem with its meaning "soon" or "without delay." However, if the reference is to the yet future second advent, then it must be understood as expressing imminency rather than temporal proximity. For the believer, the "short while" is an undetermined length of time. The Christian community is to live with the constant expectation of the personal return of Christ, as if ταχύ literally meant "short while" for its generation.

Adverbs of Place

Adverbs of place answer the question "Where?" and generally follow the word modified. Some examples are ἐκεῖ (there), κύκλῳ (around), and ὧδε (here). In Matthew 28:6 the angel told the women, "He is not here" (ὧδε). The adverbial suffix -θεν denotes "place from which," as in ἐκεῖθεν (from there). Sometimes, however, the -θεν has lost its particular force. The interrogative adverb of place is ποῦ (where?).

In John 3:3 Jesus tells Nicodemus, "Except a man be born again (ἄνωθεν), he cannot see the kingdom of God" (AV). The ἄνωθεν has been interpreted two different ways: adverb of time (again) or adverb of place (from above). Those who argue for the temporal meaning stress that the idea is not mere repetition of the first birth, but the recreation of a new life in Christ, a life that reflects humankind's original relationship with God (cf.

Westcott 1975:63). This idea is partially conveyed by the translation "anew" in some versions (RSV, Weymouth). Nicodemus, however, understood it in a more literal temporal sense. Those who argue for the spacial meaning note that the other occurrences of ἄνωθεν in John's Gospel mean "from above." The spacial idea would also harmonize with the common Johannine motif of being born of God. The focus would then be on the supernatural origin of the birth (cf. John 1:12). The temporal meaning seems to accord more with the Pauline concept of the new creation. Both Barrett (1978:205–6) and Brown (1966:130–31) argue that it means both, but that the primary meaning is "from above." This is reflected in Barclay's translation, "Unless a man is born again from above, he can have no experience of the Kingdom of God."

Adverbs of Manner

Adverbs of manner answer the question "How?" They can either precede or follow the word modified. Some examples are δωρεάν (freely), καλῶς (well), οὕτως (thus), ὁμοθυμαδόν (with one accord), and ἀκριβῶς (accurately). In Acts 16:37 Paul remarks that since the authorities had flogged them openly (δημοσίᾳ), they should not release them privately (λάθρᾳ) (cf. Col. 2:9). An interrogative adverb of manner is πῶς (how?). Interrogative adverbs can be used in either direct or indirect questions. In John 9:15 the Pharisees again asked the man born blind "how (πῶς) he received his sight." As an indirect question, it has no question mark.

Adverbs of manner are often formed with a -ως suffix. This suffix can be attached to adjectives, pronouns, and participles to construct adverbs. For example, the positive degree adjective δίκαιος (just, righteous) would become the adverb δικαίως (justly), and the passive participle ὁμολογού-μενος (being confessed) can be turned into the adverb ὁμολογουμένως (confessedly). It is conceivable, though unlikely, that ὁμολογουμένως in 1 Timothy 3:16 could be divided ὁμολογοῦμεν ὡς (We confess how great the mystery of godliness is).

Combinations involving ἔχω and an adverb function as idiomatic expressions. In English the construction is often transformed into a noun, adjective, or adverbial phrase following a copulative verb. For example, Matthew 4:24 τοὺς κακῶς ἔχοντας (those who were sick); Mark 5:23 ἐσχάτως ἔχει (she is at the point of death); Mark 16:18 καλῶς ἕξουσιν (they will get well); and Acts 21:13 ἑτοίμως ἔχω (I am ready). Such constructions should not be translated literally (e.g., "having badly").

Adverbs of Degree

Adverbs of degree answer the questions "How much?" and "To what extent?" Some examples include λίαν (very), μάλιστα (especially), σφόδρα (extremely), and μᾶλλον (more): Matthew 4:8 εἰς ὄρος ὑψηλὸν λίαν (into a very high mountain).

Particles

Particles include those words not easily classified as being another part of speech (i.e., nouns, verbs, prepositions, conjunctions, adverbs, adjectives). It is the miscellaneous file of Greek grammar. There are three basic categories of particles: emphatic, indefinite, and negative.

Emphatic Particles

ἀμήν — The English "amen" is a transliteration of the Greek ἀμήν, which, in turn, is a transliteration of a Hebrew word which is regularly translated γένοιτο (may it be) in the LXX. Ἀμήν has several functions in the New Testament. First, in the Gospels it is used only by Jesus (in the phrase "Amen, I say to you") as an authority formula. The only exceptions are found in alternate readings where it has a liturgical function (Matt. 6:13; Mark 16:20). In using it, Jesus exercises His divine authority to confirm the truth of what He said (cf. Mark 3:28). In John's Gospel ἀμήν is repeated for emphasis (John 3:3). The doublet also occurs in the Old Testament using γένοιτο (Num. 5:22). Second, in the Epistles ἀμήν is used as a liturgical formula to express personal affirmation of benedictions (Rom. 15:33) and doxologies (Rom. 11:36). There is also evidence it was used in public worship to express one's affirmation of a prayer, praise, thanksgiving, or statement made by another (1 Cor. 14:16; 2 Cor. 1:20; cf. Rev. 5:14; 19:4). Third, in Revelation it can stand with the article as a designation of Christ, the embodiment of truth (Rev. 3:14). The first two functions are capable of various translations: "truly," "indeed," "so be it," "I tell you the truth," "it is true that," or "indeed, this is true."

γέ — The particle γέ is often translated "indeed," "even," or "at least," but is sometimes left untranslated: Romans 8:32 (who did not even [γε] spare his own Son). It is commonly found in combination with other particles and conjunctions, such as εἴ γε (if indeed), εἰ δὲ μήγε (otherwise), καί γε (even), καίτοιγε (and yet), or μενοῦνγε (rather). It sometimes adds emphasis in such combinations.

δή — Δή usually gives urgency to commands and exhortations (Luke 2:15; Acts 13:2; 15:36; 1 Cor. 6:20). Its translation in such cases would be "now," "then," "therefore," or "by all means." It also affirms the veracity of a statement and can be translated "surely," "indeed," or "really" (Matt. 13:23).

ἴδε/ἰδού — Ἴδε is the aorist active imperative of εἶδον that has been stereotyped as a particle. It occurs only a few times as an imperative (e.g., John 1:46; 7:52; 11:34; 20:27; Rom. 11:22). The plural ἴδετε, however, is only used as an imperative. Ἰδού is the aorist middle imperative of εἶδον except that the circumflex is changed to an acute. The imperative form ἰδοῦ does not occur in the New Testament. The two particles occur most often in narrative discourse. The basic idea conveyed by ἴδε and ἰδού is that of "pay attention." The following are the four basic functions of the particles (adapted from Van Otterloo 1988:34–64).

(1) Ἰδού is used as a discourse marker to focus attention on the introduction of a major participant into the episode, as when Matthew introduces the Magi in Matthew 2:1 (cf. Matt. 8:2; 9:18; Luke 5:18). The particle usually occurs in the introduction of the episode, just after the background material. It alerts the audience to pay attention to a particular participant as the plot unfolds.

(2) A second discourse function of ἰδού is to introduce an unexpected turn in the story, as in Matthew 8:32 when the pigs rushed down the bank and were drowned in the water (cf. Matt. 2:9; 3:16–17; 8:29; 17:5; 27:51). The use of ἰδού in Matthew 8:24 should probably be understood as introducing a sudden, unexpected turn in the story as well: "Suddenly a fierce storm hit the lake" (TEV). The first two functions of ἰδού are easily distinguished from the third and fourth functions since they are inserted by the writer into the story. They are not found in direct quotations except in extended discourses by a speaker (e.g., Matt. 13:3).

(3) Both ἴδε and ἰδού are used by a speaker to direct attention to something contrary to the expectation of the audience. One example is Luke 1:31 when the angel told Mary she was going to have a child. Mary certainly did

not expect this since she was a virgin (cf. Matt. 20:18; Luke 1:20, 36). This function normally occurs in direct speech that is quoted by the writer. The speaker wants to make sure that the world view of the listeners does not hinder the understanding of what is being said (Van Otterloo 1988:46).

(4) Ἴδε and ἰδού are also used by a speaker to direct attention to something that the audience is expected to respond to. One example is Matthew 28:7, where the angel told the women, "Behold, he is going ahead of you to Galilee." The implicit response that is expected would be for them to follow Jesus into Galilee so they can meet Him (cf. Matt. 7:4; 12:41; 25:6; Mark 16:6). Again this is only found in direct speech. The response may be to perform an action or to draw a conclusion. The ἴδε in John 1:29 Ἴδε ὁ ἀμνὸς τοῦ θεοῦ (Look! Here is the Lamb of God) seems to introduce something that is both contrary to the expectation of the audience and something to which a response is expected.

The words ἰδού and ἴδε are usually translated with such expressions as "look," "see," "here is," "now," or left untranslated. The AV regularly translates them with "behold." Caution should be exercised when interpreting ἰδού and ἴδε, since versions often dissipate their force by translating them as regular imperatives, suggesting that we are to look at an object. The NIV, for example, translates Mark 16:6 ἴδε ὁ τόπος ὅπου ἔθηκαν αὐτόν as "See the place where they laid him." However, τόπος (place) is in the nominative case, not the accusative. It cannot be the object of an imperative verb.

μέν—The particle μέν can be used various ways. First, it can be used correlatively with δέ (and sometimes ἀλλά) to denote contrast. One example is Matthew 9:37 Ὁ μὲν θερισμὸς πολύς, οἱ δὲ ἐργάται ὀλίγοι (The harvest is plentiful, but the workers are few). The μέν clause in such cases often has a concessive force. Depending on the focus, the construction can be translated with either "although" introducing the μέν clause or "but" introducing the δέ clause. Sometimes μέν tends to emphasize or affirm the statement in its clause. The words "surely" or "indeed" could thus be added, as in Matthew 3:11 (I indeed [μέν] baptize you with water, but [δέ] there is one coming after me who will baptize with the Holy Spirit). Second, μέν can be used correlatively as part of a series with no contrast or concessive force (Eph. 4:11). Third, μέν can function alone as a particle of affirmation, as in Acts 9:31 (The churches indeed had rest; cf. John 11:6, 2 Cor. 12:12). This third usage may also have a discourse function to link thoughts together.

ναί — *Ναί* gives an emphatic affirmative response to questions or statements. It could be translated "yes, indeed," "yes, it is true," or simply "yes": Revelation 22:20 (Yes, indeed, I am coming soon).

Other emphatic particles include μενοῦν, μήτιγε, πάντως, and compound words with -περ or -τοι.

Indefinite Particle

Ἄν adds the sense of indefiniteness or potentiality to a construction. The translation of the construction will thus be affected by the presence of ἄν and will vary according to the other words involved. It is commonly used with the subjunctive, but may also be used with the indicative and optative. First, it adds indefiniteness in relative and temporal clauses, as in Matthew 5:19 ὃς ἐὰν οὖν λύσῃ . . . ὃς δ' ἂν ποιήσῃ (whoever should break . . . but whoever should do). The translation "-ever" will suffice in most of these cases. Second, it adds potentiality in the apodosis of contrary-to-fact conditions, as in John 8:42 where Jesus said, "If God were your Father, you would love (ἠγαπᾶτε ἄν) me." Potentiality is also found in other constructions, such as in Luke 9:46, where there was a discussion among the disciples as to which might be (ἂν εἴη) the greatest.

Negative Particles

The two basic negative particles are οὐ and μή. Other negatives are built off these forms, such as οὐδέ (and not), οὐδείς (no one), οὐδέποτε (never), οὐκέτι (no longer), οὔπω (not yet), οὔτε (and not), οὐχί (used as a question tag), μηδέ (and not, not even), μηδείς (no one), μηκέτι (no longer), μήποτε (lest), μήτε (and not), and μήτι (used as a question tag). Οὐ is used for negating alleged factual statements, and μή for negating potential statements. Thus οὐ is generally found with the indicative, and μή is generally found with other moods, participles, and infinitives, but there are exceptions with either form. The following are some of the specialized uses of Greek negatives.

Question tags — Most languages have a way of tagging yes/no questions, so that the speaker can convey to the listener what kind of reply is expected (i.e., a leading question). An example in English would be, "You want to pass the test, don't you?" or "You don't want to fail, do you?" In the first the speaker elicits a positive answer and in the second a negative answer.

In Greek this is done by beginning questions with οὐ or οὐχί if the speaker expects a "yes" answer and μή or μήτι if he expects a "no" answer. In yes/no questions that do not begin with negative particles, the speaker does not reveal what kind of an answer is anticipated (Matt. 9:28). Question tags only apply to real questions where a reply is expected. The same four negative particles can also introduce rhetorical questions, but since no answer is expected, the particles must serve different functions (cf. chapter 15). An example of a real question using οὐ is Matthew 27:13 Οὐκ ἀκούεις πόσα σου καταμαρτυροῦσιν (You do hear what they are saying against you, don't you?). Jesus, however, did not oblige Pilate with the "Yes" answer he was expecting. For other real yes/no questions using οὐ, see Matthew 17:24, John 9:8, and 18:26. An example of a real question using μή is John 21:5 Παιδία, μή τι προσφάγιον ἔχετε (Friends, you haven't caught any fish, have you?). The disciples, as expected, replied, "No." This could be considered further evidence of Jesus' omniscience. For other real yes/no questions using μή, see John 6:67, 7:52, 9:40, 18:17, 25.

Οὐχί and μήτι are found more often in rhetorical questions than in real questions. In real questions they anticipate a strong response. When Jesus told His disciples at the Passover supper that one of them would betray Him (Matt. 26:21–22), each one asked Μήτι ἐγώ εἰμι, κύριε (Surely you don't mean me, do you?). Judas had to ask using the same tag, otherwise he would reveal his hypocrisy (Matt. 26:25). Imagine Judas starting his question with οὐ (You mean me, don't you?). Jesus, however, sees through the hypocrisy and responds with a positive reply (You said it!) as if Judas had actually framed his question with οὐ instead of μήτι like the others (cf. NIV). See Matthew 13:27 for an example of οὐχί functioning as a question tag in a real question.

Μήτι also introduces questions in which there is doubt about the answer, as in Matthew 12:23 (Could this be the Son of David?). However, these are best considered to be rhetorical conveying a statement of incertitude (Perhaps this is the Son of David). The μήτι would then not function as a question tag.

Negative answer—The accented οὔ means "no." It is used as a negative answer to a yes/no question or to a proposed course of action. In Matthew 13:29 the householder responded to his servants' question whether they should pull up the weeds by saying *Οὔ* (cf. Jas. 5:12). The more emphatic *οὐχί* is also used to answer a yes/no question. When the neighbors and kinsfolk suggested that Elizabeth's baby be called Zechariah after his father, she answered *Οὐχί* (Luke 1:60). This could be rendered "absolutely not" or "by no means" (cf. Luke 12:51; 13:3).

Double and triple negatives—A double negative in English makes the statement positive, that is, one negative cancels the other. While this is sometimes true in Greek (Acts 4:20; 1 Cor. 9:6; 12:15), usually it is not. Double and triple negatives normally strengthen the force of the negative. An example of a double negative is 1 John 1:5 *σκοτία ἐν αὐτῷ οὐκ ἔστιν οὐδεμία* (there is no darkness in him at all; cf. Rom. 13:8). There is a triple negative in Mark 5:3 *οὐδὲ ἁλύσει οὐκέτι οὐδεὶς ἐδύνατο αὐτὸν δῆσαι* (No one could keep him bound in chains any longer; cf. Luke 23:53).

A type of double negative can also occur when a negative particle is linked with a negative verb (such as verbs of hindering or denying): 1 John 2:22 *Τίς ἐστιν ὁ ψεύστης εἰ μὴ ὁ ἀρνούμενος ὅτι Ἰησοῦς οὐκ ἔστιν ὁ Χριστός*. The literal translation "Who is the liar, if it is not the one who denies that Jesus is not the Christ" is misleading. All believers in Christ should deny the statement that Jesus is not the Christ. Versions will either leave out the negative in the last clause (AV, NIV) or substitute "says" for "deny" (TEV).

Intensive Negatives—Emphatic negation of propositional statements can also be achieved by certain negatives that have an intensive force. *Οὐχί* and *μήτι*, for example, are somewhat more emphatic than *οὐ* and *μή*. Stronger emphatic negation can be achieved by *οὐ μή* (discussed in chapter 9) and *οὐδαμῶς* and *μηδαμῶς* (no indeed, most certainly not, by no means). These latter forms are rare in the New Testament. Emphatic negation can also be achieved when the negatives are combined with certain particles. For example, there is a slight emphasis when *οὐδέ* and *μηδέ* are not used as conjunctions: Matthew 6:29 (not even [*οὐδέ*] Solomon was dressed like one of these).

Universal Negatives—A universal negative occurs when *πᾶς* modifies the subject and the verb is negated. Galatians 2:16 *ἐξ ἔργων νόμου οὐ δικαιωθήσεται πᾶσα σάρξ* literally reads "all flesh will not be justified by works of law." This gives the false notion that many will be justified by works and that some will be justified other ways. The construction, however, is that of a universal negative where the expression "all persons are not" means "absolutely no person is." Thus "absolutely no one will be justified by doing what the law requires." See also Matthew 24:22, Luke 1:37, Ephesians 4:29, 2 Peter 1:20, 1 John 2:21, 3:15, 4:3, 5:18, 2 John 9, Revelation 18:22, 21:27, and 22:3. This construction should be distinguished from that in which πᾶς is negated rather than the verb. In this construction πᾶς normally functions substantively rather than as an adjective: 1 Corinthians 10:23 Πάντα ἔξεστιν ἀλλ᾽ οὐ πάντα συμφέρει· πάντα ἔξεστιν ἀλλ᾽ οὐ πάντα οἰκοδομεῖ (All things are lawful, but not all things are beneficial; all things are lawful, but not all things edify). These are not universal negatives, since "not all are" means "some are and some are not." See also Matthew 19:11, John 13:11, and Romans 10:16.

Prohibitions—Prohibitions using μή with the aorist subjunctive and present imperative are discussed in chapter 9.

Exercises

Interpret the following adverbs and particles and then translate the passage so as to bring out the function you have selected.

1.	Matt. 5:18	ἀμήν, οὐ μή (review section in chapter 9)
2.	Matt. 10:11	ἄν (both occurrences)
3.	Matt. 12:46–49	ἰδού, ἰδού, ἰδού
4.	Matt. 13:55	οὐχ, οὐχ
5.	Luke 16:30	Οὐχί
6.	Luke 22:35	μή
7.	John 15:5	οὐ . . . οὐδέν
8.	Rom. 1:8	μέν
9.	Eph. 5:5	οὐκ
10.	Heb. 1:5–6	πάλιν, πάλιν

14 Sentence Structure

A sentence can be defined as a grammatically complete unit consisting of one or more words. The traditional definition that a sentence expresses a complete thought is now being discarded by linguists as a misleading and erroneous idea. Complete thoughts are expressed by larger discourse units within situational contexts.

The structure of Greek sentences can be analyzed in various ways. Perhaps the most rewarding for the exegete is *transformational grammar*, since it not only logically breaks down the surface structure into smaller units but also is concerned with the underlying deep structure from which the surface structure forms are generated. Transformational grammar consists of rules that can generate every possible sentence in a language from the deep structure. There are two kinds of rules: phrase structure rules and transformational rules. The phrase structure rules are used to analyze the structure of both the deep and surface levels; the transformational rules are used to analyze the changes that take place as the underlying kernel clauses are encoded into the surface structure of a language.

We must not be overly optimistic regarding the value of transformational grammar for exegesis. Different approaches do offer fresh insights, but the simple fact remains that all grammars "leak." That is, no single grammatical approach is broad enough to cover the entire communication act. With transformational grammar many important features (such as emphasis) are lost as the surface structure is decoded into basic kernel clauses. The following discussion presents a modified version of transformational grammar that is appropriate for Greek and other inflected languages that do not follow English word order.

Sentence Patterns

Sentences are structurally divided into simple, compound, complex, and compound/complex types. Simple sentences contain a single clause (John runs fast). Compound sentences contain two or more main clauses and are usually linked with coordinate conjunctions (John runs fast, and Mary watches). Complex sentences contain a main clause and at least one subordinate clause (John runs fast because he saw a snake). Compound/complex sentences contain two or more main clauses and one or more subordinate clauses. Sentences may also be classified by function (declarative, interrogative, imperative, exclamatory).

Simple Sentences

Sentences are made up of various constituents. The most basic constituents are a noun phrase (NP) which functions as the subject and a verb phrase (VP) which functions as the predicate. A predicate can be defined as that part of a sentence that asserts something about the subject. Some of the following examples are actually parts of compound and complex sentences, but we will treat them as simple sentences for illustrative purposes.

(1) ἐδάκρυσεν | ὁ Ἰησοῦς
     VP | NP[SU]

John 11:35, "Jesus wept."

(2) παραδώσει | ἀδελφὸς | ἀδελφὸν | εἰς θάνατον
     VP | NP[SU] | NP[DO] | ADVP

Matthew 10:21, "Brother will deliver brother to be put to death."

(3) δώσει | αὐτῷ | κύριος ὁ θεὸς | τὸν θρόνον Δαυίδ
     VP | NP[IO] | NP[SU] | NP[DO]

Luke 1:32, "The Lord God will give to him the throne of David."

(4) μετὰ ταῦτα | εὑρίσκει | αὐτὸν | ὁ Ἰησοῦς | ἐν τῷ ἱερῷ
     ADVP | VP | NP[DO] | NP[SU] | ADVP

John 5:14, "After these things Jesus found him in the temple."

The subject noun phrase does not need to be present in Greek surface structure. It would be present, however, at the deep structure level. The deep subject would have undergone a transformation to merge it into the pronominal suffix of the surface structure verb.

(5)   ἐξῆλθεν | πάλιν | παρὰ τὴν θάλασσαν

       VP | ADVP | ADVP

Mark 2:13, "He went again along side the sea."

The phrase structure rules for the above active simple sentences would be:

(1)   s → VP + NP[SU]

(2)   s → VP + NP[SU] + NP[DO] + ADVP

(3)   s → VP + NP[IO] + NP[SU] + NP[DO]

(4)   s → ADVP + VP + NP[DO] + NP[SU] + ADVP

(5)   s → VP + ADVP + ADVP

Some constituents are obligatory, and some are optional. We could combine all these into one rule to create Greek active sentences (optional elements are indicated by parentheses):

s → (ADVP) + VP + (NP[SU]) + (NP[DO]) + (NP[IO]) + (ADVP)

The next group will be nonactive sentences (also called copulative or stative sentences). A nonactive sentence is one in which there is a verb of being, such as εἰμί. It will express a state rather than an action. There are four types of nonactive sentences: descriptive (6), equative (7), adverbial (8), and existential (9). The predicate complement will be an adjective phrase, noun phrase, adverb phrase, respectively, for the first three. There is no predicate complement in existential sentences.

(6)   ἐγὼ | ἀγαθός | εἰμι

      NP[SU] | ADJP[PC] | VP

Matthew 20:15, "I am good."

(7)   Ἐγώ | εἰμι | ὁ θεὸς Ἀβραάμ

      NP[SU] | VP | NP[PC]

Matthew 22:32, "I am the God of Abraham."

(8)   ἐγὼ | μεθ' ὑμῶν | εἰμι

   NP[SU] | ADVP | VP

Matthew 28:20, "I am with you."

(9)   ἐγὼ | εἰμί

   NP[SU] | VP

John 8:58, "I am."

The structure of sentences can also be displayed using tree diagrams. The following example will use sentence (4) above. Note that the major constituents of the sentence can be broken down into smaller constituents. Articles and demonstratives are commonly classified as determiners (DET).

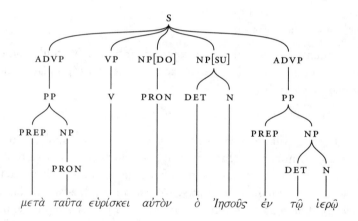

Compound Sentences

Compound sentences consist of two or more simple sentences joined with coordinating conjunctions (and, but, or).

(10)   ἐν τῷ κόσμῳ ἦν, | καὶ | ὁ κόσμος δι' αὐτοῦ ἐγένετο

    s | CONJ | s

John 1:10, "He was in the world, and the world was made by him."

Complex Sentences

Complex sentences contain one sentence embedded within another; that is, one sentence is a constituent of another. For example, the sentence "John said that it is raining" has a noun phrase direct object (a complement clause) that consists of a complementizer (that) and an embedded sentence (it is raining) as its immediate constituents. Embedded sentences occur in three different types of clauses: complement clauses, adverbial clauses, and relative clauses.

Complement clauses—Complement clauses are noun phrases that usually contain a complementizer, such as ἵνα or ὅτι, preceding an embedded sentence. The noun phrase will function as a nominal (e.g., subject, direct object).

(11) ἡμεῖς | οἴδαμεν | ὅτι μεταβεβήκαμεν ἐκ τοῦ θανάτου εἰς τὴν ζωήν
      NP[SU] | VP | NP[DO]

1 John 3:14, "We know that we have passed from death to life."

The noun phrase direct object consists of the complementizer ὅτι and the embedded sentence μεταβεβήκαμεν ἐκ τοῦ θανάτου εἰς τὴν ζωήν (we have passed from death to life). The embedded sentence is further broken down into a verb phrase and two adverb phrases, as shown on the tree diagram.

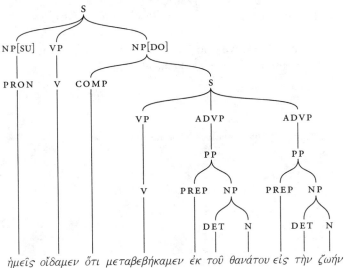

ἡμεῖς οἴδαμεν ὅτι μεταβεβήκαμεν ἐκ τοῦ θανάτου εἰς τὴν ζωήν

Adverbial clauses—What we commonly call adverbial clauses (e.g., when John came home) are in transformational grammar adverb phrases that consist of an adverbial conjunction (when) and an embedded sentence (John came home).

(12)   ὅτε ἀνέτειλεν ὁ ἥλιος | ἐκαυματίσθη
        ADVP | VP

Mark 4:6, "When the sun came up, it was burned."

The adverb phrase consists of ὅτε (when) and the embedded sentence ἀνέτειλεν ὁ ἥλιος (the sun came up). In the tree diagram the adverbial conjunction fills the COMP node.

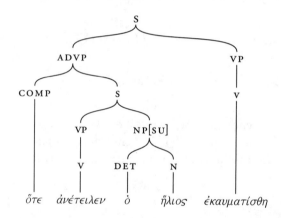

Relative clauses—A relative clause is an adjective phrase that is embedded in a noun phrase and that modifies the head noun.

(13)   αὕτη | ἐστὶν | ἡ ἐπαγγελία ἣν αὐτὸς ἐπηγγείλατο ἡμῖν
        NP[SU] | VP | NP[PC]

1 John 2:25, "This is the promise which he promised to us."

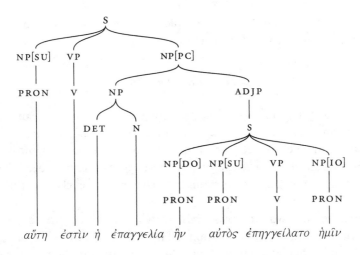

We could analyze the relative clause, like a complement clause, with an introductory word (complementizer) and an embedded sentence. The COMP node, however, does not really contain a complementizer. By means of a transformation, a nominal (in this case the direct object of the embedded sentence) is moved into the empty COMP node. This is why the word "which" in the above tree is labeled as the NP[DO]

Phrase Patterns

We have encountered five different types of phrases in the above examples (NP, VP, ADVP, ADJP, PP) and many configurations of each. A phrase may be defined in transformational grammar as one or more words that do not have a subject and predicate as its immediate constituents. We can represent phrases with phrase structure rules, as we did with sentences. For example, the noun phrase τὴν ζωὴν τὴν αἰώνιον (eternal life) in 1 John 1:2 would have the phrase structure rule NP → DET + N + DET + ADJ. The following phrase structure rules illustrate some of the other ways a noun phrase could be formed.

NP → N (e.g., book)

NP → DET + N (e.g., the book)

NP → DET + ADJ + N (e.g., the good book)

We could also make phrase structure rules for adverb phrases, verb phrases, adjective phrases, and prepositional phrases.

Basic Transformations

The above tree diagrams were based on the surface structure. Transformational grammar also posits a deep structure with certain transformational rules that rearrange the deep structure to form the surface structure of the particular language. Knowledge of basic transformations will help the exegete decode the surface structure and arrive at the kernel clauses at the linguistic deep structure.

An exegete must work on two levels, analyzing both the surface structure forms and the deep structure meaning. The surface structure is more easily analyzed and provides a window into the deep structure. Sometimes what appears on the surface to be a phrase is actually a kernel clause (or proposition) at the deep structure level. For example, the surface structure phrase using the participle εἰσελθών (having entered) represents a kernel clause (He enters) at the deep level. The deep sturcture clause has been transformed by a transformational rule into what we see in the surface structure. This is why we can translate the adverbial participle phrase εἰσελθὼν πάλιν εἰς Καφαρναούμ into an adverbial clause "When he entered again into Capernaum" (Mark 2:1).

The following is a simplified overview of a few transformations that apply to New Testament Greek. We will not be writing formal rules to describe the transformations. Instead, we will simply give prose descriptions.

Focus Rule

The focus rule changes the deep structure word order for emphasis. Most changes for emphasis involve moving the highlighted constituent before the verb. When we see this we will say that a transformation took place. We will call this transformation *focus* or *fronting*.

Relative Pronoun Movement

The sentence "The ball which John hit went over the fence" contains a relative clause, "which John hit." As we observed before, this is an embedded sentence with its own subject, verb, and object. The deep structure form of the embedded sentence was "John hit [the ball]." The object in the embedded sentence has been moved into the COMP node at the beginning of the sentence and replaced with a relative pronoun in the accusative case.

WH *Movement*

WH words refer to question words, such as what, where, who, why, or when. They all introduce content questions, not yes/no questions. Question words may function as interrogative pronouns, such as τίς (who, whom, what), interrogative adverbs, such as ποῦ and πότε (where, when), or interrogative adjectives, such as πόσος (how much). At the linguistic deep structure they occur in the kernel clause according to the normal word order. They will then be moved to the front of the sentence by a transformation rule to account for the Greek surface structure (WH words are normally clause initial in Greek). For example, the interrogative adverb ποῦ in John 1:38 ποῦ μένεις (Where are you staying?) has been moved from the regular placement for local adverbs (after the verb) to the initial position.

The Passive Shift

To understand the passive shift, it is beneficial to review thematic roles: the agent is the person who performs an action, and the experiencer is the person or thing affected by the action. Thus in Mark 1:9 "Jesus was baptized by John," John is the agent, and Jesus is the experiencer.

On the deep level, the agent is the subject and the experiencer is the object: "John baptized Jesus." This represents the kernel clause. In order to go from the deep structure to the surface structure we need the transformational rule called the *passive shift*. This involves changing the deep structure object into the subject (Jesus), inserting the preposition ὑπό (by), making the deep structure subject its object (by John), and changing the voice of the verb from active to passive (was baptized).

Translators often work from kernel clauses to generate the surface structure in the language they are working with. Thus what appears passive in Greek may not always be passive in translation. Sometimes the agent is absent and must be supplied, as in Ephesians 2:8 "By grace you are saved through faith." This could be rendered "God saves you by his grace, through faith." "God" must be supplied. This does, however, result in a shift of focus.

The Participle Rule

The participle rule transforms a finite adverbial clause at the deep structure (When John arrived, he ate dinner) into a nonfinite expression using a participle (John, having arrived, ate dinner). The deep structure actually contains two kernel clauses (John arrived; John ate dinner) linked by a relational designator (when). To go from the deep structure to the surface structure, we drop the relational designator and change the verb into a participle with the same case as its subject. The dropping of the relational designator challenges the exegete to analyze the semantic relationship between the clauses to determine the meaning the author intended.

Word Order

It is commonly thought that since Greek word order appears more or less random, there are no fixed rules. Greek is obviously freer than English. There are, however, recognizable patterns, such as certain conjunctions being postpositive, genitive modifiers following their head noun, and prepositions coming before their object. Blass and Debrunner (1961:248) even suggest that the basic word order for koine Greek is vso (verb-subject-object).

Although it might be somewhat hazardous to make generalizations on Greek word order, it does seem that some progress has been made in this direction with computer technology and discourse analysis. These tools offer the potential to determine Greek word order patterns and to explain why variations take place. Many word order variations appear to be conditioned by higher levels of discourse and therefore lie beyond the scope of sentence-based grammars. The following discussion is still provisional since many variations have not been accounted for. Furthermore, research is still needed to establish that the observations are applicable to all genres, styles, and authors. Thus it serves only as a working hypothesis. The discussion is primarily based on the work of Friberg (1982) and Randolph (1982) with comments by J. Callow (1983). Both Friberg (working on Luke) and Randolph (working on Hebrews) made use of computerized databases and discourse analysis. Other studies consulted include Dover (1960), Davies (1976), and Jung (1985).

Active Sentences

The basic order of sentences that do not have linking verbs (such as ∈ἰμί) is VSO (verb-subject-object). The order in expanded sentences with modifying elements would be: (1) Adverb (time, manner), (2) Verb, (3) Subject, (4) Direct Object, (5) Indirect Object, (6) Prepositional Phrase, and (7) Adverb (place). The following variations in the basic word order are considered normal (i.e., they do not trigger any kind of emphasis or prominence).

Pronouns move forward—If the subject is a pronoun, its normal order will be in front of the verb. Personal pronouns functioning as the subject are always somewhat emphatic since the information is already carried by the verb ending. It is the redundance, not the placement of the pronoun, that triggers emphasis. If the direct or indirect object is a pronoun, its normal order will be immediately following the verb. If both are pronouns, then the normal order prevails with the direct object preceding the indirect object.

Complex nominal forms move to the rear of the sentence—If the subject, direct object, or indirect object is an embedded clause (containing a verb), such as a relative or complement clause, it usually comes after the nonclausal elements (individual words and phrases).

Negative adverbs precede the verb—The only exception to this rule occurs in double negatives. If the negative is immediately before the verb, then it signals the negation of the whole clause. If the negative precedes nonverbal elements, then it is that element which is negated and not the whole clause. The negative particle will draw the negated element (subject, object, etc.) forward before the verb. This could be considered as a marked order.

WH *words are clause initial*—Relative pronouns and interrogative words (those introducing content questions) come first in their clause, regardless of their grammatical function (direct object, indirect object, or subject). In English these words begin with a "wh" (who, whose, whom, which, why, what, etc.).

Modifiers follow the noun—Genitives, adjectives, adjectival participles, and other modifiers normally follow the head noun they modify. The order of modifiers in noun phrases appears to be: (1) Head noun, (2) Demonstratives, (3) Indefinitives, (4) Numerals, (5) Descriptives, and (6)

Participles. Demonstratives are οὗτος, ἐκεῖνος, πᾶς, ὅλος, and μόνος, and indefinitives are τις and ὅστις.

Subordinate clauses follow or precede the main clause—Subordinate clauses rarely break up the main clause. They either precede or follow depending on their semantic classification. When a clause is shifted to the opposite position, it will signal prominence. The following chart depicts the normal order of subordinate clauses (cf. Turner 1963:344–45):

Condition	Main Clause	Purpose
Concession		Result
Temporal		Cause
		Complement
		Temporal
		Local
		Comparative

Subordinate clauses containing finite verbs are introduced with various kinds of conjunctions, such as conditional (εἰ, ἐάν), concessional (εἰ καί, καίπερ), temporal preceding verb (ὅτε, ὅταν), purpose (ἵνα, ὅπως), result (ἵνα), causal (ὅτι, ἐπεί, γάρ), complement (ἵνα, ὅτι), temporal following verb (ἕως, ἄχρι), local (ὅπου), and comparative (καθώς, ὡς).

Regarding the position of adverbial clauses in the sentence, it does not make any difference whether the clause is formed with a finite verb (indicative or subjunctive) or with a non-finite verb (participle or infinitive). The same placement pattern applies to both. For example, conditional participles normally precede the main clause, and result participles normally follow the main clause.

When there is an adverbial participle in the nominative case followed by a nominative case substantive and then by a finite verb, the nominative case substantive usually belongs to the adverbial clause, not to the main clause. For example, in Matthew 8:10 ἀκούσας δὲ ὁ Ἰησοῦς ἐθαύμασεν (When Jesus heard, he marveled), we would divide the two clauses so that they demonstrate normal word order (vs): [ἀκούσας δὲ ὁ Ἰησοῦς] [ἐθαύμασεν]. This suggests that participles syntactically do have subjects (cf. Matt. 9:2, where the participial clause has a vso order).

Nonactive Sentences

In sentences with linking verbs, such as εἰμί and γίνομαι, the most common word order is: (1) Verb, (2) Subject, (3) Complement. If the subject is a pronoun, its normal order will be before the verb. All six possible variations of the three elements occur. The variations are difficult to explain. The reasons given below for word order variations refer primarily to active sentences.

Reasons for Variations in Normal Word Order

Practically all variations involve fronting, i.e., the moving of an element (usually a nominal) forward in the sentence (usually before the verb) (cf. Moule 1968:166). In general, this "marked order" highlights information of importance to a larger discourse unit. Fronting is done for various reasons:

Contrast—When an element in one clause is contrasted with an element in another clause, both of the contrasted elements are placed before their respective verbs. In Matthew 19:6–7 "God" and "Moses" are placed in contrast, and both precede their verbs. Fronting of both elements makes it clear which ones are being contrasted.

Contraexpectation—A word which constitutes a contraexpectation is placed before its verb, i.e., "Although they went to the restaurant, Mary did not eat." In Greek, "Mary" would be placed before the verb (cf. Col. 2:5).

Comparison—Both parts of a comparison are placed before their verbs in their respective clauses, i.e., "Just as all cats are fond of birds, so all birds are fond of worms." In Greek both subjects (cats and birds) would precede their verbs (cf. John 5:21; Eph. 4:32; 5:2).

Topicalization—The topic is the subject being discussed. The introduction of a new topic is often marked by fronting it before the verb.

Motif—Fronting can also be used to highlight the first mention of a motif in a particular segment of discourse. A motif is an item other than the major theme that occurs throughout the discourse unit (such as a character or idea). The supporting motif contributes essential information to the theme of the larger unit. The fronted motif is often in the accusative case.

Rhetorical emphasis—Rhetorical emphasis expresses the emotion or expectation of the speaker (K. Callow 1974:63). The emphasized word will be fronted before the verb.

Focus—Focus refers to narrowing the reader's attention to specific, important information. Although focus would include topicalization and motif, we are using it in a general way to refer to the spotlighting of other information, such as the peak in a narrative or an important participant.

Notes on Word Order Universals

Greek follows word order universals quite well. For example, if the object of the preposition follows the preposition (as in Greek), then the language will have a sentence word order of vo. If the object of the preposition precedes the preposition, then the language will have an ov word order. Also if modifiers follow the head noun, then the sentence word order will most likely be vo; but if the modifiers precede the head noun, the word order will often be ov. Greek modifiers generally follow the head noun: τὸ τέκνον σου (the son of you).

Another observation of language universals is that adverb phrases rarely come between the verb and object. They will be on either one side or the other (v-o-advp or advp-v-o). This has led linguists to posit marginal and nuclear elements of a sentence: the adverb phrase being marginal, the nuclear element usually remaining together. Where the subject occurs has little to do with language universals. The most common word order patterns are svo (English), vso (Greek), and sov (Persian, Turkish) (cf. Comrie 1981:32).

Finally, all languages that have vso as their primary word order, such as Greek, also have svo as an alternate word order. The reverse, however, is not true. Languages, such as English, that have a svo order do not have the vso alternative. See Friberg (1982:285–334) for further discussion.

Exercises

1. Write phrase structure rules for the sentences in John 4:43, 5:16, and 14:6. Writing phrase structure rules for the phrases within the sentences is optional.
2. There are two embedded clauses in the first part of 1 John 5:13 *Ταῦτα ἔγραψα ὑμῖν ἵνα εἰδῆτε ὅτι ζωὴν ἔχετε αἰώνιον.* Translate the segment and make a tree diagram.
3. How would you analyze the relative clauses in John 2:22 and 1 Peter 3:19? What is the antecedent of the relative in 1 Peter 3:19?
4. In the following passages, note the elements that occur before the verb (omitting conjunctions, vocatives, and negatives) and then evaluate the significance of the marked order: Matthew 7:17, 19:4, John 3:16, 1 Corinthinans 15:3, and Ephesians 5:25.

15 Special Sentences and Clauses

There are several sentence types that call for special attention because their intended meaning often depends more on extra-linguistic, pragmatic factors than on linguistic factors. Some sentences, such as rhetorical questions and conditionals, may be used by the speaker apart from the normal meaning of the form to accomplish something altogether different. This kind of skewing commonly occurs in language. To return to the example used in the introduction, a wife may mention to her husband, "The car is dirty." The wife was not really making a declarative statement but politely issuing a command, "Please wash the car." Non-linguistic, pragmatic factors caused the wife to frame her command in a more indirect way. Thus, what appears as one type of sentence (statement, question, command) may be intended by the speaker to accomplish something else. Merely analyzing the surface structure of such sentences therefore will not suffice. This type of study is called *pragmatics.*

Rhetorical Questions

Questions function as either real or rhetorical. There are about seven hundred rhetorical questions in the Greek New Testament as compared to three hundred real questions. In real questions the speaker is requesting information that he or she does not know and expects a reply. In rhetorical questions, on the other hand, the speaker usually knows the answer. The question is used either to draw out information from the listener or to convey new information. Rhetorical questions often function like statements, but with the added advantage of evoking the listener to ponder the implications of what was said. The precise meaning is contingent on the intent of the speaker, the situation, and the speaker/audience relationship.

The characteristics that distinguish rhetorical questions from real questions are: (a) they are usually not directly answered; (b) sometimes they are answered by the speaker (Rom. 3:1–2, 6:1–2); (c) when answered by another person, they are more of a comment on the situation than a reply to the question (Luke 13:7–8); (d) sometimes the speaker is expecting a response (e.g., evaluation) other than a direct answer to the question (John 7:19). Rhetorical questions may be used in various ways: as emphatic declarations, evaluations, commands, or as other discourse functions.

Emphatic Declaration

The question Jesus raises in Matthew 6:30 "Will he not much more clothe you?" is actually a positive declarative statement meaning "God will surely clothe you." His question in Matthew 16:26, however, is intended as a negative declarative statement. The question "What shall it profit a man if he should gain the whole world yet lose his soul?" means "The person that gains the whole world at the expense of his soul will surely not profit anything." A negative declaration also occurs in Hebrews 2:3, "How shall we escape if we neglect such a great salvation?" When understood as a strong negative affirmation, it becomes "We will surely not escape if we neglect such a great salvation."

Evaluation of the Situation

Often a speaker will use a rhetorical question as a way to express his or her evaluation of the immediate situation. At the birth of John the Baptist the neighbors remarked, "What manner of child shall this be?" (Luke 1:66). The context and situation suggest that this is a positive evaluation. The idea behind it would be, "This is surely an unusual child. He will undoubtedly do a great work."

Negative evaluations are also possible. They may express various dispositions, such as rebuke, ridicule, disappointment, and belittlement. In Matthew 26:8 the disciples became indignant and remarked, "What was the purpose for wasting this ointment?" This is a softened rebuke. The direct rebuke, "You shouldn't have wasted the ointment like that," would not have been appropriate for the disciples in speaking to Jesus.

In Mark 3:23 Jesus responds to the charge that He casts out demons by the power of Satan by asking, "How can Satan cast out Satan?" This is actually a mollified ridicule. A direct ridicule might have turned the discussion into a heated argument. The idea being expressed is "It would be ridiculous for Satan to cast himself out." In using a rhetorical question Jesus keeps the discussion under control and evokes reflection on the charge against Him.

Negative evaluations can also express disappointment. In Mark 8:21 Jesus asks His disciples, "Do you still not understand?" In Mark 6:3 the rhetorical question is a negative evaluation that expresses belittlement. The people of Nazareth remarked, "Isn't this the carpenter?" What they are saying is "This man is only the local carpenter. He cannot be who he claims to be."

Commands

Rhetorical questions can be used as a softened command, as when an inferior is speaking to a superior. If a servant wanted to tell his master he should not be doing something, he cannot come right out with it, "Don't do that." A rhetorical question is very suitable in such situations. In Mark 5:35 some members of Jairus' household reported to him, "Your daughter has died, why bother the teacher any longer?" The command behind the rhetorical question is "Stop bothering the teacher." Negative commands or prohibitions can also be framed in a rhetorical question. In John 18:21 Jesus asks the high priest, "Why do you ask me?" This means "Don't ask me."

Discourse Functions

Rhetorical questions can introduce a new topic or a conclusion. In Mark 3:33 Jesus shifts the discussion to a new but related thought by asking, "Who is my mother? Who are my brothers?" In Romans 8:31 Paul uses a rhetorical question to introduce a conclusion, "What then shall we say to these things?" This question is basically equivalent to "therefore," although more provocative. Paul also uses rhetorical questions as a linking device between sections as he shifts to a new topic (Rom. 4:1; 6:1, 15; 7:7).

Other Rhetorical Questions

Rhetorical questions can also express (a) amazement or astonishment, as in Mark 4:41 "Who is this man?"; (b) uncertainty, as in Luke 16:3 "What shall I do?"; and (c) conditionals, as in 1 Corinthians 7:27 "Are you married?" which means "If you are married." Some rhetorical questions could be classified as "teacher questions" in that the speaker wants the listeners to think out the answer for themselves rather than being told.

Rhetorical Questions Using οὐ and μή

Since rhetorical questions do not expect an answer, the presence of οὐ or μή in the initial position is not intended to elicit a yes/no response. Rhetorical questions starting with οὐ indicate either an affirmative statement or an evaluation (sometimes pointing out what should have been done). Those starting with μή indicate either a negative statement or a statement of incertitude in which the word "perhaps" could be used (Beekman and Callow 1974:353–57).

An example of μή conveying a negative statement is 1 Corinthians 12:29–30, "Are all apostles? Are all prophets? Are all teachers? Do all work miracles? Do all possess gifts of healing? Do all speak in tongues? Do all interpret?" (NRSV). There are seven rhetorical questions, and each one starts with a μή. We should understand them as negative statements, "Not everyone in the church is an apostle, prophet, or teacher. All do not have the power to perform miracles, heal diseases, speak in tongues, or interpret the tongues." This makes it clear that Paul did not teach that tongues was a necessary gift to prove that one has the indwelling Spirit. The church is one body composed of different members, with each member performing a different gift for the proper functioning of the whole. If all had the same gift, the church could not operate as God intended. There are various combinations of form and meaning when negatives are used with rhetorical questions.

With οὐ/οὐχί — (i) οὐ conveying an affirmative statement (Matt. 22:31–32), (ii) οὐ conveying an evaluation (Matt. 26:40; Mark 7:18), (iii) οὐχί conveying a strong affirmative statement (Matt. 6:25; 18:12; 20:13; Luke 14:28, 31; Acts 5:4).

With μή/μήτι — (i) μή conveying a negative statement (Matt. 7:9; Rom. 3:3; Jas. 2:14), (ii) μή conveying a statement of incertitude (Acts 7:28), (iii) μήτι conveying a strong negative statement (John 18:35; Acts 10:47), (iv) μήτι conveying a statement of incertitude (John 4:29; 8:22).

In Luke 6:39 both μήτι and οὐχί are used: Μήτι δύναται τυφλὸς τυφλὸν ὁδηγεῖν οὐχὶ ἀμφότεροι εἰς βόθυνον ἐμπεσοῦνται (A blind person cannot really lead another blind person. If he tries, both will surely fall into a pit; cf. TEV). Brown (1966:173) interprets the μήτι in John 4:29 (Could this be the Messiah?) to mean that although the woman had hope, her faith was not complete. Others say that her faith was complete and that she used μήτι to avoid controversy and raise curiosity (Chamberlain [1941] 1979:159). The translation "Perhaps this is the Messiah" would fit either view.

With οὐ μή — Οὐ μή is also used in rhetorical questions to make a strong affirmative statement: John 18:11 τὸ ποτήριον ὃ δέδωκέν μοι ὁ πατὴρ οὐ μὴ πίω αὐτό (I will surely drink of the cup which my Father has given me). The reverse μὴ οὐ also expresses a strong affirmative statement (cf. Rom. 10:18–19; 1 Cor. 9:4, 5; 11:22).

Conditional Sentences

Conditional sentences are composed of two parts. The first part (the "if" clause) is called the *protasis*. The protasis sets forth a condition which, when fulfilled, issues into what is conveyed by the main clause. The second part (the "then" clause) is called the *apodosis*. The apodosis is the main clause that states the consequence that follows if the condition is fulfilled.

Grammarians divide conditional sentences into anywhere from three to six (or more) groups, four being the most common. There is an ongoing controversy concerning what the basis of classification should be and how the meaning of the constructions should be determined. Some classify conditional sentences according to tense, others according to mood. The main problems with these approaches are the assumptions that form always dictates meaning and that meaning can be derived within the confines of a sentence. However, the author's intent often differs from the form used. We have already observed this pragmatic skewing with rhetorical questions. The same happens with rhetorical conditional sentences. Another problem is the assumption that morphology determines temporal distinctions. Perhaps the major shortcoming with most approaches is the failure to remove sentences with a conditional form but which semantically express other relations from the corpus of examples being studied.

Traditional Classification

One of the most common approaches to conditional sentences follows the classification scheme of A. T. Robertson. Robertson patterns his system after that of Gildersleeve, a classical Greek grammarian, in identifying four classes of conditionals based on mood.

First class: determined as fulfilled—The first class condition is identified by having εἰ (if) with an indicative verb in the protasis. The apodosis can have a verb of any tense and mood. There are about three hundred examples of first class conditions in the New Testament. Romans 8:9 εἰ τις πνεῦμα Χριστοῦ οὐκ ἔχει, οὗτος οὐκ ἔστιν αὐτοῦ (If anyone does not have the Spirit of Christ, he does not belong to him).

By using the indicative mood in the protasis, it is said that the speaker assumes the reality of his or her premise. The premise may not actually be true. If it is true, then it can be rendered with "since." Otherwise, the speaker is assuming the reality of the premise for the sake of argument.

Second class: determined as unfulfilled—The second class condition is identified by having εἰ (if) with a secondary tense (imperfect, aorist, pluperfect) indicative mood verb in the protasis and normally ἄν with another secondary tense verb in the apodosis. There are about fifty examples of this construction in the New Testament.

The speaker is of the persuasion that the premise which he or she sets forth is contrary to fact. The premise may be either contrary to fact (John 5:46) or contrary to what the speaker assumes to be the facts (Luke 7:39). The indicative is again used because the speaker is asserting something concretely: Galatians 1:10 εἰ ἔτι ἀνθρώποις ἤρεσκον, Χριστοῦ δοῦλος οὐκ ἄν ἤμην (If I were still pleasing men [which, of course, I am not], then I would not be a servant of Christ). Other examples include Matthew 11:21 and John 18:30.

Third class: undetermined with prospect of determination—The third class condition is identified by having ἐάν (if) with a subjunctive mood verb in the protasis. The apodosis can have a verb of any tense (usually present or future) and mood (usually indicative). There are about three hundred examples of this construction in the New Testament: Matthew 21:3 ἐάν τις ὑμῖν εἴπῃ τι, ἐρεῖτε ὅτι Ὁ κύριος αὐτῶν χρείαν ἔχει (If anyone should say anything to you, say [imperatival future], "The Lord is having need of them").

The subjunctive is said to convey a future condition (yet undetermined). The speaker believes that the premise has a greater possibility of becoming true than the fourth class conditions, which use the optative mood.

Fourth class: undetermined with remote prospect of determination — The fourth class condition is identified by having εἰ (if) with an optative verb of any tense in the protasis. The apodosis is introduced by the particle ἄν with another optative verb. No complete construction exists in the New Testament which has both the protasis and apodosis.

First Peter 3:14 εἰ καὶ πάσχοιτε διὰ δικαιοσύνην, μακάριοι ("If perchance you should happen to suffer on account of righteousness, [you are] blessed). The use of the optative means that the speaker views the premise as future (undetermined) with less chance of fulfillment than that of a third class condition.

Semantic Analysis of Conditional Sentences

The problem with the above analysis is that it fails to provide exegetically plausible interpretations in every case. A more satisfying analysis is to follow a two-step approach. First, the exegete must determine whether the sentence under consideration is in fact a conditional sentence. As noted in chapter 12, there are many semantic relations conveyed by the particles εἰ and ἐάν, such as grounds, concession, and time. Sentences in which the "if" clause (protasis) states a condition and the "then" clause (apodosis) states the consequence that will result when the condition is fulfilled are properly classified as conditionals. Second, if the sentence under consideration semantically expresses a condition-consequence relation, then the exegete must determine whether the condition is real or rhetorical.

Real conditions — In a real condition the speaker sets forth a possible condition on the real world of action or thought that one may have to deal with. Real conditions are further divided into two subsets: confrontation and projection.

(1) *Confrontation.* Real conditionals having an indicative mood verb in the protasis seem to posit a situation or premise that the speaker perceives a

person will have to resolve or confront in some fashion. Not all conditionals with an indicative in the protasis, however, are classified as confrontational. Exceptions include conditionals with a second class form which are contextually past referring (some second class forms are future referring, such as Mark 13:20) and conditionals with a future indicative in the protasis. Past referring second class conditions appear to be all rhetorical.

(2) *Projection.* The second subset includes conditionals with a subjunctive, optative, or future in the protasis. In general, the speaker seems to project the situation beyond what is normally expected or experienced. Further analysis is possible for each subset based on aspect (cf. Porter 1989:291–320). Boyer (1982:167–70) has shown that it is fallacious to argue for degrees of objective or theological probability with third class conditions. They range from certainty of fulfillment to certainty of nonfulfillment. Some are just as certain of fulfillment as first class conditions (cf. John 14:3). The difference in subtypes, however, is primarily one of mood, and mood reflects one's subjective attitude. Therefore the question of objective probability does not really enter the picture.

The difference between the two types of real conditions is seen in the two conditionals in Galatians 1:8–9. The first has a subjunctive in the protasis: καὶ ἐὰν ἡμεῖς ἢ ἄγγελος ἐξ οὐρανοῦ εὐαγγελίζηται ὑμῖν παρ᾽ ὃ εὐηγγελισάμεθα ὑμῖν, ἀνάθεμα ἔστω (Even if we or an angel from heaven should preach to you a gospel that is different from what we preached to you, let him be accursed). The second has an indicative in the protasis: εἴ τις ὑμᾶς εὐαγγελίζεται παρ᾽ ὃ παρελάβετε, ἀνάθεμα ἔστω (If anyone preaches to you a gospel that is different from the one you received, let him be accursed). The difference is that in the first one Paul projects the thought beyond what one might expect, whereas in the second he represents a situation that he perceives the readers might have to resolve. Are there indeed false teachers in the churches? If so, then they must be dealt with.

Rhetorical conditions—Rhetorical conditions are those in which the speaker is not raising a condition on the real world. Instead, the speaker is using the form and logic of a conditional sentence for other purposes, such as to make a strong assertion, to manipulate the listener, to ask something in a polite way, to express a respectful rebuke, or to convey a lament. These are no more real conditions than rhetorical questions are real questions. They can have either a first or second class form.

(1) *Assertion*. Strong assertions are made when the "then" clause does not logically follow the "if" clause. For example, "If Hitler was a military genius, then I'm a monkey's uncle." The "then" clause is so obviously false that it turns the "if" clause into a strong negative assertion: "Hitler was not a military genius." Most cases in the New Testament are a form of Hebraic oath in which only the "if" clause is present. The "then" clause is omitted because it would be unthinkable, abominable, or the like. Hebrews 4:5 *Εἰ εἰσελεύσονται εἰς τὴν κατάπαυσίν μου* literally reads, "If they shall enter into my rest. . . ." An idiomatic translation that captures the assertive mood of the speaker would be preferred: "They will never enter into my rest." See also Mark 8:12 and Hebrews 3:11.

(2) *Argumentation*. In the speaker's mind there is usually nothing conditional in the premise that is set forth to argue a point. The speaker is either convinced it is false and is trying to persuade listeners of its falsity, or the speaker is convinced it is true and using it as a basis for a conclusion. It would be helpful at this point to review the two rules of inference in logic: (a) if the antecedent (the "if" clause) is true, then the consequent (the "then" clause) is true (*modus ponens*—method of affirming); or (b) if the consequent is false, then the antecedent is false (*modus tollens*—method of denial). Nothing can be said regarding the truth of the other element if the antecedent is false or if the consequent is true.

Modus tollens is used in Luke 7:39 *Οὗτος εἰ ἦν προφήτης, ἐγίνωσκεν ἂν τίς καὶ ποταπὴ ἡ γυνὴ ἥτις ἅπτεται αὐτοῦ* (If this man were a prophet, he would know what sort of woman this is who is touching him). The Pharisee is arguing from an apparently false conclusion to affirm his belief that his premise is also false. He is not merely assuming the "if" clause to be false for the sake of argument, he is contending that Jesus cannot possibly be a prophet. There is no essential difference between the first and second class forms of this type of condition (cf. Matt. 12:26; Gal. 2:21). Argumentation using *modus ponens* will be first class in form and grounds-conclusion in classification. For further discussion, see (Baima 1986).

(3) *Manipulation*. Speakers often use the conditional form to manipulate their listeners. For example, "If you're not a good boy, Santa won't come." Often there is an imperative in the consequent, but the presence of an imperative does not make it manipulative: Matthew 4:3 *Εἰ υἱὸς εἶ τοῦ θεοῦ, εἰπὲ ἵνα οἱ λίθοι οὗτοι ἄρτοι γένωνται* (If you are the Son of God, tell these stones to become loaves of bread). Satan is questioning Jesus' character

in order to force Him to do something contrary to His will. The translation can use either "if" or "since." "Since" would suggest that Satan is using flattery to manipulate Jesus. See also Philemon 17.

(4) *Request.* To make a request or command in a polite and socially acceptable way, we often frame it in a conditional sentence. This is especially true when addressing a superior. We would not think of directly asking or commanding a raise from our employer. Instead, we would preface our request with "If it is possible," or the like: Matthew 17:4 εἰ θέλεις, ποιήσω ὧδε τρεῖς σκηνάς (If you wish, I will make here three shelters).

(5) *Mockery.* Some people have a tendency to boast of being correct and mock or deride others for being wrong. The ridicule is even more caustic when it is framed in a conditional sentence: Luke 23:35 σωσάτω ἑαυτόν, εἰ οὗτός ἐστιν ὁ Χριστὸς τοῦ θεοῦ ὁ ἐκλεκτός (If this one is God's chosen Messiah, then let him save himself; cf. Matt. 27:40, 43; Luke 23:37). This cannot be manipulation because the Jews do not believe that Jesus was able to come down from the cross. It is pure mockery. The Jewish rulers are ridiculing Jesus for His "false" assessment of Himself and indirectly boasting that they were right all along. His hanging helpless on the cross proves for them that He cannot be the divinely chosen Messiah.

(6) *Rebuke.* When a person you respect does something that you believe is wrong, you cannot directly rebuke that person to his or her face. The rebuke needs to be softened and made more respectful. This can be done by masking it with a conditional sentence or some other rhetorical device: John 11:21 εἰ ἦς ὧδε οὐκ ἂν ἀπέθανεν ὁ ἀδελφός μου (If you had been here, my brother would not have died). Pragmatic elements in the context suggest that the same utterance by Mary (John 11:32) is a lament rather than a rebuke, e.g., her kneeling and weeping.

(7) *Lament.* Both rebukes and laments refer to past events and therefore employ a second class form: Matthew 11:21 "Woe to you, Chorazin! Woe to you, Bethsaida! For if the mighty works which were done in you, had been done in Tyre and Sidon, they would have repented long ago in sackcloth and ashes."

(8) *Justification.* Conditionals may also be used to justify one's behavior (Matt. 23:30; John 18:30). For further discussion of rhetorical conditions, see Young (1989:29–49).

Relative Clauses

Greek relative clauses can at times display other relations besides identifying a head noun (i.e., restrictive clauses) or describing a head noun (i.e., nonrestrictive). Many have observed other relational properties, such as purpose, means, and condition (BDF 1961:191–92; Burton 1898:116–26; DM 1955: 271–73; Moule 1968:131–32; BAG 1957:588). Although A.T. Robertson (1934: 956) recognizes the existence of various semantic functions of the relative clause, he expresses reluctance in leaving surface structure explanations. He states, "The relative clause may indeed have the resultant effect of cause, condition, purpose or result, but in itself it expresses none of these things. It is like the participle in this respect. One must not read into it more than is there." However, when syntactical argumentation is expanded to the deep structure, this phenomena is easily explainable.

The relational markers that were present at the linguistic deep structure level were lost in the transformation to the surface structure. The same has already been observed with the participle transformation, where various adverbial relations present at the deep structure were lost in the process of generating the surface structure of a participle. The various nuances of the relative clause therefore involve deep structure syntax, not pragmatics, as was the case with certain rhetorical questions and conditionals.

Condition

There are approximately seventy-five occurrences in the New Testament of a relative clause functioning as the conditional proposition in the condition-consequence relation. This often (but not always) happens when the relative does not refer to a specific person or event (i.e., functions as an indefinite relative). Conditional relatives therefore are usually formed with ὅστις or ὃς ἄν, as in Mark 10:44 ὃς ἄν θέλῃ ἐν ὑμῖν εἶναι πρῶτος, ἔσται πάντων δοῦλος (If anyone among you wishes to be first, then he must be servant of all). The NIV translates the following relative constructions as conditional: Matthew 5:39, 41, 10:42, 18:6, 23:16, 18, Mark 6:11, 9:42, and Luke 9:26. Sometimes ὅς alone (without ἄν) can introduce a condition, as in Matthew 7:9 and 2 Corinthians 2:10a (cf. NIV). There is good evidence that the indefinite relative clause can be semantically equivalent to a conditional proposition.

Occasionally alternate readings point to a confusion between conditional and relative clauses. In Mark 8:34 the UBS³ text adopts the reading Εἴ τις θέλει ὀπίσω μου ἀκολουθεῖν (If anyone wishes to follow after me), whereas the TR adopts the reading Ὅστις θέλει ὀπίσω μου ἐλθεῖν (Whoever wishes to come after me). Both say the same thing.

Sometimes parallel passages in the Gospels differ, one having the relative clause, the other an explicit conditional clause. Compare Matthew 15:5 with Mark 7:11; Mark 10:44 with Mark 9:35; and John 7:17 with Mark 3:35.

Often the relative clause that expresses condition is in a context with several explicit conditions. Perhaps the relative was chosen to offer surface structure variation (cf. John 14:13–14; 2 Cor. 2:10).

A construction similar to a relative clause is the article with the participle, such as ὁ πιστεύων (the one who believes). This construction can also function as the semantic equivalent to a conditional clause (if one believes). For example, Matthew 5:40 τῷ θέλοντί σοι κριθῆναι καὶ τὸν χιτῶνά σου λαβεῖν, ἄφες αὐτῷ καὶ τὸ ἱμάτιον (If anyone wants to sue you for your tunic, let him also have your cloak). This is part of a chain of five conditionals in Matthew 5:39–42, three with an article and participle and two with a relative (cf. NIV, TEV). C. B. Williams translates all five as conditional. See also Matthew 7:8, 26, 10:39, 40.

Concession

There are about nine occasions in the New Testament where a relative clause could function as a concessive proposition in a concession-contraexpectation relation. Romans 2:23 ὃς ἐν νόμῳ καυχᾶσαι, διὰ τῆς παραβάσεως τοῦ νόμου τὸν θεὸν ἀτιμάζεις (Although you boast about having God's law, you dishonor God by transgressing the law; cf. Mark 2:26; Rom. 4:25; 7:15 (twice); 11:7; Gal. 3:1; Jas. 4:13–14).

Purpose

Several times a relative clause functions as a purpose proposition: Matthew 11:10 ἀποστέλλω τὸν ἄγγελόν μου πρὸ προσώπου σου, ὃς κατασκευάσει τὴν ὁδόν σου ἔμπροσθέν σου (I am sending my messenger before you that he might prepare your way; cf. TEV.) Other examples include 1 Corinthians 2:16 (NIV) and Hebrews 8:3 (NIV).

Reason

Relative clauses may also function as a reason proposition in a reason-result relation: Matthew 19:12 εἰσὶν γὰρ εὐνοῦχοι οἵτινες ἐκ κοιλίας μητρὸς ἐγεννήθησαν οὕτως (For there are men who cannot perform the sex act because they were born like that; cf. NIV) and Romans 1:24–25 Διὸ παρέδωκεν αὐτοὺς ὁ θεὸς . . . οἵτινες μετήλλαξαν τὴν ἀλήθειαν τοῦ θεοῦ ἐν τῷ ψεύδει (Therefore God delivered them over . . . because they exchanged the truth of God for a lie; cf. NJB, NEB, RSV). See also Romans 5:11.

Grounds — Conclusion

Relative clauses may also function as a grounds (evidence) proposition in a grounds-conclusion relation: Matthew 19:6 ὃ οὖν ὁ θεὸς συνέζευξεν ἄνθρωπος μὴ χωριζέτω (Therefore, since God has joined them together, no one should separate them). In Romans 6:2 the rhetorical question that forms the conclusion is interpreted as an emphatic negative declaration: οἵτινες ἀπεθάνομεν τῇ ἁμαρτίᾳ, πῶς ἔτι ζήσομεν ἐν αὐτῇ (Since we have died to sin, we certainly cannot continue living in it). John 1:47 Ἴδε ἀληθῶς Ἰσραηλίτης, ἐν ᾧ δόλος οὐκ ἔστιν (Here is a true Israelite, since in him there is no deceit). Other examples include Luke 7:4, Acts 10:47, Romans 8:32, Ephesians 5:18, Colossians 3:5, and Revelation 3:21. See Argyle (1955) for further discussion of the causal use of relatives (both reason and grounds).

Exercises

In the following examples, interpret the rhetorical question, sentence containing ϵἰ, or relative in light of the above discussions. Translate the construction in such a way as to convey the function you have chosen. For sentences with ϵἰ, you may have to review the discussions in chapter 12, since not all will be conditional.

1.	Matt. 10:14	Relative
2.	Matt. 12:34	Rhetorical question
3.	Matt. 13:32	Relative
4.	Luke 18:7	Rhetorical question
5.	John 5:46	Sentence with ϵἰ
6.	John 13:14	Sentence with ϵἰ
7.	1 Cor. 3:17	Sentence with ϵἰ
8.	Gal. 5:4	Relative
9.	Heb. 6:9	Sentence with ϵἰ
10.	1 John 4:1	Sentence with ϵἰ

16 Figurative Language

A figure of speech is an expression that uses words in an unusual or non-literal sense for the purpose of emphasis, clarity, or freshness of thought. Figures of speech depart not only from expected lexical meanings but also from expected syntactical structures. Thus one may find a genitive in a figure of speech that seemingly defies classification. The figure has to be unraveled before sense can be made of the genitive. For example, in 1 Peter 1:13 "gird up the loins of your mind" the genitive is obscure because the mind does not have loins. However when the figure "girding up the loins" is decoded as meaning "preparation," then we have an objective genitive, "prepare your minds" (cf. NIV, TEV).

Figures of speech are usually language specific, that is, figures in one language are not necessarily figures in another. Therefore, English speakers will not innately know all the figures used by the writers of the Greek New Testament. In the process of interpretation and reducing the surface structure to its deep structure counterpart, the exegete should seek to decipher the figures. However, one should not ignore the observation that most figures are used as rhetorical devices and have specialized connotations, such as emotional impact or emphasis.

Some figures make comparisons (simile, metaphor), others use associated words (metonymy, synecdoche), still others involve personal attributes (personification, apostrophe, anthropomorphism). Traditionally, figures of speech have been divided into two groups: (1) grammatical/syntactical figures and (2) rhetorical figures. The distinction, however, is not always clear. The following list of figures is presented without any attempt at categorization. For a plausible classification scheme along with other figures, see Nida (et al. 1983:172–91) and Snyman and Cronje (1986:113–21).

Simile

A simile is an explicit comparison using the words "like" or "as." Similes usually present no difficulty for the interpreter. There are three aspects to a simile (and metaphor): (1) the topic which is being discussed, (2) the image with which the topic is compared, and (3) the point of similarity in the particular context. In a simile both the topic and image must occur; the point of similarity may or may not occur.

For example, in Matthew 24:27 Jesus says, "For as lightning that comes from the east is visible even in the west, so will be the coming of the Son of Man" (NIV). The topic is the coming of the Son of Man, the image is the lightening, and the point of similarity is that both are visible to all. In describing the angel at the tomb Matthew writes, "His appearance was like lightning, and his clothes were white as snow" (Matt. 28:3, NIV). At Pentecost the people heard a sound "like the blowing of a violent wind" and saw something "like cloven tongues of fire" (Acts 2:2–3).

Similes are common in the Book of Revelation because John is expanding the human language to describe something that no one had ever seen before or transcribed in language symbols. To communicate so we could catch a glimpse of what he saw, John used the word "like" quite often (over twenty-four times) in similes to draw comparisons with something we could identify with.

Metaphor

A metaphor is a comparison that does not use the words "like" or "as." One thing is said to be another. For example, "You are the salt of the earth. . . . You are the light of the world" (Matt. 5:13–14). Metaphors are more common in the New Testament than similes. As with similes, a metaphor has three aspects: the topic, the image, and the point of similarity. Unlike a simile, a metaphor may sometimes be missing the topic, the point of similarity, or both. This gives us three forms of metaphors:

Topic and Image

In Matthew 5:13 (You are the salt of the earth) only the topic (You) and the image (salt) are present. The point of similarity is absent. The point of similarity could be either the preserving or seasoning qualities of salt. Just as salt makes food palatable, so Christians make the world a more hospitable place to live; but then perhaps the presence of believers in the world is preserving it from immediate disintegration. Because the point of similarity is absent, the interpreter must supply one, hopefully the one Jesus intended.

Image and Point of Similarity

In Mark 14:27 (The sheep will be scattered) only the image (sheep) and the point of similarity (will be scattered) are present. The topic is absent; but here supplying the topic is no problem. Jesus is referring to His disciples. He is saying that His disciples are like sheep who will be scattered when the shepherd is killed.

Only the Image

In Luke 13:32 (Go tell that fox) only the image (fox) is present. The topic (presumably Herod Antipas) and the point of similarity are absent. Supplying the point of similarity here poses somewhat of a problem. In what way is Herod like a fox? Well, what is a fox like? A fox has whiskers, red hair, kills, steals, is crafty, and barks. Jesus was probably not saying that Herod had red hair, whiskers, and barks. Although there could be many points of similarity shared by the topic and image, usually only one is relevant to the context. Our cultural response might be the idea of craftiness or slyness (He is sly as a fox). For the Hebrew speaker, it probably referred to treachery (with specific reference to his killing John the Baptist).

Metonymy

Metonymy is the substitution of one word for another with which it is associated. Sometimes we use the term "the White House" to refer to the President: "The White House vetoed the bill." "White House" can be used as a metonymy for "President" due to the mental link we have between the terms.

In Luke 16:29 Abraham responds to the rich man in Hades, "They have Moses and the prophets; let them listen to them." Moses and the prophets were long since dead; their writings were being discussed. The one suggests the other. If they would not believe the Word of God, neither would they believe the miracle of resurrection, even if they saw it with their own eyes. In 1 Corinthians 10:21 Paul says, "You cannot drink the cup of the Lord and the cup of demons." The reference is to the contents of the cup, not to the cup itself. It is another metonymy. The figure suggests more than participating in pagan rituals. It implies the actual partaking of Satanic doctrines and entering into a covenantal relation with demons. Also God's loving Jacob and hating Esau means that He poured out blessings on the nation of Judah rather than the nation of Edom (Rom. 9:13; cf. Mal. 1:2–3). "Jacob" and "Esau" are examples of metonymy, whereas "hate" is an example of hyperbole.

The associations expressed in a metonymy may be (1) causal, as when a writer stands for his book (Luke 16:29), when tongues stand for languages (Rev. 10:11), or a sword stands for the power to punish (Rom. 13:4); (2) spacial, as when heaven is used for God (Mark 11:30–31), world or earth is used for people (Matt. 5:13–14), a city is used for its inhabitants (Luke 13:34), the cross being used for the death of Christ (1 Cor. 1:17–18), or throne being used for one's rule (Luke 1:32); (3) temporal, as when day stands for events associated with it (2 Pet. 3:12, God's judgment), hour stands for the specific event associated with it (Matt. 26:45, time to die); or (4) attributive, as when an attribute is used for one who possesses it (Luke 1:35, power of the Most High means the Holy Spirit).

Synecdoche

Synecdoche refers to the use of the whole for a part or a part for the whole. The first type (whole for a part) is represented by Luke 2:1, where we read that the whole world was to be taxed. It does not include China, only the Roman Empire. Perhaps Matthew 12:40 is a synecdoche when the Lord speaks of three days and three nights in the earth. It could refer to a portion of the first and third days and all the second. When Jesus tells the disciples to preach the gospel to every creature, He means every human being (Mark 16:15, TEV). Also the Jews in John 1:19 mean only the Jewish leaders (cf. TEV).

The second type (part for the whole) is represented by Acts 27:37, where Luke says that there were 276 souls aboard the ship taking Paul to Rome. Luke is not talking about a ghost ship with disembodied spirits (cf. NIV,

NRSV). The same idea is seen when the Lord tells Peter that flesh and blood (meaning people) did not reveal Jesus' true identity to him (Matt. 16:17; cf. TEV, REB). Other examples where a part of a person stands for the whole person include heads (Acts 18:6, TEV), feet (Rom. 3:15, TEV), bodies (Rom. 12:1, TEV, REB), tongue (Rom. 14:11, TEV), and hearts (Eph. 6:22, NIV). Other examples of synecdoche include necks standing for lives (Rom. 16:4, NIV) and bread standing for food (Matt. 6:11, TEV).

Personification/Apostrophe

A personification portrays a thing or idea as a person, or at least doing what people do. In Matthew 6:34 we read, "Do not worry about tomorrow, for tomorrow will worry about itself" (NIV). Here a period of time is said to be worrying. The idea is that there are enough real troubles today. It is foolish to worry about things that may never happen. When trusting God and seeking His righteousness (6:33), tomorrow may turn out better than expected. Often there is a deep structure actor behind the figure. When Paul says in 1 Corinthians 13:4 that love is patient, he means that the person who loves is patient.

An associated figure is called *apostrophe*. This refers to a thing or animal being addressed as if it were a person or when an imaginary person is being addressed. Paul exclaims, "O death, where is your sting" (1 Cor. 15:55).

Anthropomorphism

Anthropomorphism is the attributing of human or bodily characteristics to God. Although God is spirit (John 4:24) and does not have a physical body like we do, He is often portrayed with human characteristics. In John 10:29 no one is able to pluck the redeemed out of the Father's hand, and in 1 Peter 3:12 the eyes of the Lord are on the righteous, His ears attentive to their prayers, and His face is against those who do evil. Does God have hands, eyes, ears, or a face? Besides being anthropomorphisms, some are also examples of metonymy. God's hand in John 10:29 speaks of strength. Anthropomorphisms could be thought of as accommodations to our human limitations, to help us have some mental conception of God.

Ellipsis/Aposiopesis

Some figures involve omissions that the interpreter must fill in to arrive at the meaning. Ellipsis is the omission of words that are necessary for complete grammatical construction. The omitted words can usually be supplied from the context. For example, "John jumped into the pool, Jim into the river, and Joe into the tub." It is perfectly acceptable in English to omit the verb in the second and third clauses. Most all languages are able to communicate without having to supply every word. Individual languages, however, will differ in the ellipses they will tolerate. When working with the Greek text, the exegete must exercise care in supplying the missing words. Sometimes several options are possible with differing interpretations.

In Acts 18:6 the Greek reads, "Your blood upon your head." The verb is absent. It makes a difference whether we supply "is" or "Let . . . be." Saying "Your blood is upon your head" is a factual declaration; saying "Let your blood be upon your head" is an imprecatory prayer for something evil to happen to the people.

Aposiopesis is the suppression of part of the sentence because of emotion, an unpleasant conclusion, or because the writer wants to gain a certain rhetorical effect. In Exodus 32:32 Moses says, "Yet now, if thou wilt forgive their sin — and if not, blot me, I pray thee, out of thy book" (AV). Here Moses does not finish his statement in the first sentence because of deep emotion. This is similar to Mark 11:32, where the Jewish religious leaders were pondering how to respond to Jesus' question regarding where John the Baptist came from. They expressed the consequence of their first option, "If we say from God," but they did not express the consequence of their second option, "If we say from men," because they were afraid of the people. This shows that they feared people more than God. See also Luke 19:42 and Hebrews 4:5.

Euphemism

A euphemism is the substitution of a less offensive word for the more direct but harsh one. Euphemisms abound in all languages in order to allow people to express themselves without sounding unpleasantly crude or socially distasteful. We do not put the mentally unbalanced into nut houses, but into sanitariums. When close friends die, we do not say they kicked the bucket, but rather they passed on, went home, or went to be with the Lord. Although euphemisms are often culturally conditioned, they do seem to focus on certain semantic domains:

1. Death: fall asleep, sleep, gathered to fathers (e.g., Acts 7:60)
2. Sex: know, lie with, go in unto, touch (e.g., Luke 1:34)
3. Pregnancy: with child, with her (e.g., Luke 1:36)
4. God: heaven, most high, passive voice (e.g., Luke 15:21)
5. Finance (giving): ministry, grace (e.g., 2 Cor. 8:1–4, 9:1–4)

In Acts 1:25 Luke says that Judas went to his own place. That is a nice way of saying he went to hell. The NIV replaces it with another euphemism, "Judas left to go where he belongs." In Judges 3:24 the people said that Eglon must be covering his feet, which using an English euphemism would mean he was going to the bathroom. Robes stopped above the ankles, except when one squats down. We normally clothe sexual discussions in euphemistic terms, just as the Hebrews and Greeks do. Mary said in Luke 1:34 that she never knew a man. What she means is that she never had relations with a man (to use another English euphemism).

Litotes

Litotes occurs when an assertion is made by negating its opposite. For example, we might respond to the question "How many came to the party?" by saying, "Well, it wasn't exactly a huge crowd." What we mean is that only a few showed up. In Acts 15:2 there was "no small dissension." What Luke means is that there was a sharp dispute, bordering on a full scale riot (cf. Acts 19:23). In Acts 17:4 "not a few" of the leading women were saved, meaning quite a few. When Eutychus recovered from his accident, the people "were not a little comforted" (Acts 20:12). This means that they were overcome with joy. In Romans 1:16 Paul says that he is not ashamed of the gospel. He does not mean that he was simply not ashamed of it, but that he was very proud of it or had complete confidence in it (cf. TEV). Other examples include "not many days" standing for "in just a few days" (Acts 1:5), "no mean city" standing for "a very important city" (Acts 21:39), and "I do not want you to be ignorant" standing for "I want you to know" (Rom. 1:13).

Hyperbole

A hyperbole is an overstatement or exaggeration used to gain a certain effect and should not be taken literally. For example, we might say, "I'm freezing to death." Well, not really, but it sure is cold. John 21:25 is a classic example: "And there are also many other things which Jesus did, the which, if they should be written every one, I suppose that even the world itself could not contain the books that should be written" (AV).

Matthew 19:24 is best explained as being a hyperbole: "It is easier for a camel to go through the eye of a needle, than for a rich man to enter into the kingdom of God" (AV). This is definitely an overstatement because it is impossible for a camel to go through such a small opening. However, the point is strongly made: it is going to be very difficult for rich people to enter the kingdom. Another type of hyperbole is the use of "all" or "whole world" where only "many people" or "most" is meant (Matt. 10:22). The word "hate" in Romans 9:13, as mentioned earlier, is a hyperbole, meaning to bestow less favors. Another hyperbole is when John came neither eating or drinking (Matt. 11:18). It only means that John regularly fasted and abstained from wine (cf. TEV). Other examples include Matthew 5:29–30 and 23:24.

Meiosis

Meiosis is a deliberate understatement used to call attention to something. It is the opposite of hyperbole. Less is said than is intended to be understood. For example, in Acts 7:24 Moses smote (struck) the Egyptian. The Egyptian, however, was not simply hit, he was killed (cf. Mark 14:27). In Acts 16:28 Paul tells the jailer, "Do not harm yourself" (he was about to kill himself rather than face the Roman penalty for allowing prisoners to escape).

Irony

In an irony what is really meant is the opposite of what is said. It is commonly used in sarcasm or mockery. One example is Elijah's mocking of Baal's nonresponse to his worshipers, "He is a god; either he is talking, or he is pursuing, or he is in a journey, or peradventure he sleepeth, and must be awakened" (1 Kings 18:27, AV). Another is the soldiers' mockery of Christ, "Hail! King of the Jews" (Matt. 27:29). This is exactly the opposite of what they meant.

Hendiadys

Hendiadys is the expression of one idea with two or more similar words; that is, two words are used for the same thing. Judas left vacant this ministry and apostleship (Acts 1:25). Judas did not vacate two positions, only one. The words "ministry" and "apostleship" refer to the same thing (cf. NIV, TEV). In 2 Timothy 1:10 Paul speaks of life and immortality. The two words say the same thing, eternal life (cf. TEV). When used in adverbial phrases, the repetition may serve to intensify the concept. For example, "with reverence and awe" means "very reverently" (Heb. 12:28), and "in need and hungry" means "very hungry" (Mark 2:25, TEV).

Epizeuxis

Epizeuxis is the repetition of the same word(s) for emphasis. Isaiah writes, "Comfort ye, comfort ye my people" (Isa. 40:1, AV). In Revelation 14:8 and 18:2 we read, "Fallen, fallen is Babylon the Great." Did Babylon fall twice? The idea is that Babylon will surely fall. Also Isaiah's "Holy, holy, holy, is the Lord of hosts" (Isa. 6:3; cf. Rev. 4:8) simply emphasizes God's holiness, that He is very, very holy. It probably does not refer to the Trinity.

Chiasmus

Chiasmus is a series of two or more elements followed by a series of corresponding elements in reverse order. The simplest form involves four elements: the first corresponding to the fourth, and the second corresponding to the third. This could be considered an inverted parallelism. For example, in Mark 2:27, "The Sabbath was made for man, not man for the Sabbath." The first and fourth elements are the same, and the second and third are the same. In Galatians 4:12 Paul says, "Be as I am, for I am as ye are."

This figure helps our understanding of Philemon 5. Paul mentions Philemon's "love and faith" toward "the Lord Jesus and all saints." Was Philemon's love and faith directed toward both? Or did he have love for the saints and faith toward the Lord? The latter is correct, as the first element goes with the fourth and the second with the third (cf. NIV). Another passage in which chiasmus helps the interpretation is Matthew 7:6: "Do not give dogs what is sacred; do not throw your pearls to pigs. If you do, they may trample them under their feet, and then turn and tear you to pieces" (NIV). The NIV has both the dogs and pigs trampling the sacred things under their feet and attacking the person. The TEV unravels the chiasmus so that only the dogs attack while the pigs trample underfoot.

Anacoluthon

Anacoluthon refers to an author's breaking off a sentence partway through and starting a new sentence without finishing the first one. Sometimes this is due to the author's thoughts racing ahead of his ability to express them. Most examples of anacoluthon are unintentional. Nevertheless, they do emphasize the urgency or importance of the matter at hand. This is evident in Galatians where Paul is greatly stirred because of the encroachment of Judaizers in the churches. In Galatians 2:6 Paul begins by saying, "But those who seemed to be important," but then breaks it off and starts afresh, "whatever they were makes no difference to me."

Exercises

Identify, interpret, and translate the following figures of speech.

1. Matt. 11:10   Face
2. Luke 7:35   Wisdom is justified of her children
3. John 1:29   Lamb of God
4. John 12:19   The world
5. Acts 17:12   Not a few
6. Rom. 1:5   Grace and apostleship
7. 1 Cor. 7:1   Touch
8. 1 Cor. 15:32   I fight with wild beasts
9. 1 Thess. 4:13   Asleep
10. 1 Pet. 3:22   The right hand of God
11. Translators will supply the missing words of an ellipsis to make the sentence grammatically acceptable, but their insertions are sometimes misleading. The AV indicates the filling in of ellipsis by italics; other versions do not. Compare 1 Corinthians 14:2, Hebrews 2:1, Hebrews 2:16, and 1 Peter 5:13 in the Greek text with the AV, NIV, and other versions. Note how the words in italics can totally change the meaning of the verses.

17 Discourse Analysis

The meaning of any word, syntactical construction, sentence, or paragraph cannot be understood apart from its linguistic and situational contexts. For example, without a context the most we can say for the word λόγος is that it has a range of possible meanings. In isolation it cannot mean anything in particular. The same is true for syntactical constructions. The phrase ἡ ἀγάπη τοῦ θεοῦ cannot mean anything definite standing alone. It can only take on meaning when placed within a larger linguistic and situational setting. This even applies to sentences. The situational context reveals that the exact same sentence uttered by Mary and Martha has different meanings (John 11:21, 32).

This calls our attention to an inherent weakness of traditional sentence grammars for exegetical purposes. Because they focus only on isolated sentences, they cannot possibly be considered definitive to analyze meaning. Linguists are now recognizing that "sentence grammar will not work unless it is part of a discourse grammar, because certain factors are needed for the understanding of elements in sentences that are not available within those sentences themselves but only elsewhere in the discourse" (Grimes 1975:8).

Discourse is best defined as the communication of ideas through a set of signs (e.g., spoken or written words) within a situational context. In normal usage, discourse refers to units of speech longer than a sentence because it usually takes more than a sentence to communicate a complete thought. Moreover, a complete thought cannot be communicated merely by an artificial string of sentences lacking a situational setting. Discourse analysis therefore must be extended to include the study of language use in communicative situations. The meaning of a discourse is discerned from analyzing a set of interrelated features, such as genre, structure, cohesion, propositions, relations, prominence, and setting.

Genre

Literary genre can be simply defined as "discourse type." Some common genres in the New Testament are poetry, narrative, and parable. Each genre is characterized by certain grammatical, structural, and lexical features that help convey the meaning and purpose of the discourse.

Genre Types

There are four primary genres, each one based on the purpose of the author or speaker: (a) exposition (to explain or argue a thesis), (b) hortatory (to exhort others to fulfill certain duties), (c) narrative (to recount a past event), and (d) procedural (to prescribe how something is to be done). The procedural genre is rare in the Bible. One example is the tabernacle instructions in Exodus.

	- Prescription	+ Prescription
- Chronological	EXPOSITION	HORTATORY
+ Chronological	NARRATIVE	PROCEDURAL

It is customary in New Testament books to find a mixture of the principle text types along with embedded subtypes. Subtypes include epistles, miracle stories (pronouncement texts), parables, allegories, apocalyptic, conversations (repartee), speeches (teaching, sermons, legal pleas), liturgical fragments (songs, prayers, confessions of faith), and quotations (cf. Nida et al. 1983:60–61). The most common approach to New Testament genres recognizes three text types: narrative, epistle, and apocalypse. Although the epistle is prominent in the New Testament, it should probably not be considered a major genre, since it always serves as a vehicle for another genre. That is, the epistolary salutation and closing serve to bracket a particular genre that pertains to the author's purpose. Also, the Book of Revelation is best considered as hortatory (cf. Rev. 2–3) with the basis for the appeal in the apocalyptic subtype.

Genre Structure (Schema)

The basic structure of a discourse depends on its genre. Each genre will employ a unique structural pattern to achieve its communicative task. An exhortation, for example, would consist of the basis for the appeal, the appeal, and ways to achieve the appeal. The major divisions of a particular genre are called *schema*. On the highest level a discourse will usually have an opening rapport, the main body, and a closing. The divisions (schema) within the body will vary according to the genre. The +/- designations in the charts below indicate whether the division was obligatory. Capital letters indicate the most prominent element.

Expository discourse—The body of an expository discourse has the following schema (not necessarily in the order presented):

+/-	orientation	Define terms
+	THESIS	Case to be discussed or argued
+	evidence	Support for the thesis by illustration, emotion, logic, refutation, absurdity
+/-	inference	The deduction, verdict, or conclusion

Hortatory discourse—The body of a hortatory discourse has the following schema (again not necessarily in the order presented):

+/-	rapport	Establish sympathetic relationship
+	basis	Support for the appeal (authority, emotional, evaluative, etc.)
+/-	tension	By defense, emotional display, etc.
+	APPEAL	The command, suggestion, etc.
+/-	enablement	Means to carry out suggestion

Narrative discourse—The body (or plot) of a narrative will depend on whether or not there is a problem:

Problem-Resolution Plot		Occasion-Outcome Plot	
+	setting	+	setting
+	problem	+	occasion
+/-	complication	+	OUTCOME
+/-	resolving incident	+/-	sequel
+	RESOLUTION		
+/-	sequel		

Classical Rhetoric

One should not expect New Testament rhetoric to fit exactly into the classical mold. Classical rhetoric was predominantly a rhetoric of demonstration, whereas New Testament rhetoric is more of a rhetoric of proclamation (kerygma). Nevertheless, there is some correspondence, especially with the expository and hortatory schema. Paul and Luke were probably familiar with classical rhetoric, since it was part of Greek culture. Classical rhetoric consisted of an *exordium* (introduction that aroused attention of the audience and put them in the proper frame of mind), *narratio* (statement of the case to be considered), *propositio* (setting the concern directly before the audience), *divisio* (outline of argument), *confirmatio* or *probatio* (presentation of proofs), *confutatio* (refutation of counter-arguments), and *peroratio* (conclusion). All parts do not need to be present.

Classical rhetoricians distinguished three types of support *(confirmatio)* for the appeal or thesis: *ethos* is an ethical appeal based on the character of the speaker, *pathos* is an appeal to the emotions, and *logos* is a rational appeal.

EXAMPLE: The genre structure of Philemon using both classical and modern schema:

Opening (1–3)	Epistolary opening bracket
BODY (4–22)	Hortatory discourse
Exordium (4–7)	[rapport] Philemon's love and faith
Narratio (8–11)	[APPEAL] I appeal for Onesimus
Propositio (12)	[tension] I am sending him back to you
Probatio (13–17)	[basis for the appeal]
Pathos (13–14)	I would not keep him without your consent

Logos (15–16)	Onesimus is now a Christian
Ethos (17)	I am your partner
Confutatio (18–19)	[enablement] I will repay anything owed
Peroratio (20–22)	I know you will do more than what I say
Closing (23–25)	Epistolary closing bracket

See Wanamaker (1990) for a similar treatment of the Thessalonian Epistles and Kennedy (1984) for further discussion of using classical rhetoric in interpretation.

Structure

Structure refers to the manner of constructing something in an organized way. If human communication were not organized, it would be nothing more than a string of meaningless sounds. The entire speech activity is organized from the lower levels of phonology and morphology to the higher levels of syntax and discourse. Genre structure, as discussed above, pertains only to the major divisions of a discourse. The discussion that follows analyzes discourse structure in general. The three basic features of discourse structure are groupings, hierarchy, and boundaries. Since organization is essential for the understanding of a communication, it cannot be ignored in the exegetical process.

Groupings

Individual units of a discourse must be grouped together in clusters of manageable size. Units at any level that are grouped together to form a cluster are called *constituents* of that group. There are two basic constituents in a sentence, a noun phrase and a verb phrase. Each of these in turn can be broken down into their own constituents, as illustrated by the tree diagrams in chapter 14. The same can occur at higher levels of discourse, with sentences, for example, being constituents of paragraphs, and paragraphs being constituents of larger sections.

Arranging constituents in groups is not a random process. Within a sentence, groupings are more or less dictated by the conventions of grammar (e.g., the constituents of a subject noun phrase are not scattered all over the sentence). Larger elements are grouped together on the basis of their mutual relationship. Our minds naturally group related things together into clusters of manageable size. Since this is how the mind operates, it is also how meaningful communication operates. We simply cannot handle an endless array of unrelated fragments. There are several clues that help the exegete isolate clusters or groupings.

Referential clues (spans)—A *span* is a stretch of text in which "there is some kind of uniformity" (Grimes 1975:91). Spans are normally of paragraph length or greater. There are four types of spans. (1) *Grammatical.* Examples of grammatical spans include "person" spans, such as Romans 5:1–11 (1st person span) and Romans 5:12–21 (3rd person span); "tense" spans, such as Romans 1:21–28 (aorist span) and Romans 2:1–29 (present active span); and "vocative" spans, such as Colossians 3:18–4:1. Each vocative (nominative of address) starts a new paragraph, but the paragraphs are constituents of the same section. (2) *Lexical.* A lexical span contains the repetition of a word or related words. Examples include "Abraham" in Romans 4 and "Spirit" in Romans 8:1–27. Lexical spans may also be from the same semantic domain, such as the bad traits in Colossians 3:5–11. (3) *Informational.* Reference to the same participants, concept, events, setting, or the like, can signal a span. (4) *Teleological.* A span will have a sameness of purpose. There are three kinds of purposes: (i) to exchange information (usually 3rd person), (ii) to influence people (usually 2nd person), and (iii) to express yourself (usually 1st person).

Organizational clues—A grouping can also be marked off by its unique organization. (1) *Sandwich structure.* A sandwich structure occurs when the author states the same thing at the beginning and end of a discourse unit. This is sometimes referred to as bracketing. For example, Colossians 1:3–8 is bracketed by the mention of the Colossian's love in 1:4 and 1:8. (2) *Chiasmus.* A chiasmus is an inverted correspondence where the first element corresponds to the fourth and the second to the third (A B B′A′). It can be used to mark the extremities of a single discourse unit. A chiasmus can range in size from a clause to a whole section. (3) *Parallelisms.* Parallel structures signal constituents that belong together in a larger discourse unit. The constituents may belong to the same paragraph, as in Colossians 3:1–2 (Set your hearts on things above . . . Set your minds on things above) or to the same section, as in Colossians 2:20 and 3:1 (Since you have died with Christ. . . . Since you have been raised with Christ).

Relational clues—Discourse units are also tied together by conjunctions, participles, prepositional phrases, relative clauses, appositional elements, and the like. These units cluster around a central thought to form a dependency chain.

Hierarchy

Associated with grouping is the idea of hierarchy. Hierarchy refers to the ranking of constituent groups into a "tree-like" structure. It also stems from the need of the human mind to break long strings of items down into smaller packages so that the mind can handle them. Understanding will be impaired when the number of constituents in a group exceeds a certain number (usually about seven). If a long discourse, say the Book of Romans, were broken down into seven groups, those groups would probably contain more than seven constituents, and the message of the whole would still be lost. Thus it becomes necessary for the author to divide those groups into even smaller groups, and so on, making sure that no group had more constituents than the mind can easily process. Human language must reveal such a grouping and hierarchical structure if it is to be understood. Thus it is incumbent on the exegete to analyze these features of discourse to help uncover the meaning of a text.

Boundaries

It is very useful for exegetes of the Greek text to know where one unit (e.g., a paragraph) stops and where another begins. It is necessary for the listener of a discourse to know this as well. Therefore the speaker often inserts clues in the discourse to signal a change to another unit. An exegete should be aware of the devices used in koine Greek to mark the beginning and end of a discourse unit.

Initial Markers—(1) *Orienters*. "I do not want you to be ignorant" (1 Cor. 10:1) and "I beseech you" (1 Cor. 1:10). (2) *Vocatives*. Vocatives or nominatives functioning as vocatives are rarely found within paragraphs (Col. 3:18–4:1). (3) *Topic Statements*. "Now Concerning" (1 Cor. 7:1). (4) *Conjunctions*. Some conjunctions occur more frequently at the beginning of a unit than others (οὖν, διό). In narrative δέ often serves as a boundary marker. It is δέ rather than καί that is primarily used to carry the narrative forward by introducing a new development, a new character, or a new time frame. Καί simply holds the narrative in place. (5) *New setting* (in historical narrative). New participants, new location, or a new time frame will often signal a boundary. As mentioned earlier, genitive absolutes often signal a change of setting and a new paragraph.

Final markers—(1) *Doxologies.* Doxologies tend to close off larger units (Rom. 11:33–36). (2) *Summaries* (Heb. 11:39–40). (3) *Tail-head links.* A writer may anticipate what will be taken up next as he or she closes a section. Thus something will be mentioned at the close of one section and at the start of the next. This is often done in James and 1 John.

Cohesion

Another major feature of discourse, in addition to genre and structure, is cohesion. Cohesion refers to the need for the parts of a discourse to be connected or woven together. Since language is produced and received in a linear sequence, there must be some way of tying the pieces of this long sequence of words together. There are many cohesive devices in language that refer to something else in the text and thus form a mental link between elements. Without these connective links or bridges, the listener would be unable to keep the developing text together and would fail to grasp the meaning. Cohesion, you may say, is the glue that holds a discourse together. It refers to the chain of discourse elements that forms a linear thread throughout the whole discourse rather than to those elements that bond constituents together in a hierarchical tree. That is, cohesion is linear linkage rather than hierarchical linkage (through chains of subordination).

Cohesion is often displayed by intentional redundancies, as in James 1:2–5 "Count it all joy my brothers when you fall into various trials, for you know that the testing of your faith produces perseverance. Perseverance, however, must be allowed to develop fully so you will lack nothing. If anyone lacks wisdom. . . ." This chain of links can be followed further in the first chapter of James. A shorthand device to make redundancies more economical is to use *proforms*. A proform is a word used in place of another word, the most common being pronouns.

There are four kinds of cohesion. (1) *Grammatical cohesion* is conveyed by agreement between subject and verb, nouns and adjectives, and the like. (2) *Lexical cohesion* is the use of the same or similar words from the same semantic domain, as in James 1:2–5 above. (3) *Relational cohesion* is signaled by conjunctions and other relational devices in discourse (e.g., adverbial participles, adverbial infinitives). (4) *Referential cohesion* refers to coreferential links between an element in the immediate text and something else.

There are three types of referential cohesion. (a) *Anaphora* is a referential link to a prior element in the text. Anaphoric devices include pronouns and other proforms, such as the pro-clause words "thus" and "so," which refer back to a previous clause or paragraph. The repetition or paraphrasing of a discourse unit when moving to another unit is also classified as anaphoric reference. In Greek grammar the article of previous reference is sometimes called an anaphoric article. (b) *Cataphora* is a coreferential link to a subsequent element in the text. It is much less frequent than anaphora and not as cohesive. Pickering (1980:32) notes that "since its effect is precisely to keep the decoder in suspense until the requisite referent is supplied, it places an added burden upon the short-term memory." (c) *Exophora* is a referential link to some element outside the text. They are just as cohesive as anaphoric signals to hearers "in the know" (Pickering 1980:33).

Propositions

Another feature of discourse is that it operates on two levels; that is, the speaker's thoughts have been encoded into the surface structure of a particular language. Since the aim of discourse analysis is to uncover the speaker's intended meaning, it is necessary to work with the deep structure as well as the surface structure. The surface structure represents the phonological, lexical, and grammatical manifestations of an underlying semantic structure.

One way of unraveling the surface structure and arriving at the deep structure is by back transformations. Transformational grammar, however, gets rather complex for exegetical purposes. Nida and Taber (1974) have developed what may be considered a simplified version of transformational grammar for use in Bible translation. It is called "propositional (or kernel) analysis." Instead of writing formal transformational rules, linguists classify surface structure concepts by semantic class: T (thing), E (event), A (abstraction), or R (relation). Applying these categories to Ephesians 2:8a we have:

R	R	E	T	E	R	E
For	by	grace	you	are saved	through	faith.

Each event word is the verb of a deep structure event proposition (there are also state propositions; e.g., "John is in the desert"). An event word could be a surface structure verb, participle, infinitive, verbal noun, or verbal adjective, since they all contain a verbal idea. In Ephesians 2:8a there are three event words and thus three event propositions.

God shows grace. / God saves you. / You believe.

The relation concepts, such as "by" and "through" tie the propositions together. The underlying structure is therefore represented by a chain of propositions along with the appropriate relational designators. A proposition could be defined as a grouping of concepts (e.g., Jim, ball, hit) into the smallest and simplest predication unit (e.g., Jim hit ball). Concepts are not always expressed by single words. A concept is the smallest recognizable unit of meaning in any language. Morphemes, idioms, word order, and even voice inflection also convey concepts. Nouns can even be made up of more than one concept. For example, the word "judge" consists of two concepts, "person" (thing concept) and "to judge" (event concept): thus "a person who judges."

Decoding a long stretch of text back into its underlying kernels is rather time consuming, cumbersome, and not necessarily productive in every case for exegetical purposes (Cotterell and Turner 1989:197). It may even obscure exegetically significant information. A better procedure would be to partially decode the surface structure into a simplified form called *nuclear sentences,* which are roughly equivalent to surface structure finite clauses without clausal expansions. Thus an adverbial participle (e.g., εἰσελθὼν πάλιν εἰς Καφαρναούμ) becomes the nuclear sentence "[When] he entered again into Capernaum." Nuclear sentences retain their tense markers, simple modifiers, and relational terms.

Sometimes, however, it may be exegetically profitable to decode the surface structure all the way back to its underlying kernels. This is especially true when the meaning of the surface structure is obscure, as in Mark 1:4.

T	E		E	E	R	E
John	appeared	. . .	preaching	a baptism	of	repentance.

There are four event concepts (expressed by a verb, a participle, and two verbal nouns) that represent four deep structure kernels: John appeared / John preached / Someone baptizes people / People repent. When these kernels are encoded into a meaningful English equivalent, we have "John appeared and preached that people should repent and be baptized" (cf. TEV).

Relations

As mentioned in the previous section, propositions are tied together by relational designators. To be more precise, every discourse unit, beginning at the proposition level, is tied together in a hierarchical fashion by semantic relations. These relations are not always indicated in the surface structure by lexical or grammatical items (such as conjunctions). Also the relational pairs in the following discussion are not necessarily presented in the order in which they are found in the Greek New Testament. The member that is prominent will be in upper case (as is the convention in semantic structure analysis, to be discussed in chapter 18). Sometimes the prominent member(s) is labeled HEAD. If the elements are of equal prominence, they are both in upper case. The prominence is based on semantic considerations, not on the taxis (subordination and coordination) of surface structure grammar.

Relations with Equal Natural Prominence (Addition Relations)

Chronological—There are two relations that relate to time and are of equal prominence: sequential and simultaneous. In sequential relations one event follows another:

```
 ┌─ SEQUENTIAL HEAD₁ ──── He came
─┼─ SEQUENTIAL HEAD₂ ──── took her by the hand
 └─ SEQUENTIAL HEAD₃ ──── and lifted her up (Mark 1:31)
```

In simultaneous relations there is some overlap in the events:

```
┌─SIMULTANEOUS HEAD₁ ──────── A very strong wind came up
├─SIMULTANEOUS HEAD₂ ──────── the waves broke over the boat
└─SIMULTANEOUS HEAD₃ ──────── Jesus was sleeping on a cushion (Mark 4:37–38)
```

Non-Chronological—There are two types of non-chronological relations of equal prominence: conjoining and alternation. Conjoining relations are linked with "and," while the alternation relations are linked with "or."

```
┌─ALTERNATE HEAD₁ ──────── Is it lawful to pay tax to Caesar
└─ALTERNATE HEAD₂ ──────── or (is it) not (lawful)? (Matt. 22:17)
```

Relations with Unequal Natural Prominence (Support Relations)

Orientation—There are two basic types of orientation relations. The orienter-CONTENT relation includes topic introductions, such as in Mark 12:26 (Now about the dead rising, have you not read), but more commonly consist of communicative introductions:

```
┌─ orienter ──────── Jesus said to them
└─ HEAD ──────── Follow me (Mark 1:17)
```

The second type of orientation relation is circumstance-HEAD in which the time, setting, location, or other background information is provided.

```
┌─ circumstance ──────── After John was put in prison
└─ HEAD ──────── Jesus went into Galilee (Mark 1:14)
```

Chronological—There are two categories of relations that relate to time and are of unequal natural prominence: step-GOAL and stimulus-RESPONSE. Each can be divided into subtypes. The step-GOAL types denote a progression of events where one event does not precipitate the next event.

```
┌─ step ──────── They left the boat
└─ GOAL ──────── and followed him (Matt. 4:22)
```

The disciples' following Jesus is semantically more prominent than their leaving the boat (cf. Mark 1:35). In stimulus-RESPONSE types the stimulus event precipitates the RESPONSE event. This usually involves dialogue (e.g., question-answer, remark-evaluation) or plot structure (occasion-outcome, problem-resolution). Both step-GOAL and stimulus-RESPONSE types are found primarily in narrative and dialogue. For additional relations and explanation of these categories, see Beekman, Callow, Kopesec (1981:77–113) and Larson (1984:271–345).

Logical—There are six logical relations. The first three are direct cause/effect relations and may sound confusing at first. Grammarians have long recognized two kinds of result (unintentional and intentional). The causal side of these two results are reason (the unintentional cause) and means (the intentional cause). Thus the first two cause/effect relations are REASON-RESULT and means-RESULT. The third relation (MEANS-purpose) is also intentional, and thus it also has means for its causal proposition. Normally one element in each pair will be signaled by a familiar form in the surface structure (e.g., ἵνα + subjunctive = purpose; ὥστε + infinitive = result; διά + infinitive = reason).

(1) REASON-RESULT. Something happened that was not intended. Why it happened is expressed by the reason proposition; what happened is expressed by the result proposition. Either proposition could be semantically prominent, depending on surface structure clues and context. Semantic prominence often follows grammatical taxis. For example, in Mark 4:6 "Because it did not have deep roots, it withered away," the reason is a subordinate clause formed with διά + infinitive, and the RESULT is the main clause. Conversely, in Luke 5:7 "The disciples filled their boats with so many fish that the boats began to sink," the REASON is the main clause, and the result is a subordinate clause formed with ὥστε + infinitive. Both main clauses in these examples represent the semantically prominent element.

The surface structure main clause does not always correspond to what is semantically prominent. For example, the result clause in Mark 2:2 "Many people gathered together, so that there was no room left in the house" is formed with ὥστε + infinitive and is therefore grammatically subordinate. Yet the ensuing context develops the information in the result clause rather than that in the main clause. Thus the result is semantically prominent. In summary, a result proposition is not prominent if it serves only to intensify or amplify the reason proposition (as in Luke 5:7); it is prominent if the ensuing context builds on the idea in the result proposition (as in Mark 2:2). For discussion, see Fedukowski (1985:25–32).

Reason and result are simply different sides of the same relational pair. For example, we could reverse Mark 2:2 to read, "Because so many people gathered together, there was no place left in the house." This would make the semantically prominent proposition correspond to the main clause.

(2) Means-RESULT. Something happened that was intended. The means by which it was brought about is expressed in the means proposition, and what happened is again expressed by the result proposition. In 2 Thessalonians 2:4 the man of sin exalts himself over everything divine, so that (ὥστε + infinitive) he sets himself up as God. This could be restated as "By means of exalting himself over everything divine, the man of sin sets himself up as God." For another example, see Matthew 12:22.

(3) MEANS-Purpose. A particular action (the means) is consciously undertaken in order to achieve an intended goal (the purpose). Normally the goal is not yet realized, as in Romans 1:11 "I want to see you in order to share spiritual blessings with you." In Mark 7:9 the context assumes the goal to have been fulfilled: "You set aside the commandments of God in order to observe your own traditions." Both purpose propositions in the above examples are clearly indicated in the surface structure. There has always been confusion between intended result (2) and purpose (3), because when a purpose is achieved, it becomes an intended result. Natural result (1) does not cause problems. It is best to follow the surface structure clues as much as possible to discern between intended result and purpose.

(4) Grounds-CONCLUSION. The grounds proposition presents the basis or evidence for a conclusion. 1 John 3:14 "We know that we have passed from death to life, because we love our brothers." Loving other believers is not the cause of passing from death to life, but the evidence of it. The conclusion may be a statement or exhortation: Hebrews 4:14 "Since we have such a high priest, let us hold fast to the faith." The conjunction οὖν often introduces the conclusion proposition in a grounds-CONCLUSION relation, as in Romans 12:1. This suggests that Romans 12–16 could be semantically more prominent than Romans 1–11.

(5) Condition-CONSEQUENCE. The condition proposition states a supposition or hypothesis that when fulfilled issues into the consequence. James 2:9 "If you show partiality, you are committing sin." It would be mis-

leading to define a conditional as stating a premise that "must be fulfilled before the action of the main verb can take place" (BW 1979:148). If that were the case, then the only way to commit sin would be to show partiality. The consequence is not contingent on the fulfillment of the condition, since it could happen other ways.

(6) Concession-CONTRAEXPECTATION. The first proposition states a situation that normally turns out a certain way. The second proposition expresses an unexpected result: Colossians 1:21–22 "Although you were formerly alienated from God (concession), he has now reconciled you (CONTRAEXPECTATION)". One would expect that alienation from God would result in judgment, not reconciliation.

Clarification—There are two groups of clarification relations based on whether there is overlap of information. If there is overlap, we have clarification by restatement. If there is no overlap, we have clarification by expansion.

First, there are three relations that clarify by restatement: (1) HEAD-equivalence is where the two units convey the same meaning, as in Semitic parallelism: Matthew 5:12 "Rejoice and be glad." (2) HEAD-amplification is where one unit repeats some information of the other but adds further information: Acts 10:2 "He is a devout person; he worships God, he generously gives to those in need, and he regularly prays to God." (3) In a GENERIC-specific relation, the generic unit conveys information of a general nature that receives more precise detail in the specific unit. Mark 6:48 "He went out to them [generic], walking on the sea [specific]." When there is only one specific, as in Mark 6:48, the HEAD proposition could be either the generic or specific element.

Second, there are two relations that clarify by expansion (i.e., no overlap of information): (1) HEAD-comparison: James 1:6 "He who doubts is like a wave in the sea." This relation can link larger units, such as those found in parables. (2) Contrast-HEAD: Matthew 19:26 "With men this is impossible [contrast], but with God all things are possible [HEAD]." Syntactically, adversatives are coordinate (because they link units of equal structural rank), but as in Matthew 19:26, most introduce a semantically prominent proposition.

Relations between a Proposition and Concept

Most relations are between propositions (or semantic units). Sometimes a proposition relates to only one concept in another proposition, such as when a relative clause modifies a single word in the previous clause. There are two types: identification and description. These relations are self-explanatory.

Prominence

Prominence refers to the state of standing out from the surroundings so as to be easily noticed. Discourse must have prominence. Longacre remarks, "If all parts of a discourse are equally prominent, total unintelligibility results. The result is like being presented with a piece of black paper and being told, 'This is a picture of black camels crossing black sands at midnight'" (cited by Pickering 1980:40). Pickering (1980:40) notes, "We can only perceive something if it stands out from its background. Whether in music, art, or discourse, we look for 'the point,' a theme, a plot—if we fail to find any, our reaction will predictably be negative; our legitimate expectations will not have been met." There are two kinds of prominence in a discourse: natural and marked.

Natural Prominence

Natural prominence pertains to those elements which are semantically more significant for the development of the discourse. In narrative the naturally prominent elements are those that pertain to the plot structure (i.e., the event line or backbone of the episode). In expository discourse the naturally prominent elements are those that pertain to the development of the theme. Supporting elements are semantically less prominent. Thus a conclusion is more prominent than its grounds. As discussed earlier, natural prominence does not necessarily correspond to surface structure taxis (subordination and coordination). A grammatically subordinate element may have more prominence than the main clause. Natural prominence was indicated on the relations in the previous section by using all capitals. In the next chapter we will study a type of structural diagram that is based on propositional relations at the deep structure level. It will display those elements which are more prominent, taking into consideration both natural and marked prominence.

Marked Prominence

The author may use various devices in the surface structure to highlight portions of the discourse. This is called *marked prominence.* This is done for various reasons, such as to mark the theme or major motifs in expository discourse or the foreground material in narrative (thematic prominence). The author may also use surface structure devices to highlight surprising, unexpected, or emotional information. There are a number of ways in Greek an author can call attention to a particular part of a discourse.

Word order — Generally, any element placed before the verb signals prominence.

Certain morphemes — (-περ, παρα-)

Certain words — Emphatic particles, emphatic pronouns, and superlatives mark prominence; e.g., ἰδού, ἴδε (behold), λίαν (very), σφόδρα (extremely).

Grammatical features — Finite verbs, passive voice, relative clauses, and historical presents often mark prominence. The passive will keep the topic as subject.

Figures of speech — Some figures that trigger prominence include hyperbole ("All Jerusalem went out . . . "), hendiadys ("rejoice and be glad" means "be very glad"), epizeuxis ("holy, holy, holy" means very holy), and litotes ("no mean city" means "a very important city").

Prominence orienters — For example, "I do not wish you to be ignorant that," "Haven't you read that," and "verily, verily, I say to you."

Repetition — Sometimes repeated words are used for discourse cohesion rather than prominence.

Rhetorical questions — Rhetorical questions often trigger prominence.

Cataphoric devices — These are devices that refer to something yet to come in the discourse (τοῦτο, εἰς τοῦτο, "For this reason I have come, namely . . . ").

Discourse proportion — Romans 1–11, for example, is much larger than Romans 12–16.

Asyndeton — This is the lack of a conjunction at the beginning of a sentence.

Personal names — The use of personal names when not a new participant tends to highlight that person.

Situation

Another feature of discourse is that it always has a real-life setting. The study of language usage in light of its situational context is called *pragmatics*. Pragmatics refers to how non-linguistic features of discourse, such as social environment and shared knowledge, influence the meaning and structure of an utterance. Brown and Yule (1983:26) remark that "'doing discourse analysis' certainly involves 'doing syntax and semantics', but it primarily consists of 'doing pragmatics.'" The situation affects the meaning and structure of discourse in various ways: influencing what is said, how it is said, what the words mean, and what is meant by what is said. Three areas of recent development that study the relation between the situation and utterance are conversational maxims, speech act theory, and sociolinguistics.

Conversational Maxims

Effective exchange of information follows certain principles formulated by H. P. Grice (1975:45–47). They are (1) the co-operative principle, where the information that participants contribute is in keeping with the common purpose of the exchange; (2) the principle of quality, where the participants generally avoid saying things they know to be false; (3) the principle of quantity, where the information contributed is only as informative as required by the purposes of the exchange; (4) the principle of relevance, where the information contributed is relevant to the discussion; and (5) the principle of manner, where the participants normally attempt to be brief and orderly, avoiding obscurity and ambiguity.

Of particular exegetical significance is Grice's third principle. Many things are left unsaid or unexplained because of the shared pool of knowledge between the speaker and listener. Such implicit information is an integral part of the total discourse, for without it the communication enterprise would fail. If the information were included, the discourse would contain so much baggage that the main points would become obscured. This implicit yet necessary information is called *implicature*. Implicatures pertain not only to the deletion of information necessary for word meanings but also to the deletion of entire propositions from an exchange. Some of Jesus' obscure sayings could be clarified by the insertion of these unspoken propositions (cf. Gutt 1987:31–58). As expected, there are more implicatures in informal conversation than in formal speeches.

Speech Act Theory

Speech act theory is concerned more with what people do with language than with what the words mean. For example, an utterance may request, instruct, assert, or command something. Also the form may not necessarily correspond to the function. In Mark 15:18 the soldiers were not honoring Jesus when they cried out, "Hail, King of the Jews"; they were mocking Him. The words were used to perform a particular act. What the words literally mean is something quite different from what the speaker meant by them. As McCarthy (1991:9) says, "Form and function have to be separated to understand what is happening in discourse." The difference between what the words mean at face value and what was meant by them is due to an interplay of various extra-linguistic, pragmatic factors, such as the situational context, the relation between speaker and hearer, and the speaker's intent. In previous chapters we have evaluated some rhetorical questions and conditionals by this theory. For further discussion, see Austin (1962) and Searle (1969, 1979).

Sociolinguistics

Sociolinguistics investigates the relation between language and society. It studies actual language usage rather than what proper language is supposed to be according to prescriptive grammars. The study of sociolinguistics includes such things as the social status of the speaker (e.g., age, sex, class, education), the social situation in which a discourse takes place (e.g., frozen, formal, casual, intimate, consultative), the relation between the speaker and audience, dialects (such as the type of Greek in the New Testament), the general sociocultural context, and idiomatic speech. The first two are called *code* and *register*, respectively.

Talking is a social activity performed by social beings. When people enter into a communicative exchange, a social relationship must be posited, a specific social situation must be recognized, and a general sociocultural milieu must be reflected. This will affect what is said, how it is said, and even the meaning of words and grammatical constructions.

Diagraming

Diagraming is a method of language analysis; but not all diagraming is the same. The best methods for exegetical purposes include more than simply the structural patterns of a discourse. They also recognize skewing between form and meaning and therefore work with deep structure kernels and relations. In addition, they incorporate genre schema and prominence into the diagrams. Some of the methods that have been suggested for exegesis are as follows:

Word-by-word line diagraming—This method excels at what it was designed to accomplish, to analyze the grammatical relation of each word in a sentence. Beyond that, its value is dubious. It is a tool designed for sentence-based grammar and is not capable of handling large segments of text without becoming *overly* cumbersome. Since it adheres rigidly to the surface structure, it ignores possible skewing between form and meaning. Hence, line diagraming fails to provide semantic perspective to the text and is therefore inadequate for exegetical purposes. The following example of line diagraming is from Mark 1:12:

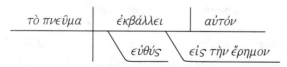

Thought-flow diagraming—This method is also called block diagraming or sentence-flow diagraming (cf. Fee 1983:60–76; Kaiser 1981:149–81). It is a vast improvement over line diagraming primarily because it plots clauses rather than individual words. Yet it also focus on surface structure forms and relations and ignores the possible skewing between form and meaning. This can be partially overcome by plotting nuclear sentences (e.g., interpreted adverbial participles) instead of surface structure clauses. Another weakness that can be overcome is the tendency not to specify the type of relation between elements. The surface structure taxis, however, may still pose a problem, since it does not always correspond to semantic prominence.

Colon diagraming—The colon diagraming of J. P. Louw (1982:91–158) offers a corrective to both of the above methods in that it is sensitive to deep structure relations. Simple and complex sentences are regarded as single colons, while compound sentences with two or more independent clauses are regarded as multiple colons. Colons are roughly equivalent to an independent clause along with its dependent expansions. Expansions within a colon are plotted with lines pointing to the element it modifies. Related colons are then grouped together as the paragraph is laid out. The major weaknesses are that neither the relations between parts nor the prominent units are specified.

Semantic structure analysis (ssa) —The best way to diagram a paragraph with a view to understanding its meaning is by semantic structure analysis. This method rigorously diagrams semantic units and interrelates them at the deep structure level. It was developed by members of the Summer Institute of Linguistics (cf. Beekman, Callow, and Kopesec 1981, Barnwell 1984, and Larson 1984). It is similar to the diagraming presented by Nida (1983:99–109). The following sections outline the method for both thought-flow diagraming and semantic structure analysis. In each, the paragraph (or pericope in narrative) is the unit of analysis. Since a paragraph is the smallest recognizable, cohesive whole that develops a single theme, it is considered as the basic building block of a discourse and the most practical unit of discourse to diagram.

Thought-Flow Diagraming

A thought-flow diagram visually displays the progression and development of the author's argument. Independent clauses (presumably the author's main points) are set off to the left, while supporting elements are indented to the right. This method is quick, gives the exegete a reasonable understanding of a passage, and provides structure for expository messages. Its shortcomings, however, should be kept in mind. There are six basic steps to follow:

Step 1: *Put the First Main Clause at the Upper Left Margin.*

If the paragraph begins with a main clause, then it should be placed at the upper left margin of your page. The diagrams come out better if the 8½ x 11 inch page is turned sideways. The main clause consists of the subject, verb, and usually a direct object. Our example is James 1:2–8:

Πᾶσαν χαρὰν ἡγήσασθε, ἀδελφοί μου

The main clause is actually χαρὰν ἡγήσασθε ([You] consider joy). The subject is embedded in the verb ending. For the sake of simplicity, the singular adjective πᾶσαν (all) and the vocative of address ἀδελφοί μου (my brothers) are included on the same line.

Step 2: *Indent All Subordination.*

All subordination is to be indented. Subordinate elements in discourse are essentially the modifiers. Nouns can be modified by individual adjectives (the good man), adjective phrases (the man in the house), and adjective clauses (the man who is in the field). Verbs can be modified by individual adverbs (He ran fast), adverbial phrases (He ran to the store), or adverbial clauses (He ran because the dog was after him). Continuing our example from James 1:2–8 we have:

Πᾶσαν χαρὰν ἡγήσασθε, ἀδελφοί μου

    ⌐ ὅταν πειρασμοῖς περιπέσητε ποικίλοις

    ∟ γινώσκοντες ὅτι τὸ δοκίμιον ὑμῶν τῆς πίστεως κατεργάζεται ὑπομονήν

The adverbial clause ὅταν . . . ποικίλοις (when you fall into various temptations) modifies the verb ἡγήσασθε (consider), telling when we are to consider it all joy. The second adverbial clause is formed with the participle γινώσκοντες which we interpret as a grounds participle (because you know). Subordinate elements are to be placed under (or over) the word they modify with an ∟ or ⌐ shaped bracket.

Step 3: *Line up All Coordination.*

Coordination means "being of equal structural rank." Syntactical coordination is often indicated by coordinating conjunctions, such as "and" and "but." Syntactical subordination is indicated by subordinate conjunctions, such as "when," "after," "because," "if," and "although." Any kind of element (whether individual words, phrases, or clauses) can be structurally coordinate with other elements. Continuing our example from James 1:2–8 we now have:

Πᾶσαν χαρὰν ἡγήσασθε, ἀδελφοί μου

       ├─ ὅταν πειρασμοῖς περιπέσητε ποικίλοις

       └─ γινώσκοντες ὅτι τὸ δοκίμιον ὑμῶν τῆς πίστεως κατεργάζεται ὑπομονήν

ἡ δὲ ὑπομονὴ ἔργον τέλειον ἐχέτω

The coordinating conjunction δέ coordinates the first independent clause with the second independent clause. The exegete must always examine the context to determine what element the new clause is coordinate to.

Attendant circumstance participles are somewhat perplexing to diagram. In English translation they appear as coordinate with the verb in the adjoining clause. The coordination, however, is only superficial. It is actually an adverb clause modifying the adjoining verb by naming an accompanying action. As such, it should not be treated as syntactically coordinate.

Step 4: *Line up All Multiple Subjects, Objects, and Predicate Nominatives.*

All compound subjects, objects, and predicate nominatives should be placed one under another in coordinate fashion. Some compound predicate nominatives occur in the next clause of James 1:2–8:

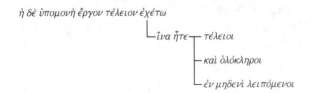

ἡ δὲ ὑπομονὴ ἔργον τέλειον ἐχέτω
            └─ ἵνα ἦτε ┬─ τέλειοι
                    ├─ καὶ ὀλόκληροι
                    └─ ἐν μηδενὶ λειπόμενοι

Step 5: Bracket Missing Information.

ἵνα ἦτε ┬─ τέλειοι

└─ καὶ ὁλόκληροι

└─ [καὶ] ἐν μηδενὶ λειπόμενοι

Step 6: Connect Related Main Clauses.

Πᾶσαν χαρὰν ἡγήσασθε, ἀδελφοί μου

└─ ὅταν πειρασμοῖς περιπέσητε ποικίλοις

└─ γινώσκοντες ὅτι τὸ δοκίμιον ὑμῶν τῆς πίστεως κατεργάζεται ὑπομονήν

ἡ δὲ ὑπομονὴ ἔργον τέλειον ἐχέτω

Step 7: Specify the Relations.

This is normally not done, but is very helpful.

Πᾶσαν χαραν ἡγήσασθε, ἀδελφοί μου

└─ ὅταν πειρασμοῖς περιπέσητε ποικίλοις [TIME]

└─ γινώσκοντες ὅτι τὸ δοκίμιον ὑμῶν τῆς πίστεως κατεργάζεται

ὑπομονήν [GROUNDS]

ἡ δὲ ὑπομονὴ ἔργον τέλειον ἐχέτω

A Thought-Flow Diagram of James 1:2–8

The following is the thought flow diagram of James 1:2–8, first in Greek, then in a rough English translation, and finally transposed into a teaching outline.

Πᾶσαν χαρὰν ἡγήσασθε, ἀδελφοί μου

     ὅταν πειρασμοῖς περιπέσητε ποικίλοις [TIME]

     γινώσκοντες ὅτι τὸ δοκίμιον ὑμῶν τῆς πίστεως κατεργάζεται
       ὑπομονήν [GROUNDS]

ἡ δὲ ὑπομονὴ ἔργον τέλειον ἐχέτω

     ἵνα ἦτε   τέλειοι [PURPOSE]

           καὶ ὁλόκληροι

           [καὶ] ἐν μηδενὶ λειπόμενοι

    εἰ . . . τις ὑμῶν λείπεται σοφίας [CONDITION]

δὲ . . . αἰτείτω παρὰ . . . θεοῦ

      τοῦ διδόντος πᾶσιν ἁπλῶς [MODIFY GOD]

      καὶ μὴ ὀνειδίζοντος [MODIFY GOD]

καὶ δοθήσεται αὐτῷ

αἰτείτω δὲ

   ἐν πίστει [MANNER]

   μηδὲν διακρινόμενος [MANNER]

     ὁ γὰρ διακρινόμενος ἔοικεν κλύδωνι [GROUNDS]

        θαλάσσης

        ἀνεμιζομένῳ

        καὶ ῥιπιζομένῳ

     μὴ γὰρ οἰέσθω ὁ ἄνθρωπος ἐκεῖνος ὅτι λήμψεταί τι

          παρὰ τοῦ κυρίου

     ἀνὴρ δίψυχος

     ἀκατάστατος ἐν πάσαις ταῖς ὁδοῖς αὐτοῦ

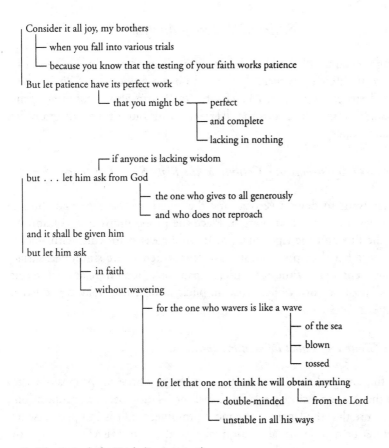

I. The Attitude for Trials (James 1:2–4)
   A. A Joyful Disposition
      1. The time of rejoicing
      2. The reason for rejoicing
   B. A Wondrous Destination
      1. Perfect
      2. Complete
      3. Lacking in nothing
II. The Wisdom for Trials (James 1:5–8)
   A. The Prayer for Wisdom
      1. From the One who gives generously
      2. From the One who does not reproach
   B. The Gift of Wisdom
   C. The Requirement for Wisdom
      1. The presence of faith
      2. The absence of doubt

Semantic Structure Analysis

Although semantic structure analysis is more demanding, it offers greater rewards for the diligent exegete. It is based on the propositional analysis and relational structure presented in chapter 17. It can also incorporate genre schema and prominence into the diagram. Work out a rough diagram first on scratch paper.

Step 1: *List Propositions in a Column at the Right Side of the Page.*

You may want to draw a vertical line the length of the page and three to four inches from the right margin. Place the propositions in a column between the line and the right margin. It will be easier to work with nuclear sentences rather than propositions. Nuclear sentences are simplified surface structure sentences without clausal expansions. Retain relational terms, such as "because" or "while." Also implicit information may be added in parentheses.

Step 2: *Group and Label Related Propositions.*

Work first at the lowest level and group the neighboring propositions together that are most closely related. Label the relation between propositions, making sure that the label for the more prominent unit is in upper case letters (either using its normal relation label or the term HEAD) and that the supporting unit is labeled in lower case. If the propositions are of equal prominence, then both labels are to be in upper case. In the following examples, the propositions are numbered (e.g., proposition 1) for instructional purposes rather than using actual text.

Example: ┌── condition ───────────[proposition 1]
          └── CONSEQUENCE ──────[proposition 2]

Step 3: *Align Properly Next Higher Level.*

The labels of the next higher level (to the left) are aligned horizontally with the HEAD element of the next lower level (to the right). If the units of the next lower level are of equal prominence, then the connecting line is placed between them. In the following example, proposition 4 supports proposition 3 in a means-RESULT relation, and proposition 3 supports proposition 5 in a grounds-CONCLUSION relation.

Example: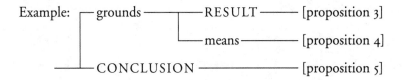

Step 4: *Connect Multiple Supporting Units to Same Vertical Line.*

When there is one HEAD unit with several supporting units, they can all be connected to the same vertical line. Use the general term HEAD when there are multiple supporting units. In the following example, propositions 6, 8, and 9 all support proposition 7 in various ways.

Example: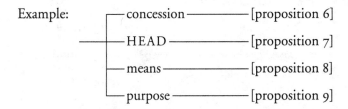

Step 5: *Make Sure Supporting Unit Relates to Proper* HEAD.

When there are several HEAD units and the supporting unit relates to all of them, attach both the HEAD and supporting units to the same vertical line. In the following example, proposition 10 supports both propositions 11 and 12 in a grounds-CONCLUSION relation.

Example: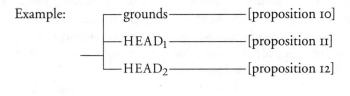

When there are several HEAD units and the supporting unit relates only to one, then it must be connected to the right of the HEAD it supports. In the following example, proposition 13 supports only proposition 12, doing so in a reason-RESULT relation.

Example:

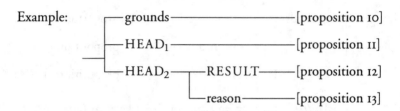

Step 6: *Note Where Propositions Relate Only to a Concept.*

Sometimes a proposition relates only to a concept rather than to an entire proposition, such as when a relative clause modifies a particular noun. It is best to arrow the proposition into the HEAD term, making sure the particular concept in the HEAD term is specified.

Example:

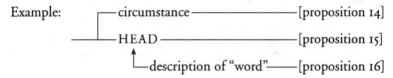

Step 7: *Insert Genre Schema.*

At the highest levels of the display (to the left), the genre schema can be inserted, either in place of the relational roles or alongside them.

Semantic Structure Analysis of James 1:2–8

The following is an SSA display of James 1:2–8. The significant differences from thought-flow diagraming are the clarification of relationships throughout and the focus on the deep structure instead of the surface structure. An optional feature is to indent the propositions to reflect the levels of thematicity (much like thought-flow diagraming).

SECTION CONSTITUENT [James 1:2–8] (Paragraph) (Role: HEAD of 1:2–18). THEME: Attitude in Trials. Considering trials as occasions for joy, developing patience, and asking God for wisdom.

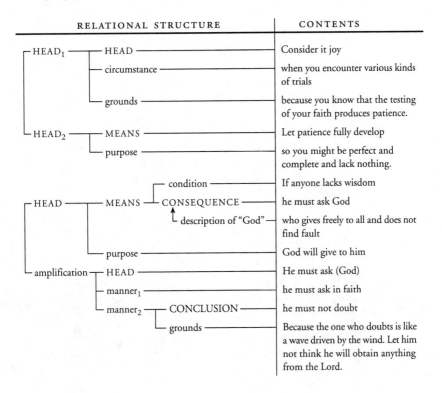

RELATIONAL STRUCTURE	CONTENTS
HEAD₁ — HEAD	Consider it joy
circumstance	when you encounter various kinds of trials
grounds	because you know that the testing of your faith produces patience.
HEAD₂ — MEANS	Let patience fully develop
purpose	so you might be perfect and complete and lack nothing.
condition	If anyone lacks wisdom
HEAD — MEANS — CONSEQUENCE	he must ask God
description of "God"	who gives freely to all and does not find fault
purpose	God will give to him
amplification — HEAD	He must ask (God)
manner₁	he must ask in faith
manner₂ — CONCLUSION	he must not doubt
grounds	Because the one who doubts is like a wave driven by the wind. Let him not think he will obtain anything from the Lord.

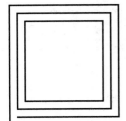

Appendix

Summary of Semantic Relations

I. Equal Natural Prominence

  A. Chronological
    1. SEQUENTIAL HEAD$_1$ — SEQUENTIAL HEAD$_2$
    2. SIMULTANEOUS HEAD$_1$ — SIMULTANEOUS HEAD$_2$

  B. Non-chronological
    1. CONJOINING HEAD$_1$ — CONJOINING HEAD$_2$
    2. ALTERNATING HEAD$_1$ — ALTERNATING HEAD$_2$

II. Unequal Natural Prominence

  A. Orientation
    1. orienter — CONTENT
    2. circumstance — HEAD

  B. Chronological
    1. step — GOAL
    2. stimulus — RESPONSE

  C. Logical
    1. reason — RESULT
    2. means — RESULT
    3. MEANS — purpose
    4. grounds — CONCLUSION
    5. condition — CONSEQUENCE
    6. concession — CONTRAEXPECTATION

D. Clarification
   1. HEAD — equivalence
   2. HEAD — amplification
   3. GENERIC — specific
   4. HEAD — comparison
   5. contrast — HEAD

III. Relations between a Proposition and Concept

   A. Identification

   B. Description

Note: These are only the relations explained in the text. For other relations which are primarily found in narrative and dialogue, see Beekman, Callow, Kopesec 1981:77–113 and Larson 1984:271–345.

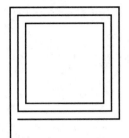

Bibliography

Argyle, A. W. 1955. The Causal Use of the Relative Pronouns in the Greek New Testament. *The Bible Translator* 6:165–69.

Austin, J. L. 1962. *How to Do Things with Words.* New York: Oxford University Press.

Baima, John K. 1986. Making Valid Conclusions from Greek Conditional Sentences. Th.M. thesis, Grace Theological Seminary.

Barnwell, Katharine. 1974. Vocative Phrases. *Notes on Translation* 53:9–17.

―――. 1984. *Introduction to Semantics and Translation.* Horsleys Green, England: Summer Institute of Linguistics.

Barrett, C. K. [1957] 1987. *A Commentary on the Epistle to the Romans.* Harper's New Testament Commentaries. Reprint. Peabody, MA: Hendrickson.

―――. [1973] 1987. *A Commentary on the Second Epistle to the Corinthians.* Harper's New Testament Commentaries. Reprint. Peabody, MA: Hendrickson.

―――. 1978. *The Gospel According to St. John.* 2nd ed. Philadelphia: Westminster Press.

Bauckham, Richard J. 1983. *Jude, 2 Peter.* Word Biblical Commentary, vol. 50. Waco, TX: Word Books.

Bauer, Walter. 1957. *A Greek-English Lexicon of the New Testament and Other Early Christian Literature.* Translated and adapted from Bauer's 4th ed. by William F. Arndt and F. Wilbur Gingrich. Chicago: University of Chicago Press.

Beekman, John, and John Callow. 1974. *Translating the Word of God.* Grand Rapids: Zondervan.

Beekman, John, John Callow, and Michael Kopesec. 1981. *The Semantic*

Structure of Written Communication. Dallas: Summer Institute of Linguistics.

Blackwelder, Boyce W. [1958] 1976. *Light from the Greek New Testament.* Reprint. Grand Rapids: Baker Book House.

Blass, F., A. Debrunner, and Robert W. Funk. 1961. *A Greek Grammar of the New Testament and Other Early Christian Literature.* Chicago: University of Chicago Press.

Boyer, James L. 1982. Third (and Fourth) Class Conditions. *Grace Theological Journal* 3:163–75.

———. 1984. The Classification of Participles: A Statistical Study. *Grace Theological Journal* 5:163–79.

———. 1985. The Classification of Infinitives: A Statistical Study. *Grace Theological Journal* 6:3–27.

———. 1987. A Classification of Imperatives: A Statistical Study. *Grace Theological Journal* 8:35–54.

———. 1988. A Classification of Optatives: A Statistical Study. *Grace Theological Journal* 9:129–40.

Brooks, James A., and Carlton L. Winbery. 1979. *Syntax of New Testament Greek.* Lanham, MD: University Press of America.

Brown, Gillian, and George Yule. 1983. *Discourse Analysis.* Cambridge: Cambridge University Press.

Brown, Raymond E. 1966. *The Gospel According to John (I-XII).* Anchor Bible, vol. 29. New York: Doubleday.

———. 1970. *The Gospel According to John (XIII-XXI).* Anchor Bible, vol. 29A. New York: Doubleday.

———. 1982. *The Epistles of John.* Anchor Bible, vol. 30. New York: Doubleday.

Bruce, F. F. 1982. *The Epistle to the Galatians.* New International Greek Testament Commentary. Grand Rapids: Eerdmans.

———. 1984. *The Epistles to the Colossians, to Philemon, and to the Ephesians.* New International Commentary on the New Testament. Grand Rapids: Eerdmans.

Burton, Ernest de Witt. 1898. *Syntax of the Moods and Tenses in New Testament Greek.* 3rd ed. Edinburgh: T. & T. Clark.

———. 1980. *A Critical and Exegetical Commentary on the Epistle to the Galatians.* International Critical Commentary. Edinburgh: T. & T. Clark.

Buth, Randall. 1977. Mark's Use of the Historical Present. *Notes on*

Translation 65:7–13.

———. 1981. On Levinsohn's "Developmental Units." *Selected Technical Articles Related to Translation* 5:53–56.

Caird, G. B. [1966] 1987. *A Commentary on the Revelation of St. John the Divine.* Harper's New Testament Commentaries. Reprint. Peabody, MA: Hendrickson.

Callow, John C. 1978. To What Do TOUTO and TAUTA Refer in Paul's Letters? *Notes on Translation* 70:2–8.

———. 1983. Word Order in New Testament Greek. Parts 1–3. *Selected Technical Articles Related to Translation* 7:3–50, 8:3–32.

———. 1984. The Function of the Historical Present in Mark 1:16–3:6; 4:1–41; 7:1–23; 12:13–34. *Selected Technical Articles Related to Translation* 11:9–17.

———. 1986. Some Initial Thoughts on the Passive New Testament Greek. *Selected Technical Articles Related to Translation* 15:32–37.

Callow, Kathleen. 1974. *Discourse Considerations in Translating the Word of God.* Grand Rapids: Zondervan.

Chamberlain, William Douglas. [1941] 1979. *An Exegetical Grammar of the Greek New Testament.* Reprint. Grand Rapids: Baker Book House.

Charles, R. H. 1920. *A Critical and Exegetical Commentary on the Revelation of St. John,* vol. 1. International Critical Commentary. Edinburgh: T. & T. Clark.

Colwell, E. C. 1933. A Definite Rule for the Use of the Article in the Greek New Testament. *Journal of Biblical Literature* 52:12–21.

Comrie, Bernard. 1981. *Language Universals and Linguistic Typology: Syntax and Morphology.* Chicago: University of Chicago Press.

Cotterell, Peter, and Max Turner. 1989. *Linguistics & Biblical Interpretation.* Downers Grove, IL: InterVarsity Press.

Cranfield, C. E. B. 1959. *The Gospel According to Saint Mark.* Cambridge Greek Testament Commentary. Cambridge: Cambridge University Press.

———. 1975. *A Critical and Exegetical Commentary on the Epistle to the Romans,* vol. 1. International Critical Commentary. Edinburgh: T. & T. Clark.

———. 1979. *A Critical and Exegetical Commentary on the Epistle to the Romans,* vol. 2. International Critical Commentary. Edinburgh: T. & T. Clark.

Dana, H. E., and Julius R. Mantey. 1955. *A Manual Grammar of the Greek*

New Testament. Toronto: Macmillan.

Daube, David. [1947] 1981. Participle and Imperative in 1 Peter. In *The First Epistle of St. Peter*, by Edward G. Selwyn, 467–88. Reprint. Grand Rapids: Baker Book House.

Davids, Peter H. 1982. *The Epistle of James*. New International Greek Testament Commentary. Grand Rapids: Eerdmans.

———. 1990. *The First Epistle of Peter*. New International Commentary on the New Testament. Grand Rapids: Eerdmans.

Davies, David P. 1976. The Position of Adverbs in Luke. In *Studies in New Testament Language and Text: Essays in Honour of George D. Kilpatrick on the Occasion of his 65th Birthday*, ed. J. K. Elliott, 106–21. Leiden: Brill.

Deissmann, Adolf. 1965. *Light from the Ancient East*. Reprint. Grand Rapids: Baker Book House.

Denney, James. 1974. St. Paul's Epistle to the Romans. In *The Expositor's Greek Testament*, vol. 2. Reprint. Grand Rapids: Eerdmans.

Dods, Marcus. 1974. The Epistle to the Hebrews. In *The Expositor's Greek Testament*, vol. 4. Reprint. Grand Rapids: Eerdmans.

Dover, K. J. 1960. *Greek Word Order*. Cambridge: Cambridge University Press.

Fanning, Buist M. 1990. *Verbal Aspect in New Testament Greek*. Oxford: Clarendon Press.

Fedukowski, Donna. 1985. On the Use of HOSTE with the Infinitive. *Selected Technical Articles Related to Translation* 14:25–32.

Fee, Gordon D. 1983. *New Testament Exegesis: A Handbook for Students and Pastors*. Philadelphia: Westminster Press.

———. 1987. *The First Epistle to the Corinthians*. New International Commentary on the New Testament. Grand Rapids: Eerdmans.

Fitzmyer, Joseph A. 1970. *The Gospel According to Luke (I-IX)*. Anchor Bible, vol. 28. New York: Doubleday.

Friberg, Timothy. 1982. New Testament Greek Word Order in Light of Discourse Considerations. Ph.D. diss., University of Minnesota.

Furnish, Victor Paul. 1984. *II Corinthians*. Anchor Bible, vol. 32A. New York: Doubleday.

Grice, H. P. 1975. Logic and Conversation. In *Speech Acts*, 41–58. Vol. 3 of *Syntax and Semantics*, Eds. P. Cole and J. Morgan. New York: Academic Press.

Grimes, Joseph E. 1975. *The Thread of Discourse*. New York: Mouton.

Gutt, Ernst-August. 1987. What is the Meaning We Translate? *Occasional Papers in Translation and Textlinguistics* 1(1):31–58.

Harner, Philip B. 1973. Qualitative Anarthrous Predicate Nouns: Mark 15:39 and John 1:1. *Journal of Biblical Literature* 92:75–87.

Harris, M. J. 1978. Prepositions and Theology in the Greek New Testament. In *The New International Dictionary of New Testament Theology*, ed. Colin Brown, vol. 3, 1171–215. Grand Rapids: Zondervan.

Hawthorne, Gerald F. 1983. *Philippians*. Word Biblical Commentary, vol. 43. Waco, TX: Word Books.

Healey, Phyllis, and Alan Healey. 1990. Greek Circumstantial Participles: Tracking Participants with Participles in the Greek New Testament. *Occasional Papers in Translation and Textlinguistics* 4:177–259.

Hughes, Philip Edgcumbe. 1977. *A Commentary on the Epistle to the Hebrews*. Grand Rapids: Eerdmans.

Hull, Sanford D. 1986. Exceptions to Apollonius' Canon in the New Testament: A Grammatical Study. *Trinity Journal* 7 (Spring):3–16.

Jung, Min-Young. 1985. The Position of Adverbs in Biblical Greek. Master's thesis, University of Texas at Arlington.

Kaiser, Walter C., Jr. 1981. *Toward an Exegetical Theology: Biblical Exegesis for Preaching and Teaching*. Grand Rapids: Baker Book House.

Käsemann, Ernst. 1980. *Commentary on Romans*. Trans. and ed. Geoffrey W. Bromiley. Grand Rapids: Eerdmans.

Kelly, J. N. D. [1969] 1988. *A Commentary on the Epistles of Peter and of Jude*. Harper's New Testament Commentaries. Reprint. Peabody, MA: Hendrickson.

Kennedy, George A. 1984. *New Testament Interpretation through Rhetorical Criticism*. Chapel Hill: University of North Carolina.

Kilpatrick, G. D. 1977. The Historic Present in the Gospels and Acts. *Zeitschrift Für Die Neutestamentliche* 68:258–62.

Knowling, R. J. 1974. The Acts of the Apostles. In *The Expositor's Greek Testament*, vol. 2. Reprint. Grand Rapids: Eerdmans.

Kuehne, C. 1973. The Greek Article and the Doctrine of Christ's Deity. *Journal of Theology* 13 (September):12–28 [Part I]; 13 (December):14–30 [Part II].

———. 1974. The Greek Article and the Doctrine of Christ's Deity. *Journal of Theology* 14 (March):11–20 [Part III]; 14 (June):16–25 [Part IV]; 14 (September):21–33 [Part V]; 14 (December):8–19 [Part VI].

———. 1975. The Greek Article and the Doctrine of Christ's Deity, Conclusion. *Journal of Theology* 15 (January):8–22.

Ladd, George Eldon. 1972. *A Commentary on the Revelation of John.* Grand Rapids: Eerdmans.

Larson, Mildred L. 1984. *Meaning-Based Translation: A Guide to Cross-Language Equivalence.* Lanham, MD: University Press of America.

Laws, Sophie. [1980] 1987. *A Commentary on the Epistle of James.* Harper's New Testament Commentaries. Reprint. Peabody, MA: Hendrickson.

Lenski, R. C. H. 1936. *The Interpretation of St. Paul's Epistle to the Romans.* Minneapolis: Augsburg Publishing House.

———. 1943. *The Interpretation of St. Matthew's Gospel.* Minneapolis: Augsburg Publishing House.

———. 1966. *The Interpretation of the Epistles of St. Peter, St. John and St. Jude.* Minneapolis: Augsburg Publishing House.

Levinsohn, Stephen H. 1981a. Notes on the Distribution of Δέ and Καί in the Narrative Framework of Luke's Gospel. *Selected Technical Articles Related to Translation* 5:39–53.

———. 1981b. Sentence Conjunctions and Development Units in the Narrative of Acts. *Selected Technical Articles Related to Translation* 5:2–39.

Lightfoot, J. B. [1879] 1959. *Saint Paul's Epistles to the Colossians and to Philemon.* Reprint. Grand Rapids: Zondervan.

———. [1913] 1953. *St. Paul's Epistle to the Philippians.* Reprint. Grand Rapids: Zondervan.

———. 1957. *The Epistle of St. Paul to the Galatians.* Reprint. Grand Rapids: Zondervan.

Lincoln, Andrew T. 1990. *Ephesians.* Word Biblical Commentary, vol. 42. Dallas: Word Books.

Lofthouse, W. F. 1955. "I" and "We" in the Pauline Letters. *The Bible Translator* 6:72–80.

Longenecker, Richard N. 1990. *Galatians.* Word Biblical Commentary, vol. 41. Dallas: Word Books.

Louw, Johannes P. 1982. *Semantics of New Testament Greek.* Philadelphia: Fortress Press.

Louw, Johannes P., and Eugene A. Nida. 1988. *Greek-English Lexicon of the New Testament Based on Semantic Domains.* 2 vols. New York: United Bible Societies.

Mantey, J. R. 1951. The Causal Use of EIS in the New Testament. *Journal of*

Biblical Literature 70:45–48.

Marshall, I. Howard. 1978a. *The Epistles of John.* New International Commentary on the New Testament. Grand Rapids: Eerdmans.

————. 1978b. *The Gospel of Luke.* New International Greek Testament Commentary. Grand Rapids: Eerdmans.

Mayor, Joseph B. 1897. *The Epistle of St. James.* London: Macmillan.

McCarthy, Michael. 1991. *Discourse Analysis for Language Teachers.* Cambridge: Cambridge University Press.

McGaughy, Lane C. 1972. *Toward a Descriptive Analysis of Εἶναι as a Linking Verb in New Testament Greek.* Society of Biblical Literature Dissertation Series, no. 6.

McKay, K. L. 1972. Syntax in Exegesis. *Tyndale Bulletin* 23:39–57.

————. 1981. On the Perfect and Other Aspects in New Testament Greek. *Novum Testamentum* 23:289–329.

————. 1985. Aspect in Imperatival Constructions in New Testament Greek. *Novum Testamentum* 27:201–26.

Metzger, Bruce M. 1975. *A Textual Commentary on the Greek New Testament.* New York: United Bible Societies.

Meyer, Heinrich August Wilhelm. [1884] 1979. *Critical and Exegetical Hand-Book to the Epistle to the Romans.* Reprint. Winona Lake, IN: Alpha Publications.

Moeller, Henry R., and Arnold Kramer. 1962. An Overlooked Structural Pattern in New Testament Greek. *Novum Testamentum* 5:25–35.

Moffatt, James. 1974. The Revelation of St. John the Divine. In *The Expositor's Greek Testament,* vol. 5. Reprint. Grand Rapids: Eerdmans.

Morris, Leon. 1988. *The Epistle to the Romans.* Grand Rapids: Eerdmans.

Moule, C. F. D. 1957. *The Epistles of Paul the Apostle to the Colossians and to Philemon.* Cambridge Greek Testament Commentary. Cambridge: Cambridge University Press.

————. 1968. *An Idiom Book of New Testament Greek.* 2nd ed. Cambridge: Cambridge University Press.

Moulton, James Hope. 1978. *Prolegomena.* Vol. 1 of *A Grammar of New Testament Greek.* 3rd ed. Edinburgh: T. & T. Clark.

Moulton, James Hope, and Wilbert Francis Howard. 1979. *Accidence and Word Formation.* Vol. 2 of *A Grammar of New Testament Greek.* Edinburgh: T. & T. Clark.

Murray, John. 1959. *The Epistle to the Romans,* vol. 1. New International

Commentary on the New Testament. Grand Rapids: Eerdmans.

Nida, Eugene A., J. P. Louw, A. H. Snyman, and J. v. W. Cronje. 1983. *Style and Discourse.* Cape Town, South Africa: Bible Society of South Africa.

Nida, Eugene A., and Charles R. Taber. 1974. *The Theory and Practice of Translation.* Leiden: Brill.

O'Brien, Peter T. 1982. *Colossians, Philemon.* Word Biblical Commentary, vol. 44. Waco, TX: Word Books.

———. 1991. *The Epistle to the Philippians.* New International Greek Testament Commentary. Grand Rapids: Eerdmans.

Pickering, Wilbur. 1980. *A Framework for Discourse Analysis.* Dallas: Summer Institute of Linguistics.

Plummer, Alfred. 1915. *A Critical and Exegetical Commentary on the Second Epistle of St Paul to the Corinthians.* International Critical Commentary. Edinburgh: T. & T. Clark.

———. 1922. *A Critical and Exegetical Commentary on the Gospel According to S. Luke.* International Critical Commentary. Edinburgh: T. & T. Clark.

Porter, Stanley E. 1989. *Verbal Aspect in the Greek of the New Testament, with Reference to Tense and Mood.* New York: Peter Lang.

Radney, J. Randolph. 1982. Some Factors that Influence Fronting in Koine Clauses. Master's thesis, University of Texas at Arlington.

Reed, Jeffrey T. 1991. The Infinitive with two Substantival Accusatives. *Novum Testamentum* 33:1–27.

Robertson, A. T. 1934. *A Grammar of the Greek New Testament in the Light of Historical Research.* Nashville: Broadman Press.

———. 1977. *The Minister and His Greek New Testament.* Reprint. Grand Rapids: Baker Book House.

Robertson, A. T., and W. Hersey Davis. 1933. *A New Short Grammar of the Greek Testament.* New York: Harper & Brothers.

Ropes, James Hardy. 1978. *A Critical and Exegetical Commentary on the Epistle of St. James.* International Critical Commentary. Edinburgh: T. & T. Clark.

Sanday, William, and Arthur C. Headlam. 1902. *A Critical and Exegetical Commentary on the Epistle to the Romans.* International Critical Commentary. Edinburgh: T. & T. Clark.

Searle, John R. 1969. *Speech Acts: An Essay in the Philosophy of Language.* New York: Cambridge University Press.

———. 1979. *Expression and Meaning*. New York: Cambridge University Press.

Selwyn, Edward Gordon. [1947] 1981. *The First Epistle of St. Peter*. Reprint. Grand Rapids: Baker Book House.

Smalley, Stephen S. 1984. *1, 2, 3 John*. Word Biblical Commentary, vol. 51. Waco, TX: Word Books.

Snyman, A. H., and J. v. W. Cronje. 1986. Toward a New Classification of the Figures (*ΣXHMATA*) in the Greek New Testament. *New Testament Studies* 32:113–21.

Stagg, Frank. 1972. The Abused Aorist. *Journal of Biblical Literature* 91:222–31.

Taylor, Vincent. 1952. *The Gospel According to St. Mark*. London: Macmillan.

Thrall, Margaret E. 1962. *Greek Particles in the New Testament*. Grand Rapids: Eerdmans.

Turner, Nigel. 1963. Syntax. Vol. 3 of *A Grammar of New Testament Greek*. Edinburgh: T. & T. Clark.

———. 1965. *Grammatical Insights into the New Testament*. Edinburgh: T. & T. Clark.

Van Otterloo, Roger. 1988. Towards an Understanding of "Lo" and "Behold" Functions of ἰδού and ἴδε in the Greek New Testament. *Occasional Papers in Translation and Textlinguistics* 2(1):34–64.

Vincent, Marvin R. 1979. *A Critical and Exegetical Commentary on the Epistles to the Philippians and to Philemon*. International Critical Commentary. Edinburgh: T. & T. Clark.

Wallace, Daniel B. 1983. The Semantic Range of the Article-Noun-καί-Noun Plural Construction in the New Testament. *Grace Theological Journal* 4:59–84.

———. 1984. The Relation of Adjective to Noun in Anarthrous Constructions in the New Testament. *Novum Testamentum* 26(2):128–67.

Wanamaker, Charles A. 1990. *The Epistles to the Thessalonians*. New International Greek Testament Commentary. Grand Rapids: Eerdmans.

Ward, Ronald A. 1969. *Hidden Meaning in the New Testament*. Greenwood, SC: Attic Press.

Waterman, G. Henry. 1975. The Greek "Verbal Genitive." In *Current Issues in Biblical and Patristic Interpretation*, ed. Gerald F. Hawthorne, 289–93.

Grand Rapids: Eerdmans.

Westcott, Brooke Foss. 1974. *The Epistle to the Hebrews.* Reprint. Grand Rapids: Eerdmans.

———. 1975. *The Gospel According to St. John.* Reprint. Grand Rapids: Eerdmans.

Young, Richard A. 1989. A Classification of Conditional Sentences Based on Speech Act Theory. *Grace Theological Journal* 10:29–49.

Zerwick, Maximilian. 1963. *Biblical Greek Illustrated by Examples.* Rome: Scripta Pontificii Instituti Biblici.

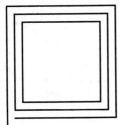

Scripture Index

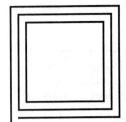

SUBJECT INDEX